Dane Ortlund has sa_____ learned much of what _____ person he was. In this book he shares his findings with us. As we read these pages, we will be led to the same internal relish for God that transformed Edwards' life, theology, and ministry. Like Edwards we will be powerfully drawn by "the beauty of holiness."

David B. Calhoun,
Covenant Theological Seminary, St. Louis, Missouri

Dane Ortlund does a marvelous job of demonstrating how the "new sense of the heart," divinely and graciously imparted by God, governs Edwards' understanding of motivation in Christian obedience. I know of no other book-length treatment of this theme in Edwards and I highly recommend Ortlund's clear and insightful study of it.

Sam Storms,
Enjoying God Ministries, Kansas City, Missouri

There are many books that promise to reveal Jonathan Edwards' insight into the Christian life. This book delivers. Dane Ortlund, artfully using the incisive and perennial thought of Edwards, points us to a Christian obedience that is indeed a whole-hearted delight.

Stephen J. Nichols,
Lancaster Bible College and Graduate School, Lancaster, Pennsylvania

Dane Ortlund's book on Christian motivation is timely and important as Christians wrestle with the problems of licence and legalism. He has combined an acute theological analysis of what motivates authentic Christian obedience with pastoral sensitivity and urgency, drawing on Jonathan Edwards' colossal vision of God. I found the book stimulating for its learning, but much more importantly spiritually searching and encouraging. Edwards encouraged his flock to live rejoicing in God and this book captures just that call.

Michael Ovey,
Principal, Oakhill College, London

By steeping himself in the writing and preaching of Jonathan Edwards, Dane Ortlund has unerringly identified the powerful themes that undergirded the Great Awakening that touched both sides of the Atlantic in the mid-eighteenth century: the Christian's inner motivation and affections, obedience and holiness, prayer and preaching, redemption and regeneration - and above all, the glory of God. As I read the author's words on America's foremost theologian of his time, I found myself praying, "Oh God, send a new awakening, and begin it in me!"

Richard Bewes,
former Rector of All Souls Church, Langham Place, London

A New Inner Relish

Christian Motivation in the Thought of Jonathan Edwards

Dane Ortlund

CHRISTIAN
FOCUS

ISBN 978-1-84550-349-9

Copyright © Dane Ortlund

10 9 8 7 6 5 4 3 2 1

Published in 2008
by
Christian Focus Publications Ltd.,
Geanies House, Fearn, Ross-shire,
Scotland, UK, IV20 1TW

www.christianfocus.com

Cover design by Paul Lewis

Printed by CPD Wales

CONTENTS

For Stacey –
Encourager and Best Friend

ACKNOWLEDGMENTS

One of the main ways God's grace washes into my life is through the people across whose path He brings me. One becomes keenly aware of this mercy in undertaking even a small writing project such as this one. The fingerprints of those whose hearts have shaped mine are etched into the fabric of this book, though perhaps only visibly to the author. So I marvel at the kindness of God in shaping me through the influence of the following saints and fellow friends of Edwards.

Phil Douglass guided and encouraged me through my first intensive exposure to Edwards and has done as much as anyone at Covenant Seminary to make my time here the richest of my life. David Calhoun set aside time during a busy semester to comb through a pestering student's manuscript and apply his kind wisdom with characteristic warmth and insight. This book would not exist without his help and encouragement – thank you, Dr. Calhoun. Sean Lucas and David Jones read an early manuscript and provided helpful suggestions. J. I. Packer kindly and thoughtfully responded to numerous personal letters concerning both Edwards and motivation. My dear friend Brian Martin, who so exemplifies authentic, delight-driven motivation, spurred me on in this project. The sharpening insights and (better yet) Christ-drenched lives of my brothers, Eric and Gavin, are endless sources of inspiration to me – David had them in mind when he wrote Psalm 133. And my dad, Ray Ortlund, Jr., who has impacted me more than anyone and who cares about all the right things in life, loves Jonathan Edwards and happily helped me think through Christian motivation. I love these nine men more than they know.

The many remaining shortcomings are due not to their suggestions but the author's stubbornness.

I am grateful to Willie MacKenzie for taking on this project and encouraging me in it. Rebecca Rine's careful editorial eye caught many errors and provided several helpful suggestions. And with a kindness that is typical of all three of them, Steve Nichols, Sam Storms, and Richard Bewes read through a late draft and graciously expressed support and encouragement.

Finally, thank You, God of history, for Jonathan Edwards. I worship this man no more than a patient the scalpel in his surgeon's hand. Edwards was a fault-laden sinner. Yet through him You have given me new eyes to look beyond the domesticated deity that is the best my puny mind can summon to see with wonder the Lord of glory. Words will not express what he means to me. Thank You for performing eye surgery with the scalpel of a skinny Northampton preacher. The cuts were painful. But the view is breathtaking.

As my first book, this project is dedicated to the person who has first place in my heart. Perhaps one day, Stacey, I'll discover words to tell you what your affirmation and encouragement mean to me.

This book exists so that the sun and center of the universe, Jesus Christ, might shine more brightly in the life of His Church. If this is accomplished in any degree, the labor has been worth it. *Soli deo gloria*.

Dane Ortlund
St. Louis, Missouri
Easter 2007

INTRODUCTION

Why should twenty-first-century Christians listen to Jonathan Edwards?

After all, Edwards was born three hundred years ago in an obscure Connecticut town. He never benefited from a laptop, a microphone, Google, or American Airlines. Colonial New England knew nothing of automobiles, credit cards, iPods, cell phones, or professional sports. The powdered wigs which grace surviving portraits of early eighteenth-century aristocrats seem to relay not only an outer sternness but an inner austerity to match. Tolerance-embracing postmoderns today would perhaps welcome him into Starbucks no more readily than Marilla Ricker a century ago, according to whom Edwards 'believed in the worst God, preached the worst sermons, and had the worst religion of any human being who ever lived on this continent.'[1]

Not only his times but his own life was obscure. Edwards never wrote a biblical commentary, nor did he travel outside his native New England.[2] After laboring for twenty-four years in a single church on what was then the

---

[1] Marilla M. Ricker, *Jonathan Edwards: The Divine Who Filled the Air with Damnation and Proved the Total Depravity of God* (New York: American Freethought Tract Society, 1918), quoted in Kenneth P. Minkema, 'Jonathan Edwards in the Twentieth Century,' *Journal of the Evangelical Theological Society* 47/4 (2004): 660.

[2] His British contemporary George Whitefield, by contrast, traveled to America seven times (Arnold Dallimore, *George Whitefield: The Life and Times of the Great Evangelist of the 18th Century Revival* [2 vols.; Edinburgh: Banner of Truth Trust, 1970, 1980], 2:438). Yet Edwards himself 'never crossed the Atlantic, remaining all his life in the American colonies, and even here he did little traveling' (Hughes Oliphant Old, *The Reading and Preaching of the Scriptures in the Worship of the Christian Church: Moderatism, Pietism, and Awakening* [5 vols.; Grand Rapids: Eerdmans, 2004], 5:248).

edge of the world, a vote of ten to one eventually expelled him from this charge. He endured his final brief years in the untamed wilderness of western Massachusetts, living with and ministering to a handful of Native Americans and a few white families before abruptly becoming 'the deadest of dead white guys' at age fifty-five.[3] One recent biographer pointedly concludes that Edwards 'by his own standards as well as those of his day had a disappointing – some might even say a failed – career.'[4] The sermon that single-handedly keeps the preacher of Northampton in high school American literature texts, moreover, proclaims neither the love nor the grace nor the power of God, but His anger. Edwards never saw his sixtieth birthday. And his family? George Marsden sums up the Edwards heritage: 'his grandmother was an incorrigible profligate, his great-aunt committed infanticide, and his great-uncle was an ax-murderer.'[5]

Perhaps we should be more eager to forget such a man than remember him, let alone learn from him.

UNYIELDING THEOCENTRISM

Yet Jonathan Edwards must be heard today. Not because he was an intellectual giant (though he was). Nor because secular academicians, owning no interest in the Savior for

---

[3] Christine Leigh Heyrman, 'Mark Noll's Master Synthesis,' *Church History* 72/3 (2003): 617. His great-grandson, Sereno E. Dwight, writes: 'He was born in an obscure village, in which the ancient reign of barbarism was only beginning to yield to the inroads of culture and civilization; in a colony comprising but here and there a settlement; and in a country literally in its infancy, constituting with the exception of now and then a white plantation, one vast continuous forest, and distant three thousand miles from Europe, the seat of arts, refinement, and knowledge' (*The Works of Jonathan Edwards* [1834; repr., Peabody, MA: Hendrickson, 2003], ccxxx).

[4] Philip F. Gura, *Jonathan Edwards: America's Evangelical* (New York: Hill and Wang, 2005), xi.

[5] George Marsden, *Jonathan Edwards: A Life* (New Haven: Yale University Press, 2003), 22.

whom he poured out his life, revere him as the greatest philosopher-theologian in American history (though they do).[6] Nor because he wrote with singular beauty of prose (he did not). Jonathan Edwards must be heard today because he exhaled the air of eternity as one intoxicated with the resplendent beauty of the immortal God in the person and work of Jesus Christ. This was his all-consuming passion as he lived under an awareness of and enthrallment with God foreign to vast portions of the church today.[7] Yes, we need the intellect of this remarkable man. More than this, though, we twenty-first-century Christians need his colossal vision of Almighty God – the God who motivates.

Edwards was a sinner. My aim is not to elevate him to superhuman status. He struggled tremendously, for example, with pride.[8] Nevertheless in two specific ways he stands uniquely qualified in deserving our attention. We

---

[6] The late Perry Miller of Yale University, for example, is principally responsible for the surge in interest in Edwards in secular academia in the late twentieth century. Yet (it appears) he never bought into the faith of the man whose mind he studied with such admiration.

[7] David F. Wells, in our time, has labored to awaken the Western church from its neglect of the pre-eminence of God. The evangelical church, says Wells, 'has lost its traditional understanding of the centrality and sufficiency of God' (*No Place for Truth: Or Whatever Happened to Evangelical Theology?* [Grand Rapids: Eerdmans, 1993], 296). 'It is one of the defining marks of Our Time,' he writes elsewhere, 'that God is now weightless. I do not mean by this that he is ethereal but rather that he has become unimportant. He rests upon the world so inconsequentially as not to be noticeable. He has lost his saliency for human life. Those who assure the pollsters of their belief in God's existence may nonetheless consider him less interesting than television, his commands less authoritative than their appetites for affluence and influence, his judgment no more awe-inspiring than the evening news, and his truth less compelling than the advertisers' sweet fog of flattery and lies. That is weightlessness' (*God in the Wasteland: The Reality of Truth in a World of Fading Dreams* [Grand Rapids: Eerdmans, 1994], 88). See also *Above All Earthly Pow'rs: Christ in a Postmodern World* (Grand Rapids: Eerdmans, 2005), 58.

[8] Marsden, *Edwards*, 5-6, 45, 51, 225, 373; Gura, *Edwards*, 230-31; editor's introduction in *The Works of Jonathan Edwards*, vol. 17, *Sermons and*

note these before returning to the overarching reason we should heed the words of Jonathan Edwards.

'THEOLOGY ON FIRE'
First, Edwards was a man of both remarkable intellect and warm piety. The rarity with which this blend is found in a single person need hardly be demonstrated. For too many geniuses, humility and holiness are sacrificed on the altar of intellect-fueled arrogance. Intelligence leads to pride – worship of the beneficiary rather than the Benefactor. Human sinfulness rarely allows genuine piety to exist, let alone flourish, in the presence of intellectual superiority. Yet Edwards was a man of both head and heart – his was 'an intellect fired by, and filled with, the Holy Spirit.'[9]

This blend is poignantly seen in the different reasons for which Edwards has been studied. On the one hand, secular academicians (such as Perry Miller) have made life pursuits out of Jonathan Edwards. It is a tragic irony that Miller – it would appear – never experienced the saving and motivating power of the God Edwards preached, the God to whom Edwards attributed any intellectual gifting he had. Yet on the other hand Edwards was himself driven by a relentless pursuit of holiness, and many are drawn to him

Discourses, 1730–1733, ed. Mark Valeri (New Haven: Yale University Press, 1999), 29. Iain Murray comments likewise: 'When Edwards ... spoke of pride as *the* sin of the human heart he was speaking from experience as well as from Scripture' (*Jonathan Edwards: A New Biography* [Edinburgh: Banner of Truth Trust, 1987], 33). Nevertheless Perry Miller doubtless overstates the point when in a chapter entitled simply 'Hubris,' he describes Edwards as 'proud and overbearing and rash' and, alluding to the metaphor in 'Sinners in the Hands of an Angry God,' calls him 'a fiendish torturer of writhing spiders' (*Jonathan Edwards* [New York: William Sloane, 1949], 210, 221).

[9] D. Martyn Lloyd-Jones, 'Jonathan Edwards and the Crucial Importance of Revival,' in *The Puritan Experiment in the New World* (Huntington, Cambs.: Westminster Conference, 1976), 113. 'What makes Edwards such a brilliant star on the horizon of American Christianity,' concurs H. O. Old, 'is his conjunction of learning and piety' (*Reading and Preaching of the Scriptures*, 5:249).

not by his mind but his heart. His desire to promote godly living in both himself and others colors his language through and through, bringing one biographer to comment that 'his studying was another kind of worship.'[10] In Warfield's words, 'the peculiarity of Edwards' theological work is due to the union in it of the richest religious sentiment with the highest intellectual powers.'[11] Perhaps the secret to his intellectually rigorous piety was resolution number forty-four: 'Resolved, that no other end but religion, shall have any influence at all on any of my actions; and that no action shall be, in the least circumstance, any otherwise than the religious end will carry it.'[12] Light and heat, to use his own frequently employed metaphor, are not meant to exist at odds but to mutually reinforce one another as inseparable elements of healthy Christianity. Edwards possessed both, vindicating Martyn Lloyd-Jones' memorable metaphor: his was a 'theology on fire.'[13]

REASON AND REVELATION

The second unique blend in this man has to do with *reason* and *revelation*, those two channels of knowledge so often set against each other. On the one hand, Edwards thought hard about the subjects on which he wrote. He elevated reason almost as high as anyone.[14] At the same time, he was utterly childlike in his attitude toward the Bible, ever

---

[10] Marsden, *Edwards*, 432.

[11] B. B. Warfield, 'Edwards and the New England Theology,' *Biblical and Theological Studies: Vol. 10*, 527-28.

[12] Jonathan Edwards, *The Works of Jonathan Edwards*, vol. 16, *Letters and Personal Writings*, ed. George S. Claghorn (New Haven: Yale University Press, 1998), 756.

[13] 'Jonathan Edwards,' 119. 'It was not only Edwards' intellectual might,' concurs Harold Simonson, 'but also his gigantic heart including imagination and vision that enabled him to achieve the rare combination of clarity of thought and depth of insight' (*Jonathan Edwards: Theologian of the Heart* [Grand Rapids: Eerdmans, 1974], 85).

[14] Paul Helm writes that Edwards shared with many of his opponents, such as John Taylor, against whom he wrote his treatise on *Original Sin*,

bowing his rational powers at the foot of God's Word. This is why I say he elevated reason *almost* as high as others. The Word of God always held the last word for him, so that, as John Gerstner put it, 'back to Edwards is back to the Bible.'[15] Edwards was convinced that 'the Word of God should certainly be our rule in matters ... above reason and our own notions.'[16] Yet he did not allow this to excuse him from employing every last ounce of brain power God had given him. We see this balance in his resolutions: 'Resolved, when I think of any theorem in divinity to be solved, immediately to do what I can towards solving it, if circumstances don't hinder' along with 'Resolved, to study the Scriptures so steadily, constantly, and frequently, as that I may find, and plainly perceive myself to grow in the knowledge of the same.'[17] Edwards loved the Bible and he loved to think hard – *in that order*. For him, Scripture 'is the fundamental and primary pillar.'[18] This approach to theology is evident in the title of one of his sermons, as he shows that

---

'a confidence in human reason. Not because he believed that it was the only reliable source of human knowledge, but because he believed that it was God-given, and that properly used it corroborated and undergirded the teaching of God's special revelation, the Bible.' Helm later comments: 'I suppose that if Edwards had been asked to rank Scripture, reason, and experience in order of importance for theology, he would undoubtedly have ranked Scripture first. But he would have thought that the choice that we were offering him was rather unnecessary, and indeed superficial' ('The Great Christian Doctrine (*Original Sin*),' in John Piper and Justin Taylor, eds., *A God Entranced View of All Things: The Legacy of Jonathan Edwards* [Wheaton: Crossway, 2004], 177).

[15] John H. Gerstner and Jonathan Neil Gerstner, 'Edwardsean Preparation for Salvation,' *Westminster Theological Journal* 42 (1979): 30.

[16] Jonathan Edwards, in Alexander Grossart, ed., *Selections From the Unpublished Writings of Jonathan Edwards* (Ligonier, PA: Soli Deo Gloria 1992), 43. Reprint from 1865.

[17] *Letters and Personal Writings*, 754, 755. The resolutions are numbers 11 and 28, respectively.

[18] Stephen J. Nichols, *An Absolute Sort of Certainty: The Holy Spirit and the Apologetics of Jonathan Edwards* (Phillipsburg, NJ: Presbyterian &

'A Divine and Supernatural Light' given to the human heart is 'both a Scriptural, and Rational Doctrine.'[19] It is this dual (albeit asymmetrical) approach to the theological endeavor which prompted Gerstner to label his three-volume work of Edwards' theology *The Rational Biblical Theology of Jonathan Edwards*.[20]

CAPTIVATED WITH DIVINE MAJESTY

Both of these distinctive character blends – head and heart, reason and revelation – are subsumed under the umbrella of what was said at the start of this introduction. Jonathan Edwards is so needed by the Church in the twenty-first century because of his immense vision of God. He was gripped with the glory of the King of Ages in a way foreign to almost all of us. Again, this does not mean he deserves our attention because he looks down on the rest of us. Rather he is one of the few among us who persistently focused his gaze upward. 'Edwards's piety continued on in the revivalist tradition,' wrote Mark Noll in 1983, 'his theology continued on in academic Calvinism, but there were no successors to his God-entranced world-view.'[21]

Edwards knew God. He knew God because he had seen God. And what he had seen held him spellbound. We are confronted with the pre-eminence of God at every turn in Edwards' writings: in human choice, in *Freedom of the Will*;

Reformed, 2003), 131; see also 41-44. One might say, then, that Edwards' response to the Catholics of his day (who emphasized tradition over the Bible) was that we do not need *more* than Scripture; to the Enthusiasts of his day (who emphasized experience over the Bible), we do not need *less* than Scripture; and to the rationalists of his day (who emphasized reason over the Bible), *we need Scripture*.

[19] *Sermons and Discourses, 1730–1733*, 406.

[20] John H. Gerstner, *The Rational Biblical Theology of Jonathan Edwards* (3 vols.; Orlando: Ligonier Ministries, 1991).

[21] Mark A. Noll, 'Jonathan Edwards, Moral Philosophy, and the Secularization of American Christian Thought,' *Reformed Journal* 33/2 (1983): 26.

in human emotion, in *Religious Affections*; in human history, in *A History of the Work of Redemption*; in human depravity, in *Original Sin*; in human conversion, in *Narrative of Surprising Conversions*; in human morality, in *The Nature of True Virtue*; in human existence, in *The End for Which God Created the World*. All of these – choice, emotion, history, depravity, conversion, morality, even existence itself – are undeniably human realities. But Edwards saw that the God of the Bible precludes them from being only *human* choice, *human* depravity, *human* conversions, *human* morality, *human* emotion, *human* history, or *human* existence. God Himself wisely and mercifully governs each of these – such that human strivings are not emptied of, but energized with, meaning. The Creator stands behind all that happens, whether religious awakenings (Isa. 57:15) or political decisions (Prov. 21:1) or murderous tsunamis (Zech. 10:1) or a game of Monopoly (Prov. 16:33) or the next meal I am about to eat (Ps. 136:25) or the reason you picked up this book today (Prov. 16:9). This theme flavors everything Edwards wrote. *The End for Which God Created the World* is Edwards' most explicit enunciation of this thesis as he shows that one of the implications of God being the center of creation is the recognition that the purpose of everything is to display God's own supreme beauty and worth. Indeed, this treatise 'might be seen as the logical starting point for all of [Edwards'] thinking,' according to Marsden. And this is the heart of Edwards' contribution to a Western world enamored with human exploits and abilities: God is so thoroughly the center of the universe that He lies in, around, under, and above every thought and deed experienced by human beings as well as every seemingly random event of nature. Edwards inhaled Scripture and exhaled theocentrism. 'The key to Edwards' thought,' Marsden reiterates, 'is that everything is related because everything is related to God.'[22]

MOUNT EVEREST

For these reasons at least, when we emerge bleary-eyed from the study, the binders of the two bulky Banner of Truth volumes wearing thin, perhaps we will forgive – or even echo – the audacity of Lloyd-Jones' superlative comparison:

> I am tempted, perhaps foolishly, to compare the Puritans to the Alps, Luther and Calvin to the Himalayas, and Jonathan Edwards to Mount Everest! ... There are so many approaches to this great summit; but not only so, the atmosphere is so spiritually rarified, and there is this blazing whiteness of the holiness of the man himself, and his great emphasis upon the holiness and the glory of God; and above all the weakness of the little climber as he faces this great peak pointing up to heaven.[23]

The high school literature texts will not tell us that he depicts hell only to woo to heaven. So let us learn, dear fellow climbers, from Jonathan Edwards. His writing is not easy. But it is worth it. The safe consistency of munching coarse grasses in the lowlands may appear to those who do so to outweigh the monotony of so bland a diet; it is only in the mountain passes, however, among the crags and difficult labors of navigation, that one finds the choicest of fruit and flowers – and profits immeasurably thereby.

THE NEED FOR MOTIVATION

The need for the voice of Jonathan Edwards is one of two concerns fueling this book. The other is the need for motivation. It is a centuries-old dilemma:

> Close to our vineyard there was a pear tree laden with fruit. This fruit was not enticing, either in appearance

---

[22] Marsden, *Edwards*, 460.
[23] Lloyd-Jones, 'Jonathan Edwards,' 108.

or in flavor. We nasty lads went there to shake down the fruit and carry it off at dead of night, after prolonging our games out of doors until that late hour according to our abominable custom. We took enormous quantities, not to feast on ourselves but perhaps to throw to the pigs; we did eat a few, *but that was not our motive*: we derived pleasure from the deed simply because it was forbidden.[24]

So goes the ancient account of the most (in)famous fruit theft in history. Augustine of Hippo, among the Church's greatest thinkers in its two thousand-year history, later reflected on the elusive reasons behind his mischievous act by confessing, 'I feasted on the sin, nothing else, and that I relished and enjoyed.'[25] Thus one man's struggle with moral motivation. It is a problem that can be traced back to the hearts of a married couple in a tranquil Garden (Gen. 3:6) and forward to the heart of any person honest and brave enough to admit the inability to live for any length of time without straying from God's will.

There is hardly a more pressing subject for the people of God to consider than motivation. It is not peripheral. The question of why we obey God pervades the daily lives of followers of Jesus Christ. Why pursue holiness? If we are to possess and exemplify authentic Christianity, it is crucial to understand not only *that* we ought to follow God's commands but *why* we do so. For is this not the difficulty? Our failures lie not in ignorance. We know how to honor God. The Bible tells us – adequately, if not exhaustively. The problem is that, once knowing, we fail to *want* to do it. As Augustine once mused, 'The intellect flies ahead, but weak human feelings follow tardily, if at all.'[26]

---

[24] Saint Augustine, *The Confessions*, trans. Maria Boulding (New York: Vintage Books, 1997), 30. Emphasis added.

[25] Ibid, 32.

[26] *The Works of Saint Augustine, Vol. 19: Expositions of the Psalms, 99-120*, ed. Boniface Ramsey, trans. Maria Boulding (New York: New City, 2003), 376.

The issue is motivation. And it lies at the root of any relationship's vitality. Lackluster at best will be the marriage in which the wife acts lovingly toward her husband even as she wonders why she does it. The son who constantly but fruitlessly examines his heart for reasons to obey his parents will soon give up the task of obedience, even if he has a vague intuition that he ought to submit. Begrudging obedience is miserable. The human will is a strong force when driven with purpose. Without it, though, the most likely results of our attempts to live uprightly are bitterness and frustration.

Motivation is essential to authentic Christian living.

THE PATH BEFORE US

Out of these two great needs, then – our need to learn from Jonathan Edwards and our need for motivation – this book is born. Our aim is to ask what America's theologian has to say on the subject of Christian motivation.

Before delving into Edwards himself, we will begin with a brief overview of various classes into which motivation can be divided. Drawing insights from various writers, we will identify three basic categories in which believers are motivated to obey God with respect to the past, the present,

---

The comment is on Ps. 119:20. Thomas Aquinas quotes this statement of Augustine's and deals with it at length in his *Summa Theologica*, trans. Fathers of the English Dominican Province (New York: Benziger Brothers, 1947-48), 1:628-33. In another place Augustine writes of believers that God 'grants them both to know what they should do and to do what they know' ('The Grace of Christ and Original Sin,' in *The Works of Saint Augustine, Vol. 23: Answer to the Pelagians*, ed. John E. Rotelle, trans. Roland J. Teske [New York: New City, 1997], 410).

Augustine and Edwards, on the one hand, and Socrates, on the other, are diametrically opposed in their understanding of ethics and motivation if Everett Ferguson is right: 'Soctrates' basic idea was that if you know what is right, you will do it. Wrongdoing is the result of wrong thinking and wrong information' (*Backgrounds of Early Christianity*, 3rd ed. [Grand Rapids: Eerdmans, 2003], 329).

and the future. Though these categories are not air-tight and room must be left to accommodate overlap, for clarity's sake we will label them gratitude, identity, and personal benefit. They will be taken in this order, each section concluding with a few Scripture passages which implement that particular avenue of motivation. This will lead to an examination of a handful of pertinent sermons and other works by Edwards. At the end we'll tie it all together before drawing out some implications.

AUTHENTIC OBEDIENCE

One final note – a point absolutely critical to everything that follows. Reference will be made repeatedly to 'obedience' throughout this book. Unless otherwise indicated, this refers to *authentic* obedience: that is, obedience which is from the heart. It is simplistic to see only two possibilities regarding faithfulness to God: disobedience and obedience. Rather, three options are before us: disobedience, authentic obedience and inauthentic obedience. Disobedience refers, of course, to rejection of the imperatives of God. Inauthentic obedience is a bit more slippery. It is obedience driven by something other than the heartfelt love for God and his glory that characterizes authentic obedience. Legalism, for example, sees obedience as a cause of fellowship with God rather than its result. Such 'obedience' is in fact disobedience, since God demands not only that we obey but that we do it for the right reasons (Deut. 28:47; Prov. 16:2; 1 Cor. 4:5). So there is not only an external (the act of obedience) but an internal (the motivation) element to godly living. We find ourselves, then, not with two kinds of obedience and one kind of disobedience. Rather there are actually two brands of disobedience – one involving open disobedience and one involving apparent obedience accompanied by impure motives – and only one true obedience. It is the latter we are after here.

How, then, does this authentic obedience come about? The answer to that question is the reason for this book.

The LORD searches all hearts and understands
every plan and thought.
1 Chronicles 28:9

All the ways of a man are pure in his own eyes,
but the LORD weighs the spirit.
Proverbs 16:2

He will bring to light the things now hidden in darkness
and will disclose the purposes of the heart.
1 Corinthians 4:5

I

CATEGORIES OF CHRISTIAN MOTIVATION

We will look at Christian motivation from the three perspectives of past, present and future. Simply put, the past motivation is that of gratitude, the present is that of identity, and the future is that of benefit. These will be explained and explored in the following pages. Concluding each section will be a few Scripture passages supporting that category of motivation.

Here at the outset, however, it is important to recognize that these three aspects, while distinguishable, are in the end inseparable. Though it is helpful for our purposes to make a distinction between what has taken place in the past, what is now true, and what awaits us in the future as motivation to obey God, these three components are intimately connected with and mutually reinforce one another. For example, a Christian enjoys a new *present* identity as a child of God only because of what God has done in the *past* work of election (Eph. 1:3-6), and this adoption will be fully consummated only eschatologically in the *future* (Rom. 8:23). Moreover, can a Christian not be *grateful* not only for past mercies but for the (present) possession of a new identity or for the (future) pleasure promised in obedience? Of course! Salvation itself is spoken of in Scripture as being a past (Eph. 2:8), present (1 Cor. 1:18), and future reality (Acts 15:11).

Nevertheless a temporary distinction between these three categories of motivation will help us as we seek a biblical understanding of Christian motivation. To them we now turn.

Past-Looking: The Motivation of Gratitude

Christians are motivated by gratitude to God. Why? What prompts thanksgiving in the hearts of believers? In a word, Christ! We are grateful to God for the astonishing gift He has given to us of His Son, come to earth as God incarnate to take on Himself all the sin of His people. We are thankful for the forgiveness made possible in the gospel: 'There is therefore now no condemnation for those who are in Christ Jesus' (Rom. 8:1).[1] Thanksgiving results. Moreover, God has permanently cleared His people not only of the guilt but also of the reign of sin. Through union with Christ, believers are freed from sin's penalty and power (Rom. 6:1-11). For all He has done both for us and in us, believers are grateful to God.

Yet the implications of the cross of Christ do not end with emotions or feelings. Gratitude manifests itself in a life of loving obedience to God. Moreover, these acts of obedience are not done to pay God back. After all, every act of obedience is itself only a gift of God's grace (2 Cor. 9:8; 1 Pet. 4:11). Therefore if we are counting on obedience to put us right with God or to pay Him back, such moralistic strategy will backfire since it will only be putting us more in His debt. Rather, glad obedience to God is something the Christian is freed unto as a result of divine grace. After all, Christ has provided for all the righteousness before God we will ever need. We are robed in the righteousness of

---

[1] With the exception of those passages directly quoted as reproduced by Edwards (which are from the King James Version), all Scripture quotations are in the English Standard Version unless otherwise indicated.

his Son. Believers are motivated to obey God, then, out of grateful love – not legalistic catch-up.

J. I. Packer has explained this element of Christian motivation in these terms: 'The secular world never understands Christian motivation.... From the plan of salvation I learn that the true driving force in authentic Christian living is, and ever must be, not the hope of gain, but the heart of gratitude.'[2] Incentive lies not in what God will do for us if we obey, but in what He has already done for us as we believe. As John Stott puts it, 'the same cross of Christ, which is the ground of a free salvation, is also the most powerful incentive to a holy life.'[3]

In short, then, the grace of God in the cross of Christ leads to thanksgiving in His people, which in turn leads naturally to obedience. One can see why we have labeled this the 'past-looking' motivation for obedience: gratitude, by its very nature, is thankfulness for something done in the past. While the cross of Christ has, of course, enormous implications for the Christian faith we are now living (in the present) and will our whole lives long (in the future), gratitude to God is founded centrally on past displays of God's grace, seen supremely in that past event of the cross and the achieved reality that we have been brought into God's glorious kingdom. 'Thanks be to God for his inexpressible gift!' (2 Cor. 9:15)

SCRIPTURE PASSAGES[4]

Titus 2:11-14:
For the grace of God has appeared, bringing salvation for all people, training us to renounce ungodliness and worldly passions, and to live self-controlled, upright,

---

[2] J. I. Packer, *Rediscovering Holiness* (Ann Arbor, MI: Servant, 1992), 75.

[3] John R. W. Stott, *The Cross of Christ* (Downers Grove, IL: InterVarsity, 1986), 84.

[4] See also: Ps. 116:12-13; Rom. 2:4; 12:1; 1 Pet. 2:9.

and godly lives in the present age, waiting for our blessed hope, the appearing of the glory of our great God and Savior Jesus Christ, who gave himself for us to redeem us from all lawlessness and to purify for himself a people for his own possession who are zealous for good works.

Here Paul tells Titus that God's grace brings 'self-controlled, upright, and godly lives.' How? Paul cannot be speaking exclusively of the grace that progressively sanctifies because he labels it the grace that *brings* salvation.[5] So Paul is including in his understanding of grace the event of the cross in which Christ secured the salvation of the Church, and it is this that 'train[s] us to renounce ungodliness.' Grace does not encourage sin; it invigorates obedience (Rom. 5:20–6:2). Looking back at the cross ignites something in the believer that brings obedience. The grace of God in salvation fuels obedience.

Hebrews 12:28:
Let us be grateful for receiving a kingdom that cannot be shaken, and thus let us offer to God acceptable worship, with reverence and awe, for our God is a consuming fire.

The writer to the Hebrews calls his believing readers to 'be grateful' for their part in the inheritance of the kingdom of heaven. And what is the natural result? That we would 'thus ... offer to God acceptable worship.' We know from the opening words of Romans 12, which like Hebrews 12:28 employs the metaphor of sacrifice, that true Christian worship is not exhausted by a few praise choruses on Sunday morning. Rather, real worship is to 'present your bodies as a living

---

[5] We admit that Paul may indeed be speaking of 'the grace that brings salvation' as the grace which encompasses both justification and sanctification. For our purposes here we simply note that it cannot be referring *exclusively* to progressive sanctification.

sacrifice, holy and acceptable to God.' *This* 'is your spiritual worship' (Rom. 12:1). Obedience, borne out of gratitude, is worship. And such obedience ought to be accompanied with due 'reverence and awe,' says the writer to the Hebrews, for this is no tribal deity or chuckling grandfather – rather 'our God is a consuming fire.'

PRESENT-LOOKING: THE MOTIVATION OF IDENTITY

We have not only been brought into God's kingdom as citizens of that realm. We have been brought into God's family as sons and daughters of the King Himself. This too is motivation for righteous living, for a Christian is someone who has had one's fundamental self-image changed. We are no longer enemies of God, living under His wrath. We are instead children of the King, living under His fatherly care. Believers enjoy a filial relationship with a heavenly Father. A Christian's essential identity has been forever altered, going from the worst possible scenario (enemies of God the Judge) to the best possible (children of God the Father). God has conquered our treason and adopted us.

How does this fuel obedience? Our identity motivates us because it alters our whole perspective on life and holiness. No longer are sinful acts one more offense added to an ever-increasing list of shortcomings to eventually be recounted by an angry Judge. Nor are we simply indifferent to how we may offend whatever deity might exist out there. Rather, to act sinfully for the believer is to dishonor one's own Father. It is to act in a way that is not consistent with who we are. Sin is a contradiction with one's new filial relationship with God. A *sinning Christian* is an oxymoron. We obey God because we have a new identity to live out. Faithfulness to the revealed will of God is therefore simply living out who we are. One is never part of the family of God by title only; this privilege flows out into daily living.

In *Children of the Living God*, Sinclair Ferguson dwells on this very fact:

> Whenever a person is brought into the kingdom of God, and becomes a child of God, the new lifestyle follows. While God works in and through the personalities we already have ... he begins to mark those personalities with certain broad similarities. These are characteristic qualities of life shared by all of God's children; there is a certain family likeness which is always present. We expect this in any family.

Ferguson goes on to explain that those who are in Christ were once members of the family of Satan himself, which led to a life of sin:

> A new relationship with the world of sin and the dominion of darkness has been established in the life of the child of God.... Where [the Apostle John, in 1 John] describes the Christian as 'not sinning', he does so in the context of his adoption out of the family of the Evil One into the family of God. He is no longer under the dominion of the devil (in whose power John sees the whole world lying, 5:19). Freed from those family ties, and from the legal reign of sin over his life, the Christian 'no longer sins.' Sin is no longer the characteristic feature of his lifestyle.[6]

In other words, holiness is driven not only by *what has been done* (past) and *what obedience promises us* (future – see below) but by *who we are* (now). 'Adoption,' writes John Murray, 'is an act of transfer from an alien family into the family of God himself. This is surely the apex of grace and privilege.'[7] Lions don't chirp, crickets don't roar – and Christians don't sin. It's not who we are.

---

[6] Sinclair Ferguson, *Children of the Living God* (Edinburgh: Banner of Truth Trust, 1989), 40, 44.

By focusing on our *identity* as that which invigorates holiness, we are concentrating on a present reality. Thus we will call the motivation of identity 'present-looking.' Though rooted in the past and anticipatory of the future, identity is fixed on who we are now. When faced with temptation, Christians look to the present truth of their newfound identity by divine adoption and say 'no' to sin and 'yes' to righteousness.

SCRIPTURE PASSAGES[8]

1 Peter 1:14:
As obedient children, do not be conformed to the passions of your former ignorance, but as he who called you is holy, you also be holy in all your conduct, since it is written: 'You shall be holy, for I am holy.'

Peter calls his readers 'obedient children.' These two words form the crux of what it is to be driven to holiness by one's identity. We obey because we are children. The two naturally go together. Peter explains that his hearers are to live godly lives, pursuing holiness even as God himself is holy, as is consonant with the truth that they are sons and daughters of their Father in heaven.

1 John 3:1-2, 4-6:
See what kind of love the Father has given to us, that we should be called children of God; and so we are. The reason why the world does not know us is that it did not know him. Beloved, we are God's children....

---

[7] John Murray, *Redemption Accomplished and Applied* (Grand Rapids: Eerdmans, 1955), 134. John Stott similarly speaks of this motivation when he says: 'A remembrance that Jesus Christ has bought us with his blood, and that in consequence we belong to him, should motivate us as individual Christians to holiness.... Bought by Christ, we have no business to become the slaves of anybody or anything else' (*The Cross of Christ*, 181-82).

[8] See also Rom. 8:15-17; Eph. 5:1.

> Everyone who makes a practice of sinning also practices lawlessness; sin is lawlessness. You know that he appeared to take away sins, and in him there is no sin. No one who abides in him keeps on sinning.

In verses 1-2, John speaks of adoption; in verses 4-6, of obedience. The two, once again, are intimately connected. Being a child of God necessarily implies the end of sinning. In verse 10 John goes on to say, 'By this it is evident who are the children of God, and who are the children of the devil: whoever does not practice righteousness is not of God, nor is the one who does not love his brother.' The new self-image of the Christian is powerful impetus to 'practice righteousness.'

FUTURE-LOOKING: THE MOTIVATION OF PERSONAL BENEFIT

A third category of Christian motivation is that of personal benefit or profit. The phrase 'personal benefit' encompasses a range of blessings, including joy, peace of conscience, heavenly rewards, and so on.[9] In short, we are dealing with the promises of God. These divine assurances motivate Christians to obedience by promising gain to those who obey. In other words, motivation by personal benefit is the persuasion that there is a superior pleasure to be enjoyed in obedience than in sin.

In 1870 Charles Spurgeon preached a sermon entitled, 'The Profit of Godliness in this Life.' While acknowledging

---

[9] You may put your nose to rest; what you smell is not a health-wealth-and-prosperity Gospel. Quite the contrary – the Bible is clear that the faithful Christian life is a life of suffering. Nevertheless we remind ourselves especially of the book of Proverbs, which time and again lays down *general* maxims about life which (by virtue of what kind of literature they are) inform us that to live life in a God-honoring way will generally cause things to go better for us (e.g. to work hard will generally [though not always] put food on the table [Prov. 12:24]). This is not, however, to downplay the suffering which is guaranteed all true disciples of Christ (Matt. 5:10; John 16:33; Acts 14:22; 1 Cor. 15:19; 2 Tim. 3:12).

that perfect bliss awaits us only in the next life – that would be the subject of the sermon Spurgeon preached in the evening service later that same day – the Baptist preacher declared that

> you who have godliness, and live in the fear of God, let me entreat you to believe that there is provided for you in godliness, comfort, joy, and delight for the life that now is. You need not postpone your feasting upon Christ till you see him face to face.... Without exception, the whole of us can unanimously declare that we have found in godliness the highest happiness, the supremest delight, the richest consolation.[10]

John Piper in our day has written that 'the pursuit of pleasure is an essential motive for every good deed.' Regarding the obedience of love, for instance, Piper says, 'Loving your enemy doesn't earn you the reward of heaven. Treasuring the reward of heaven empowers you to love your enemy.'[11] In other words, God promises to make obedience worth it, and this personal benefit empowers obedience. Counter-intuitive though it be, joy awaits those who deny themselves and submit in humble obedience to the will of Christ. He who would obey is spurred on by the knowledge of the delight-laden results of his obedience.

The focus here, then, is on the future. Believers obey because of the blessings expected to arrive when the path

---

[10] *The Metropolitan Tabernacle Pulpit: Sermons Preached and Revised by C. H. Spurgeon* (Pasadena, TX: Pilgrim, 1970), 16:358-59. See also 'The Secret of a Happy Life' (22:409-20) and 'The Secret of Happiness' (56:589-598).

[11] John Piper, *Desiring God: Meditations of a Christian Hedonist* (3d ed.; Sisters, OR: Multnomah, 2006), 97, 163. For other clear expositors of this avenue of motivation see Daniel P. Fuller, *The Unity of the Bible: Unfolding God's Plan for Humanity* (Grand Rapids: Zondervan, 1992), 150-51, and Scott J. Hafemann, *The God of Promise and the Life of Faith: Understanding the Heart of the Bible* (Wheaton: Crossway, 2001), 167-85. 'The pursuit of a greater good in the future,' writes Hafemann, 'is the only motive strong enough to bring about self-denial in the present' (174).

of holiness, now lying open before them, is taken. It must be clarified that this focus on the human blessings of obedience does not steal glory from God or make obedience human-centered, because the blessing sought is fundamentally God Himself. Seeking spiritual enjoyment glorifies God, not ourselves, since it is an enjoyment *in Him*, not (ultimately) in His gifts.

SCRIPTURE PASSAGES[12]

Deuteronomy 10:12-13:
And now, Israel, what does the LORD your God require of you, but to fear the LORD your God, to walk in all his ways, to love him, to serve the LORD your God with all your heart and with all your soul, and to keep the statutes and commands of the LORD, which I am commanding you today for your good?[13]

After God gives Moses two new stone tablets to replace the ones smashed at the sight of Israel's idolatry, Moses addresses Israel with the above words. And the qualification he adds on to the end of his exhortation to fear, walk with, love, and serve Yahweh is that it is *for your good*.[14] Moses appeals to the personal benefit involved. To the degree that one obeys God, to that degree one will experience a full and satisfying life – though not, it must be stressed, as the world understands satisfaction. For in a cross-centered Christianity, to be weak is to be strong (2 Cor 12:10); to be poor is to be rich (Luke 6:20; 2 Cor. 9:6-11). Nevertheless the point stands: God's law is not meant to enslave but to free.[15]

---

[12] See also: 2 Chron. 24:20; Prov. 11:17; Isa. 1:19-20; 58:13-14; Amos 5:14; Heb. 11:6; James 1:25.

[13] The theme of God responding to obedience with blessing is a major motif of the book of Deuteronomy. Relevant passages include: Deut. 4:40; 6:1–3, 18, 24, 25; 7:6-11; 8:1; 10:12-13; 11:13-15, 26-28; 28:1-14; 29:9; 30:9-10, 15-18.

[14] NIV: 'for your own good.'

Hebrews 11:24-26:
By faith Moses, when he was grown up, refused to be
called the son of Pharaoh's daughter, choosing rather to
be mistreated with the people of God than to enjoy the
fleeting pleasures of sin. He considered the reproach of
Christ greater wealth than the treasures of Egypt, for he
was looking to the reward.

As the writer to the Hebrews recounts his inspiring list of
faith-filled saints, he speaks of the motivation that drove
Moses' obedience. Lasting future pleasure was what
beckoned Moses to be 'mistreated with the people of God.'
I say *lasting* because he rejected the 'fleeting pleasures of
sin.' He was after permanent, solid pleasure. I say *future*
because 'he was looking ahead to his reward.' He took the
long view. Moses saw the immensity of pleasures available
in loyalty to Yahweh and chose obedience. This is the
motivation of personal benefit.

CONCLUSION

These then are three clearly biblical categories of Christian
motivation. Let me be clear: the writers cited above must not
be limited to the categories in which they are mentioned.
Nevertheless each of the men quoted above illumines
particularly clearly the respective motivational emphases
here described.

It must also be reiterated, moreover, that while these
three motivations are logically distinguishable, they are not
finally separable. Scripture holds them all high. Occasionally
we even see all three together in one context. After Saul has
been installed as Israel's king, for example, Samuel delivers
a farewell speech to the nation in 1 Samuel 12. In response

---

[15] This is a recurring theme in Hafemann's *The God of Promise and the
Life of Faith*.

to the prophet's charge, the people realize their wickedness in asking for a king (v. 17). They plead with Samuel to pray to Yahweh for them. In his short response, Samuel assures them that they need not be afraid. Rather,

- 'serve the LORD with all your heart. And do not turn aside after empty things that cannot profit or deliver, for they are empty' (vv. 20-21). (*future: personal benefit*)

- 'For the LORD will not forsake his people ... because it has pleased the LORD to make you a people for himself' (v. 22). (*present: newfound identity*)

- 'Only fear the LORD and serve him faithfully with all your heart. For consider what great things he has done for you' (v. 24). (*past: gratitude*)

Each of these motivations, then – past, present and future – provides spiritual potency in daily Christian living. Yet my aim in this book is to hear with you Jonathan Edwards' supremely relevant message that while all three are legitimate and even crucial encouragements toward obedience, Christian motivation is fundamentally achieved by a divinely-bestowed spiritual taste.

We must be careful not to impose upon Edwards a framework which would feel foreign to him; indeed, nowhere does he speak of such a triad of motivations. We must freely acknowledge, therefore, that we are bringing certain questions *to* Edwards deductively, and not drawing our framework *from* him inductively. In stepping back and viewing his thought as a whole, however, these categories will help illumine his own mind on the subject of motivation. Edwards does, moreover, speak to each of these three kinds of motivation, as will be seen. And he consistently goes beneath these to the root of a new inclination. By this sense of the heart the believer is moved to obey God not *essentially* by any logical reasoning (such as the three mentioned thus far) but by an immediate sense of and inclination toward God. While the motivations mentioned above may be used as kindling for obedience, they cannot in themselves provide the spark. Christian motivation is, at bottom, the granting of a new inner relish.

I have diligently endeavored to find
out and use the most powerful motives
to persuade you to take care for
your own welfare and salvation.

Jonathan Edwards,
'A Farewell Sermon,' 1750

2

MOTIVATION IN EDWARDS (1): SERMONS

'June 22, 1750, the Revd Jonathan Edwards was dismissed.'[1]

With this prosaic statement the church record of Northampton Church recounts a moment more integral to church history and the welfare of numberless generations of saints than any of the two hundred-plus parishioners who drove Edwards from their church could realize. For several of his major works, such as *Freedom of the Will* and *Original Sin*, were completed during these eight years of rural exile, which was spent in the harsh wilderness of western Massachusetts ministering to Native Americans and a few white settlers. Had he not been dismissed, Edwards would probably have written much less during those final years of his life. Though he had been driven from his church by a vote of ten to one, the sovereign Lord was orchestrating events for the good of His church and the glory of His name.[2]

---

[1] Quoted in Murray, *Edwards*, 352; see also *Guided Tour*, 62.

[2] Edwards' dismissal was the result primarily of a controversy regarding who could participate in communion on Sunday mornings. For detailed accounts of Edwards' dismissal and the factors involved, see Marsden, *Edwards*, 341-74; Murray, *Edwards*, 311-49. Both conclude that the communion controversy was only one factor among many in Edwards' dismissal.

'I HAVE USED THE MOST POWERFUL MOTIVES'

We begin here, where Edwards' story (almost) ends, with his last sermon preached as stated pastor of the church he led for twenty-one years.[3] The date recorded on the Northampton church register – June 22, 1750 – was the day on which Edwards delivered a final summons to his people to pursue holiness with uncompromising single-mindedness. 'A Farewell Sermon' rings with compassion yet sternness, reminding the Northampton congregation that they would meet their pastor again one day before the judgment seat of God. Based on 2 Corinthians 1:14, Edwards formulated the following doctrine in his final attempt to impel his people on toward greater faithfulness: 'Ministers and the people that have been under their care, must meet one another, before Christ's tribunal, at the day of judgment.'[4]

I mention this sermon here at the outset simply to prepare the way for the rest of this book, pointing out that Jonathan Edwards was explicitly concerned with motivating his people. Our quest for Edwards' understanding of Christian motivation is not misplaced. He declares unambiguously as he exits his pastorate that he has labored to inspire them to tend to their souls.

> I have diligently endeavored to find out and use the most powerful motives to persuade you to take care for your

---

[3] It was not, however, the last sermon he ever preached at the church – the congregation, finding itself hard-pressed to fill the pulpit after Edwards' dismissal, often called on him to fill the pulpit before he moved west (Marsden, *Edwards*, 364)!

[4] Wilson H. Kimnach, Kenneth P. Minkema and Douglas A. Sweeney, eds., *The Sermons of Jonathan Edwards: A Reader* (New Haven: Yale University Press, 1999), 213. The full title of the sermon was: 'A Farewell Sermon, Preached at the First Precinct at Northampton, After the People's Public Rejection of Their Minister, and Renouncing Their Relation to Him As Pastor of the Church There, on June 22, 1750; Occasioned By Difference of Sentiments, Concerning the Requisite Qualifications of Members of the Church in Complete Standing.'

own welfare and salvation. I have not only endeavored to awaken you that you might be moved with fear, but I have used my utmost endeavors to win you: I have sought out acceptable words, that if possible I might prevail upon you to forsake sin, and turn to God, and accept of Christ as your Savior and Lord. I have spent my strength very much in these things.[5]

This gives us a helpful window into Edwards' own understanding of what he had been doing in Northampton as he stood reflecting on over two decades of ministry there. His central labor was the production not of theological treatises nor philosophical reflections but the advancement of spiritual growth in the lives of his parishioners. To this all his energies were channeled.

MULTIPLE MOTIVATIONS

Edwards notes in this statement, moreover, that he has employed various methods in motivating his people, sometimes with fear and sometimes by winning them. We dare not oversimplify Edwards on this important subject. He did not invariably resort to a single approach in igniting greater holiness among his people. Rather, he viewed motivation comprehensively, using whatever biblical means appropriate to give his parishioners incentive to yield themselves to God. A trio of Edwards scholars puts it this way:

There is a method to Edwards' seeming madness, and ... even his most frightening sermons were part of his larger effort to open what he took to be hard and calloused hearts to the love of his gracious and merciful God. Indeed, while the horrifying hellfire of *Sinners*[6] has become by far the best-known element of the entire

---

[5] Ibid, 231-32.
[6] That is, 'Sinners in the Hands of an Angry God.'

Edwards corpus, it is important to note that Edwards employed many other measures by which to motivate his listeners to attend to religion.[7]

The attending to religion – this was Jonathan Edwards' great interest. Even his most profound theological works ultimately aimed at this.

What then did he perceive to be the most effective means for executing this aim? We will sample Edwards' various 'measures' in a representative selection of his writings with the goal of discovering how he understood motivation for moral living and what we can learn from him. After looking at a handful of sermons, we will analyze a few pertinent treatises before trying to distill the heart of what he has to say. It is impossible to point to one particular sermon or work as a holistic explanation of his understanding of what motivates Christians to obey. That is, nowhere does one find a sermon by Edwards entitled 'Christian Motivation.' No 'Why True Saints Obey God' exists in his corpus. Yet motivation is implicit almost everywhere with Edwards. This will become evident in what follows.

The Centrality of the Sermon

I include Edwards' sermons unapologetically. Preaching was the supreme labor of his life.

Although it may seem obvious to general readers that sermons lie at the center of a preacher's vocation, most scholars have somehow failed to notice this fact as it applies to Edwards. Somewhat surprisingly, they have most often looked to Edwards' major treatises as the supreme sources of his most deeply held ideas. But sermons above all stood as Edwards' favored literary form and his most time-consuming activity.[8]

---

[7] Kimnach, et al, *Sermons Reader*, xxxix.

With these words, three scholars introduce an edited collection of fourteen sermons of the Northampton pastor. Jonathan Edwards was a preacher. As a shepherd of God's people, the principal labor to which he attended was the preparation and delivery of sermons. 'Edwards was foremost a pastor, and his primary genre was the sermon.'[9]

Over fourteen hundred sermons came from Edwards over the course of life, many of which have yet be transcribed (perhaps we will yet find that elusive sermon 'Why True Saints Obey God'!). Here we examine only a few of the more well-known which helpfully address the subject of Christian motivation. I consider these a representative sampling of his preaching.

'HEAVEN IS A WORLD OF LOVE'

In 1738 the Northampton congregation heard a message which culminated a series of fifteen sermons expounding 1 Corinthians 13.[10] The doctrine of this climactic sermon was simply that 'heaven is a world of love.'[11] After summarizing

---

[8] Kimnach, et al, *Sermons Reader*, xxxviii.

[9] Stephen J. Nichols, *Jonathan Edwards: A Guided Tour of His Life and Thought* (Phillipsburg, NJ: Presbyterian & Reformed, 2001), 189. Nichols later states: 'Very few of [Edwards's] ideas did not first find public expression in one of his sermons. This, of course, is not surprising, as Edwards's primary vocation was pastor' (195). See also his *Absolute Sort of Certainty*, 155.

[10] Specifically, vv. 8-10: 'Charity never faileth; but whether there be prophecies, they shall fail; whether there be tongues, they shall cease; whether there be knowledge, it shall vanish away. For we know in part, and we prophesy in part. But when that which is perfect is come, then that which is in part shall be done away' (Kimnach, et al, *Sermons Reader*, 242). This sermon series is what we know today as *Charity and Its Fruits* (*The Works of Jonathan Edwards*, vol. 8, *Ethical Writings*, ed. Paul Ramsey [New Haven: Yale University Press, 1989], 123-397).

[11] Ibid, 243. This is the usual structure of an Edwardsean sermon: the declaration and reading of the passage, followed by a brief exposition; then the 'doctrine,' or thesis of the sermon, upon which is built the main body of exposition; then, lastly, the application. The last two sections take up the vast majority of the sermon. This particular sermon is unique in that the doctrine is exactly the same as the title.

the sermon, we will make plain the connection to Christian motivation.

'A GARDEN OF PLEASURES'

In this sermon Edwards asserts that love is, essentially, selflessness – specifically, delighting in the joy of others. Those in lower stations in heaven will not be jealous of others, but just the opposite: they will rejoice, because they are so caught up in the desire of the well-being of others. That is, 'if the love be perfect, the greater the prosperity of the beloved is, the more is the lover pleased and delighted. For the prosperity of the beloved is, as it were, the food of love; and therefore the greater the prosperity is, the more richly is love feasted.'[12]

Heavenly love, then, is that which finds its greatest delight in the well-being of the object of love. Therefore the degree to which the object of one's love prospers, to this degree one is 'pleased and delighted.' The question may then be raised: Do those in lower positions of glory in heaven actually experience more joy than those in higher positions, since they have greater prosperity outside themselves to behold and therefore enjoy? In typical fashion Edwards anticipates and answers: 'It will be a damp to none of the saints to see them who have higher degree of holiness and likeness to God to be more loved than themselves; for all shall have as much love as they desire, and as great manifestations of love as they can bear; all shall be fully satisfied.' More specifically, 'those who are highest will not only be more beloved by the lower saints for their higher holiness, but they will also have more of a spirit of love to others.' Those in higher stations in heaven will not experience less love, because the very thing that gives them a higher station is their more profound experience of love! While selfishness

---

[12] Kimnach, et al, *Sermons Reader*, 250.

is a pervasive and profoundly subtle motive among even believers, it is non-existent in heaven, hard as this is to imagine. 'Heaven itself, the place of habitation, *is a garden of pleasures*, a heavenly *paradise* fitted in all respects for an abode of heavenly lovers, a place where they may have sweet society and perfect enjoyment of each other's love.'[13] In short, heaven will be perfect bliss because it will be full of love among the saints and their Creator, and this will in no way be diminished by the various degrees of reward experienced.

Two aspects of this sermon call for our attention as we pursue Edwards' understanding of Christian motivation. One has to do with what Edwards *explicitly* preaches and the other with what he says *implicitly*.

MOTIVATION AND THE NEW BIRTH

First, Edwards is speaking to the question of who will enjoy the everlasting paradise of heaven. In so doing he describes the life of the believer in highly relevant terms for our purposes. According to Edwards, believers will be motivated only when they experience a new inner relish for holiness. Christian motivation, Edwards says, is incalculable. In our motivation to obey God, we do not ponder the advantages and disadvantages of our actions, and make a subsequent well-thought-through decision. We do not consider and reconsider. It is immediate. It is a taste of the heart's tongue, not a decision of the mind's rationale. Those who are heaven-bound 'are those who have had a principle or seed of ... love implanted in their hearts in a work of regeneration.' In other words,

> they have been the subjects of a new birth; they have been born of the Spirit. A glorious work of the Spirit of God has been wrought in their hearts, renewing their

---

[13] Ibid, 250, 251, 257. Emphasis original.

hearts, as it were, by bringing down some of that light, and some of that holy pure flame, which is in the world of love, and giving it place in them. Their hearts are a soil in which this heavenly seed has been sown and in which it abides. And so they are changed, and of earthly are become heavenly in their dispositions. The love of the world is mortified, and the love of God implanted.[14]

Christians, then, are those who have undergone a divine operation by the heavenly Surgeon ('a glorious work of the Spirit of God') and have had new 'principles' wrought in their souls in a lasting way ('[the heavenly seed] abides'). In the above quote we find the first reference to a vital concept in this study: *regeneration*, or being born again, the act of God which inaugurates the new inner relish and which Marsden rightly defines through Edwards' eyes as 'to be given eyes to see the light of Christ in hearts that had been hopelessly darkened by sin.'[15]

Listen to how Edwards continues to explain that Christians are those who have a new sense of taste that has been awakened, a 'relish' for holiness leading to obedience.

---

[14] Ibid, 262.

[15] Marsden, *Edwards*, 55. Sam Storms gives another, broader definition of regeneration, without specific reference to Edwards, calling it 'a radical and spiritually pervasive transformation in which [one's] mind, heart, indeed [one's] entire personality has been renewed by the Spirit of God' (*Chosen for Life: The Case for Divine Election* [Wheaton: Crossway, 2007], 150). R.C. Sproul calls regeneration 'the new genesis' (*The Mystery of the Holy Spirit* [Wheaton: Tyndale House, 1990], 91). Charles Hodge, the father of the Princeton School of Reformed Theology, defines regeneration as 'a new life communicated to the soul; the man is the subject of a new birth; he receives a new nature or new heart, and becomes a new creature. As the change is neither in the substance nor in the mere exercises of the soul, it is in those immanent dispositions, principles, tastes, or habits which underlie all conscious exercises, and determine the character of the man and of all his acts' (*Systematic Theology* [Grand Rapids: Eerdmans, 1946], 3:33). Conversion can be understood as the same event from the human perspective, though it logically follows regeneration (See Anthony A. Hoekema, *Saved by Grace* [Grand Rapids: Eerdmans, 1989], 106-107).

Believers 'are those who have freely chosen that happiness which is to be had in the exercise and enjoyment of such love as is in heaven above all other conceivable happiness. They see and understand so much of this as to know that this is the best good.' For the regenerate, God does not force obedience against the will; rather it is the very will itself that is changed. Edwards continues his description of Christians:

> They do not merely assent that it is so from rational arguments which may be offered for it, but they have seen that it is so; they know it is so from what little they have tasted. It is the happiness of love, and the happiness of a life of such love, heavenly love, holy and humble and divine love; love to God, and love to Christ, and love to saints for God's and Christ's sake, and the enjoyment of the fruits of God's love, holy communion with God and Christ and with holy persons.[16]

A key concept which will resound all through this study is the statement that believers are not drawn to heavenly love 'from rational arguments which may be offered for it.' Rather, it has been seen and tasted. Edwards elaborates on what it means to taste this heavenly love, explaining that such an experience is not at odds with the will but is in fact what the will now desires and enjoys. 'This is what they have a relish for. They feel within them such a nature that such a happiness suits their disposition and relish and appetite above all others; not only above what they have, but above all that they can conceive they might have.... Their souls go out after it more than any other, and their hearts are more in pursuit of it than any other.' In other words, the selfless love that characterizes believers in heaven (perfectly) and on earth (imperfectly) is not the fruit of ordered logic.

---

[16] Kimnach, et al, *Sermons Reader*, 262.

Believers obey because it is what they 'relish.' It is their new inclination. They love to love! They 'are those who from that love which is in them are in heart and in practice struggling after holiness. Holy love makes them long for holiness. Divine love is a principle, which thirsts after [increase].'[17]

'PAINTING A PLEASING PICTURE'

We cannot, however, end our discussion of this sermon yet. For this is why, on the one hand, Edwards is difficult to nail down as exhorting Christian behavior with specific logical motivation, while on the other hand one frequently comes to the end of reading his sermons with a keen awareness of wanting to honor God in daily living. And here we arrive at the second observation to be made. There is an implicit element in Edwards' preaching that complements the explicit. Edwards arouses motivation toward obedience by portraying the human predicament and the divine solution so vividly, with such detail, and in such colorful language, while remaining thoroughly biblical, that one cannot help but be moved to obey the Lord who has made Himself and heaven available to poor sinners such as us![18] This is why another sermon is described as 'painting a pleasing picture of the joys of heaven.'[19] In 'Heaven Is a World of Love,' too, Edwards depicts the pleasures of a chocolate bar rather than analyzing the ingredients. He illustrates the lavish, unending delights of heaven instead of simply

---

[17] Ibid, 263.

[18] Consider Edwards' imaginative use of the English language in this typical utterance: 'In another world (heaven) ... all the saints enjoy each other's love in glory and prosperity in comparison with which the wealth and honor of the greatest earthly princes is sordid beggary' (Kimnach, et al, *Sermons* 256).

[19] Jonathan Edwards, *The Works of Jonathan Edwards*, vol. 14, *Sermons and Discourses, 1723–1729*, ed. Kenneth P. Minkema (New Haven: Yale University Press, 1997), 279. The sermon so described is 'The Spiritual Blessings of the Gospel Represented by a Feast.'

saying *that* it will be nice. He is showing his hearers *why* to believe, rather than just telling them *to* believe. The appeal is not only to our heads but to our hearts, and we taste the spiritual sweetness which Edwards persistently shows to be the only pathway to change and holiness.

In other words, Edwards motivates indirectly as well as directly. Instead of whipping the donkey, he holds an apple out in front of it. Instead of coming right out and exhorting his listeners in a forthright manner to pursue holiness (just because they should?), he paints an irresistibly winsome portrait of holiness. In doing so, he motivates his people on to holiness more effectively than he ever could by bland imperative. He is like the father who, striving to induce his children to do their homework, exults in the glories of learning (and the dissatisfying results of neglect) and does not say a word of imperative-driven instruction.

This sermon is a prime example of Edwards moving his listeners to change and greater obedience by sketching a portrait of the beauty of obedience rather than by bald exhortation. Edwards spends the greater part of 'Heaven Is a World of Love' painting a verbal picture of a heaven so wonderful that one comes to the end longing to experience such a place. Heavenly virtue is shown to be supersaturated with beauty and joy, and the spiritual taste buds of the reader increasingly salivate as the sermon progresses. By the time Edwards comes to what he calls his 'application,' therefore, one hardly needs it but perhaps for a little guidance. If you doubt what I'm saying, read the sermon! The pump of our hearts is so thoroughly primed that we are keenly aware of our desire for heaven and the perfect love, and absence of sadness, jealousy, or any other evil, that is to be found there. So it is with full justification that he encourages Christians toward the end of his discourse, as he begins the exhortation of the sermon, 'Let the consideration of what has been said of heaven stir you up earnestly to seek after it. If heaven be such a blessed world, then let this be our chosen country, and the inheritance we seek. Let us turn our course this way.' He then states quite simply:

> Let what we have heard of the land of love excite us all to turn our faces towards that land, and bend our course thitherward. Is not what we have heard of the happy state of that country and the many delights which are in it enough to make us thirst after it, and to cause us with the greatest earnestness and steadfastness of resolution to press towards, and to spend our whole lives in traveling in the way which leads thither?[20]

And so we see in this sermon two important truths for Edwards regarding motivation. First, God must grant a 'relish' for obedience if it is going to take place. Complementing this truth, secondly, Edwards attempts to paint a picture of heaven that is so attractive that the listener is stirred up to pursue obedient love for the sake of experiencing the glories and joys of heaven. This is not the only time we will see Edwards holding together both divine sovereignty and pastoral responsibility in motivation.

In this sermon we have laid the foundation for what follows in this book. Yet does Edwards also implement rational motivations, such as the three discussed in chapter one? In other words, how did he go about 'painting a pleasing picture' of holiness? In search of an answer we turn to a 1741 sermon on generosity.

'MUCH IN DEEDS OF CHARITY'

The doctrine of this sermon, based on Cornelius' vision in Acts 10:4-6, states that 'to be much in deeds of charity is the way to have spiritual discoveries.'[21] Practical obedience is

---

[20] Kimnach, et al, *Sermons Reader*, 267, 268.
[21] Ibid, 198.

clearly implied in the title of the sermon, making it a fitting choice for a study on motivation for obedience. We can expect to find certain ways in which Edwards attempts to motivate his people to be 'much in deeds of charity.'

The obedience in this sermon is specifically in the context of material generosity and giving to the poor, referred to at several junctures by Edwards as 'second table duties.' The sermon begins by stating two observations from Acts 10. First, Cornelius has certain 'duties' to which God is calling him. That is, Cornelius is being called to *obedience*. Secondly, says Edwards, the passage lays out specific 'benefits' to the faithful completion of these duties. That is, Cornelius is being given *motivation*.[22]

'SPIRITUAL DISCOVERIES'

Edwards makes three basic points of doctrine before applying the message. First, Christians ought to be charitable. Second, two elements confirm charity to be a valid avenue 'to obtain spiritual discoveries': the promises and the providence of God.[23] Third, he explains how exactly charitable giving connects with these 'spiritual discoveries.' By 'spiritual discoveries' Edwards is referring to the further realizations and enjoyments of God which flow from an authentic relationship with God in Christ.

At the outset, then, Edwards is laying before his people the incentive of spiritual discoveries as the *reward* of a charitable lifestyle. He is motivating his people by showing them the personal gain to be experienced by such a pattern

---

[22] Kimnach, et al, *Sermons Reader*, 198. By 'second table duties' Edwards refers to those Christian obligations which are indirectly offered to God by being directly offered to man. A 'first table duty' is a duty offered directly to God, such as prayer (Cf. Kimnach, et al, *Sermons Reader*, 197-98, 209). These designations are taken from the Ten Commandments, in which the first four refer to one's duty to God ('first table') and the last six to one's duty to man ('second table').

[23] Ibid, 198.

of living. Edwards prompts his people on toward greater generosity, not only by naked exhortation that it ought to be done, but by setting forth incentive to do it. That incentive is 'spiritual discoveries.'

Arriving at the body of the sermon, Edwards then explains (while commenting on a passage containing bountiful promises to his people, Isa. 58:7-11) that while personal profit is not the only reason to obey God, it is a valid motivation. Referring to Isaiah 58, he remarks that 'In the eighth verse 'tis promised that if we deliver bread to the hungry, etc., that our light shall "break forth as the morning." ' He explains the appropriate motivational role of such potential gain: 'Though receiving spiritual light and gracious discoveries of God's glory and mercy to the soul be not the only thing there is intended, yet it is not to be excluded, but without doubt is a principal thing by which such a promise is fulfilled.'[24]

Motivated by a Vested Interest

This is a key theme in Edwards to which we will return. Edwards has said that it is perfectly legitimate – because it is perfectly biblical – to allow oneself (and even to seek) to be motivated because of one's vested interest inextricably linked to the obedience commanded. Our existence will be a happier one if we obey. At the same time, and very importantly, Edwards says this cannot stand alone; these kinds of reasons to obey 'be not the only thing intended'. As we will continue to see, Edwards believes that on the subject of Christian motivation the gain experienced in obedience is incomplete apart from something more, something that resides not essentially in the results of the commands but in the one who commands; there is a motivation that comes

---

[24] Ibid, 199. The context of this quote is specifically an explanation of Isaiah 58:7-11, all of which Edwards reproduces in the sermon as he shows, as mentioned above, the *promises* God makes in Scripture.

simply by virtue of the worthiness of the one calling for the obedience. The reality of God and the weight of His glory beckon a certain response, quite independent of the truth that there is also good incentive for doing so.[25]

Edwards continues to urge his people toward generous giving by further explaining that these spiritual discoveries are not dry and dull but joy-filled. Joy is part of the spiritual discovery that takes place in the hearts of believers when they are submissive to God's call to charitable giving. 'Living in deeds of love ... is the way to have spiritual joy, as appears by John 15:11-12, "These things have I spoken unto you, that my joy might remain in you, and that your joy might be full. This is my commandment, That ye love one another, as I have loved you." '[26] To pursue holiness is to pursue joy. Because the desire to be happy is a universal human trait, Edwards knows he is on persuasive ground when he opens up the incentive of joy to his people.

Edwards further shows that, whereas it is material blessing that we give away to those who need it (as Cornelius did), it is spiritual blessing that we reap as a result of our obedience (as Cornelius experienced): 'When we give to others earthly good things, God will reward us with heavenly good things.... If we will feed Christ[27] with the food

[25] As an example of Edwards having a strong sense that believers simply have a duty to obey, consider this example, plucked from many such statements: 'The way in which God has directed us to seek him is the way of attending on all commanded duties. It is not only to read and to pray and to go to meeting and to meditate, but is to attend all the duties which God has required of us, both towards God and towards our neighbor' (Kimnach, et al, *Sermons Reader*, 203).

[26] Ibid, 200.

[27] By 'Christ' Edwards refers to those who stand in need today. Earlier in the sermon he has explained that 'though we can't be charitable to Christ in person as [Mary and Martha and Lazarus] were, because he is not here, nor does he now stand in need, yet we may be charitable to Christ now as well as then. For though Christ is not here, he has left others in his room to be his receivers, and they are the poor, and has told us that he shall look upon

of our houses, even outward food, Christ will reward us by feeding us with the food of his house, which is spiritual food.' Material seed sowed results in spiritual crops reaped. Edwards continues, 'As we receive all spiritual things from Christ or depend upon Him for all we hope for, we should be ready to give Him our carnal things; otherwise, how justly might he for the time to come withhold spiritual things from us.'[28] Here he is arguing the same thing in negative form. Instead of 'Obedience brings spiritual blessings,' Edwards is saying, 'Disobedience forfeits spiritual blessings.' The point is clear: If you are faithful in obedience and pour out your life by giving to those in need, God will 'richly reward you in his own time.'

MOTIVATED BY THANKFULNESS

Are there, however, other motivational categories on Edwards' lips as he seeks to cultivate generosity among his people? Edwards switches gears as he enters into the heart of the application of his sermon to show his people that *grateful* hearts are not only appropriate but vital to authentic Christian giving. Speaking of material generosity, Edwards comments, 'This would show our thankfulness to God for the blessings we have already received. What does it signify to pretend to be thankful and yet to neglect our second table duties?' We give because we are thankful. So gratitude does indeed play a role. Earlier he said, 'Let godly persons be hence exhorted to abound in deeds of charity. They who are the subject of so much of the free mercy and kindness of God are above all persons obliged to this duty.'[29] A past-looking gratitude at the magnanimous generosity of God presents motivation to obey Him. We are charitable

---

what is done to them as done to him' (Kimnach, et al, *Sermons* 202). See Matt. 25:31-46.

[28] Ibid, 206.

[29] Ibid, 207, 209, 211. In the context, the 'duty' here mentioned is alms-giving.

because we have been the subjects of God's 'free mercy and kindness.'

A New Character

This leads to the present motivation of the newfound identity of the truly regenerate believer: the grace of God leads us to give generously because to do so is simply to act in accordance with our new character. To call oneself a Christian and yet be stingy with one's resources is not consonant with one's Christian identity. Says Edwards concerning material giving, 'if they neglect it, [they] will in a peculiar manner act beside their character.'[30] A new character has been given in conversion, and to lay up treasures on earth is contrary to this new identity.

In 'Much in Deeds of Charity,' then, we see that the rewards of assurance and joy (future), gratitude for mercy received (past), and a new identity (present) all play a role in spurring hearts on to hold their financial resources loosely.

'THE DUTY OF CHARITY TO THE POOR'

This is also true of 'The Duty of Charity to the Poor,' preached in 1733 and based on Deuteronomy 15:7-11. The doctrine of this sermon was: ''Tis the most absolute and indispensable duty of a people of God to give bountifully and willingly for the supply of the wants of the needy.'[31]

Looking With Gratitude at What Christ Has Done

Eighty percent of the sermon is application, and it is here that we focus our attention, noting first the motivation of gratitude. Because of Christ's tremendous gift of death in our stead on the cross, the Christian therefore gladly obeys the precepts of the Lord. Remarking on the injunction of

---

[30] Ibid, 209
[31] *Sermons and Discourses, 1730–1733*, 373.

John 13:34 that Christians love one another, Edwards says that 'We must not only love our neighbor as ourselves, but as Christ hath loved us. We have the same again [in] John 15:12, "This is my commandment, That ye love one another, as I have loved you."' We then read a particularly clear expression of the motivation of gratitude.

> Christ has loved us so as to be willing to deny himself and to suffer greatly for our help, so should we be willing to deny ourselves, and to suffer greatly to help others. Christ loved us, and showed us great kindness, though we were far below him; so should we be willing to love others, and show them kindness, though they be below us. Christ denied himself to help us, though we are not able to recompense him; so we should be willing to lay out ourselves to help our neighbor freely, expecting nothing again. Christ loved us, and was kind to us, and was willing to relieve us, though we were very hateful persons, of an evil disposition, not deserving any good, but deserving only to be hated, and treated with indignation; so we should be willing to be kind to those that are an ill sort of person, of a hateful disposition, and that are very undeserving. Christ loved us, and laid himself out to relieve us, though we were his enemies, hated him, had an ill spirit towards him, and treated him ill; so, as we would love Christ as he hath loved us, should we love those who are our enemies, hate us, have an ill spirit toward us, and have treated us ill.

Lest we be concerned that Edwards is here speaking only of following the *example* of Christ and not necessarily of obeying out of gratitude, I point out that Edwards goes on to clarify that he is indeed speaking of 'a grateful and thankful disposition.'[32] Here then is a clear statement that because of

---

[32] Ibid, 396-397.

Christ's remarkable work of mercy on our behalf, we ought to be gratefully motivated to act likewise to those around us.

YOU ARE NOT YOUR OWN
Edwards also makes use of the Christian's newfound identity as a motive by which to prompt his people to be generous in giving material goods and money to the poor.

> First [Motive]. Consider that what you have is not your own, i.e. you have no absolute right to it, have only a subordinate right. Your goods are only lent to you of God to be improved by you in such ways as God directs you. You yourselves are not your own; 1 Cor. 6:19-20, 'Ye are not your own, for ye are bought with a price; your body and your spirit are his.'

He continues, 'You have by covenant given up yourself and all you have to God; you have disclaimed and renounced any right in your self, as in anything you have, and given God all the absolute right.'[33] In becoming a disciple of Jesus Christ, one is brought from a place of having one's identity wrapped up in material things to having one's identity wrapped up in Christ. This is a motive, says Edwards, to obey God by fulfilling our 'duty of charity to the poor.'

THE PROMISE OF REWARD
Yet personal interest also drives Christians on in faithful giving of themselves and their goods to those in greater need. 'If you give what you bestow with a spirit of true charity, you shall be rewarded in what is infinitely more valuable than what you give. For parting with a small part of your earthly substance, you shall be rewarded with eternal riches in heaven.' He continues:

[33] Ibid, 379.

If you give to the needy only in the exercise of a moral virtue, you won't be in the way to lose by it, but greatly to gain in your temporal interest. They that give in the exercise of a gracious charity, they are in the way to be gainers both here and hereafter; and those that give, in the exercise of a moral bounty and liberality, they have many temporal promises made to them.

Edwards later adds: 'God has threatened to follow them with his curse that are uncharitable to the poor; as Prov. 28:27, "He that giveth to the poor shall not lack: but he that hideth his eyes shall have many a curse." '[34] Christians are to survey the long-term results of their obedience and reflect on how God has promised to bless those who give freely of what God has given them. It goes better for those who are generous. It goes worse for those who are not. The motive of personal interest is clearly evident. Who does not want to be, to use his word, a 'gainer'?

This sermon, like the last one, employs the past-looking motivation of thankfulness, the present-looking motivation of a new, blood-bought identity, and the future-looking motivation of personal benefit as we pursue the rewards that accompany obedience and avoid the curses concomitant with disobedience.

'A Divine and Supernatural Light'

Revival came to Northampton Church in 1734, inaugurating almost two full years of divinely poured-out blessing half a decade before the Great Awakening swept more broadly across the Atlantic. In August of the previous year Jonathan Edwards preached what has rightfully become one of his most well-known sermons, 'A Divine and Supernatural Light.' Based on Matthew 16:17, the following doctrine

[34] Ibid, 384, 386.

was the thrust of the message: 'There is such a thing, as a spiritual and divine light, immediately imparted to the soul by God, of a different nature from any that is obtained by natural means.'[35] 'No sermon,' according to one Edwards scholar, 'contains more of the essential Edwards.'[36]

In this sermon we continue to crystallize our understanding of Edwards' perspective on true Christian motivation. Specifically, obedience and the motivation that drives it come as one is changed from the inside out, not from the outside in. The latter is legalism. Edwards preached rather that God must Himself change us in a fundamental way, and this in turn will 'dispose' or 'incline' us – motivate us – to obey Him. God 'must bestow the Holy Spirit by his own sovereign initiative before individuals can have a right perception of him.'[37]

The sermon is broken into thirds. The first part delineates what exactly this 'divine light' is. The second argues that this divine light is 'given immediately by God, and not obtained by natural means.' The third section attempts to 'show the truth of the doctrine.'

The central idea of the sermon is that conversion is not primarily intellectual assent to a new set of beliefs regarding God. Conversion is rather the event in which this Being who created the universe causes His light to shine into a human heart. God gives a glorious and utterly new perspective on

---

[35] *Sermons and Discourses, 1730–1733*, 123. Full title: 'A Divine and Supernatural Light, Immediately Imparted to the Soul by the Spirit of God, Shown to Be Both a Scriptural and Rational Doctrine' (406). A sermon from a decade earlier that 'anticipates in nearly every respect *A Divine and Supernatural Light*' is 'A Spiritual Understanding of Divine Things Denied to the Unregenerate' (*Sermons and Discourses, 1723–1729*, 67). The doctrine of the significance of regeneration and its implications for motivation is present in Edwards from early on, as this sermon from the early 1720s demonstrates (70-96). 'Profitable Hearers of the Word,' from late 1728 or early 1729, contains similar themes (246-277).

[36] Simonson, *Theologian of the Heart*, 37.

[37] *Sermons and Discourses, 1730–1733*, 405.

life in which the individual sees the excellencies and glory
of God in Christ and is brought to gladly love and cherish
Him. One of the reasons for the power of the sermon is
the metaphorical skill Edwards employs throughout. He
describes this new perspective by using analogies such as
a new 'light' being given to an otherwise darkened soul. A
'new sense' has been given to the convert that is similar to
the sense of taste experiencing the sweetness of honey on
the tongue, using the same metaphor the psalmist had used
in prayer centuries before: 'How sweet are your words to
my taste, sweeter than honey to my mouth!' (Ps. 119:103).

Two Kinds of Knowledge
Edwards begins by arguing that knowledge of God is the
goal of Christianity, and this includes not only (as the
Rationalists of the day mistakenly overemphasized) a
knowledge of propositional truth but also (as the Enthusiasts
mistakenly overemphasized) a felt knowledge of the heart.
Discussing the phrase 'divine light' as it is found in the title
of the sermon, Edwards explains:

> There is a twofold understanding or knowledge of good,
> that God has made the mind of man capable of. The first,
> that which is merely speculative or notional: as when a
> person only speculatively judges, that anything which by
> the agreement of mankind, is called good or excellent,
> viz. that which is most to the general advantage, and
> between which and a reward there is a suitableness;
> and the like. And the other is that which consists in
> the sense of the heart:[38] as when there is a sense of

[38] Simonson memorably writes of the 'sense of the heart' in this way:
'Edwards was a Christian thinker, and the adjective makes all the difference.
He wrote from within the full sense of the heart. His faith was like a grand
cathedral. Standing outside, one sees no glory, nor can possibly imagine
any; standing within, every ray of light reveals a harmony of unspeakable
splendors' (*Theologian of the Heart*, 32).

the beauty, amiableness, or sweetness of a thing; so that the heart is sensible of pleasure and delight in the presence of the idea of it.

'In the former,' Edwards further explains, 'is exercised merely the speculative faculty, or the understanding strictly so-called, or as spoken of in distinction from the will or disposition of the soul. In the latter the will, or inclination, or heart, are mainly concerned.'[39]

So we can know God in a 'merely speculative' way or we can know Him with 'the will, or inclination, or heart.' In the first we consent to the fact that something is beautiful. In the second we *feel* its beauty. This is central to Edwards' understanding of human experience, and we as the Church today do well to hear him lest we mistake the former kind of knowing for the latter and rest content with a faith in which truths about Christ replace love for Christ.

NEW TASTE BUDS, NEW EYES

This truth about two levels of knowing God is then illustrated in two ways: first using the sense of taste, and second using the sense of sight. Regarding the first he says:

> Thus there is a difference between having an opinion that God is holy and gracious, and having a sense of the loveliness and beauty of that holiness and grace. There is a difference between having a rational judgment that honey is sweet, and having a sense of its sweetness. A man may have the former, that knows not how honey tastes; but a man can't have the latter, unless he has an idea of the taste of honey in his mind.

---

[39] Kimnach, et al, *Sermons Reader*, 127. For Edwards, the 'will' and the 'heart' are often interchangeable. Marsden notes this: 'The will, or one's inclinations or loves, might be called the 'heart' of the whole person' (Marsden, *Edwards*, 285). Simonson has written extensively on Edwards' two kinds of knowledge. 'The distinction,' he sums up at one point, 'is between a determining intuitive knowledge and a rational or speculative knowledge' (*Theologian of the Heart*, 27).

He continues on with the second analogy, moving from the metaphor of taste to that of sight:

> So there is a difference between believing that a person is beautiful, and having a sense of his beauty. The former may be obtained by hearsay, but the latter only by seeing the countenance. There is a wide difference between mere speculative, rational judging anything to be excellent, and having a sense of its sweetness, and beauty. The former rests only in the head, speculation only is concerned in it; but the heart is concerned in the latter.[40]

There is a knowledge of God which, while seen *through* objective fact, goes well *beyond* objective fact. It is the kind of knowledge which was needed to keep 'the Gentiles who do not *know God*' from sexual immorality (1 Thess. 4:5). There is a knowledge of God that remains at a cold, safe distance; and there is a knowledge which sees doctrine not as an end in itself but a means to enjoy God.[41] And while God uses truth to inflame the heart, there is no logical process of reasoning necessary for the recipient of such enjoyment of the divine flavor.

In a sermon preached five years after 'A Divine and Supernatural Light,' Edwards further elucidates the difference between the two species of knowledge:

> There are two kinds of knowledge of the things of divinity, viz. *speculative* and *practical*, or in other terms, *natural* and *spiritual*. The former remains only in the head.

---

[40] Ibid, 127-28.

[41] See also Miscellanies 489, 540, and 628-30. The former is found in Jonathan Edwards, *The Works of Jonathan Edwards*, vol. 13, *The 'Miscellanies' Entry Nos. a-z, aa-zz, 1-500*, ed. Thomas A. Schafer (New Haven: Yale University Press, 1994), 533. The latter four are in Jonathan Edwards, *The Works of Jonathan Edwards*, vol. 18, *The 'Miscellanies' Entry Nos. 501-832*, ed. Ava Chamberlain (New Haven: Yale University Press, 2000), 88. The 'Miscellanies' were Edwards' running list of personal theological reflections.

No other faculty but the understanding is concerned in it. It consists in having a natural or rational knowledge of the things of religion, or such a knowledge as is to be obtained by the natural exercise of our own faculties, without any special illumination of the Spirit of God. The latter rests not entirely in the head, or in the speculative ideas of things; but the heart is concerned in it: it principally consists in the sense of the heart. The mere intellect, without the heart, the will or the inclination, is not the seat of it. And it may not only be called seeing, but feeling or tasting.[42]

ONE STEP, NOT TWO

William Wainwright explains that the beauty of God, to 'a spiritual person,' is a 'perception ... as immediate and direct as a perception of color or the sweetness of food.' In other words, 'only one step is involved.'[43] When the Holy Spirit fuels motivation by granting a new relish for God, the tongue of the heart tastes the doctrine simmering in the head as the feast it truly is. Like a meal taken out of the freezer and placed in the warm oven to melt into a tasty dinner, the otherwise cold doctrine of the head is meant to be swallowed down into the heart to be fed upon and enjoyed.

---

[42] From 'The Importance and Advantage of a Thorough Knowledge of Divine Truth' (Kimnach, et al, *Sermons Reader*, 30).

[43] William Wainwright, 'Jonathan Edwards and the Sense of the Heart,' *Faith and Philosophy* 7 (1990): 51. Wainwright later continues: 'the inference on which one's belief is based doesn't involve a long or complicated chain of reasoning, and is as spontaneous and compelling as our (alleged) inference to other minds or the reality of the physical world' (52). See also an analysis of Edwards' understanding of the 'sense of the heart' in Sean Michael Lucas, 'What Is the Nature of True Religion?' *Religious Affections* and Its American Puritan Context,' in *All for Jesus: A Celebration of the 50th Anniversary of Covenant Theological Seminary,* Robert A. Peterson and Sean Michael Lucas (Fearn, Scotland: Christian Focus, 2006), 117-38, especially 129-31. The discussion of the new sense comes in the context of Lucas' argument that Edwards is better understood against the backdrop of earlier American Puritanism than that of Lockean metaphysics.

While Edwards does go on to describe the pleasure to be found in such tasty living, he explains that this pleasure is itself the result of a God-given inner relish: 'When the heart is sensible of the beauty and amiableness of a thing, it necessarily feels pleasure in the apprehension. It is implied in a person's being heartily sensible of the loveliness of a thing, that the idea of it is sweet and pleasant to his soul; which is a far different thing from having a rational opinion that it is excellent.'[44]

What Edwards is saying here is vital for a proper understanding of how he viewed motivation in the life of the Christian. His point in this sermon is that objective, factual, information-based head knowledge is, to be sure, vitally necessary for true Christian living and experience. It cannot be ignored. Without, it one is certainly headed for destruction. *Yet it is utterly inadequate of itself to bring about change resulting in authentic obedience.* Christian faith that consists only of facts and not of enjoyment of these facts is not Christian faith. The divine light is an utterly new pleasure in God. It is a matter of the affections, which today we would probably call the 'emotions,' though we must be discerning as we do so. Edwards is not talking about mustering up warm fuzzy feelings inside us or sweaty palms and relying on these as evidences of a new and saving light being given us by God. He calls such things 'animal spirits.' They are merely the result of chemical processes taking place in the body. One may drink a few beers and feel affection toward God (or anything), but this is no proof of a work of the Spirit! Edwards points out that someone might be moved to tears by a well-told story of a Jew who lived centuries ago and was unjustly killed by the state, but unless supernatural light is given to the person, the story will make no lasting difference.

---

[44] Kimnach, et al, *Sermons Reader*, 128.

Authentic saving faith, then, is a gift of God in which one not only reads of the beauty of Christ but also sees Christ's beauty with one's own eyes. This gift is the impartation of a holistic knowledge: one that includes both the understanding of the mind and the sense of the heart. Yet how exactly does this truth pertain to motivation? 'This light is such as effectually influences the inclination, and changes the nature of the soul. It assimilates the human nature to the divine nature, and changes the soul into an image of the same glory that is beheld.' This new kind of knowledge

> conforms the heart to the gospel, mortifies its enmity and opposition against the scheme of salvation therein revealed: it causes the heart to embrace the joyful tidings, and entirely to adhere to, and acquiesce in the revelation of Christ as our Savior: it causes the whole soul to accord and symphonize with it, admitting it with entire credit and respect, cleaving to it with full inclination and affection. And it effectually disposes the soul to give up itself entirely to Christ.[45]

In salvation God brings sin addicts to be drawn toward godliness rather than to be repelled by it. There is a radical one hundred eighty-degree turn in the life of every true saint, and this turn is possible only because God Himself has acted.

NATURAL OBEDIENCE

But this is not all. And here we come to the crux of the importance of this sermon. Notice the language Edwards uses to describe the results of this divinely-given grace. In the above quote we see that God gives Christians a new 'inclination.' What does that mean? Edwards says it

---

[45] Ibid, 139-140.

is what 'disposes the soul to give itself entirely to Christ.' Obedience then naturally follows. In other words, only a divinely-wrought, inward change truly and lastingly motivates rebels to lay down their arms in glad obedience. God grants a new inclination.

Edwards goes on to make what we are saying even more explicit. In the last paragraph of the sermon Edwards ends (as he typically did) on a note of how his words impact daily life: 'This light, and this only, has its fruit in an universal holiness of life. No merely notional or speculative understanding of the doctrines of religion, will ever bring to this. But this light, as it reaches the bottom of the heart, and changes the nature, so it will effectually dispose to an universal obedience.' The reason for this, moreover, lies ultimately not in the new inclination but in the object of one's new inclination. The new light is motivating because it draws back the curtain of the heart. God is seen. 'It shows God's worthiness to be obeyed and served. It draws forth the heart in a sincere love to God, which is the only principle of a true, gracious and universal obedience.'[46]

Summary

We have touched on a representative sample of Edwards' sermons to cull some of his mind on Christian motivation. 'A Farewell Sermon' makes it clear that Edwards conscientiously sought to motivate his people. 'Heaven Is a World of Love' touches on the need for a new inner relish, yet at the same time Edwards lays before his people the joys of heaven, prompting them more indirectly to pursue heavenly love here and now. In 'Much in Deeds of Charity' and 'Duty of Charity to the Poor' we find Edwards making ample use of all three categories of motivation (past, present, and future) as he strives to propel his people toward practical

---

[46] Ibid, 140.

obedience in Christian living. And we reflected longest on 'A Divine and Supernatural Light,' in which we found the clearest explanation of Edwards' understanding of the foundation of true obedience as being a God-given relish.

Many more sermons could be discussed. Yet none would replace what one Edwards scholar calls a 'dominant theme'[47]: namely, the only motivation that will effectually propel toward holy living is that which is from God Himself and which changes from the inside out. The heart is transformed.

To the two most relevant treatises expressing this idea we now turn.

---

[47] Editor's introduction to *Sermons and Discourses, 1730–1733*, 4.

The first effect of the power of God in the heart in regeneration, is to give the heart a Divine taste or sense; to cause it to have a relish of the loveliness and sweetness of the supreme excellency of the Divine nature; and indeed this is all the immediate effect of the Divine Power that there is, this is all the Spirit of God needs to do, in order to a production of all good effects in the soul.

Jonathan Edwards,
A Treatise on Grace

3

MOTIVATION IN EDWARDS (2): TREATISES

RELIGIOUS AFFECTIONS

A Treatise Concerning Religious Affections in many ways sums up the very heart of Edwards' contribution to Christendom. The major themes of *The Distinguishing Marks of a Work of the Spirit of God*, *A Narrative of Surprising Conversions*, *Thoughts Concerning the Present Revival*, and *A Treatise on Grace* are subsumed within this great work second in profundity perhaps only to *Freedom of the Will*. *Religious Affections* is an attempt to get at the core of authentic Christianity, a core just beginning to experience the heart-chilling anesthetic of the impending movement later labeled the Enlightenment. In seeking to make sense of what he believed to be God-sent revival in the 1730s and 40s, Edwards asserts that a faith consisting only of 'enlightened' knowledge without an accompanying experience of the heart – in a word, 'affections' – is not Christianity.

In this 1746 work Edwards sets out to answer the question, What is authentic Christianity? How can it be distinguished from hypocrisy? How do we know if we are truly born again, or are just playing games with God? What are the signs which indicate whether one's profession of faith is truly heaven-sent or not? Boiled down into one short sentence, Edwards' point is that 'true religion, in great part, consists in holy affections.'[1] Divided into three sections, the first and shortest argues that 'affections' – that is, the engagement of the heart in religious experience as opposed to mere intellectual assent – is not only permissible but integral in saving faith. The second part delineates what are *not* necessarily signs of regeneration, such as great confidence, bodily effects, tears, felt zeal, or copious discharge of one's moral duty. Such apparent signs of holiness may exist without authentic Christian faith. Complementing the second, the third section is the engine of the book as it explains the twelve sure marks that one *has* been savingly wrought upon by the Spirit of God. Several of these marks will be addressed in what follows.

THE LEGITIMACY OF OBJECTIVE MOTIVATIONS

Edwards does write in *Religious Affections* of rational motivations in the life of the Christian. For example, he is speaking to the motivation of gratitude when he says, discussing the inevitability of this humbling effect of true grace: 'Grace and the love of God in the most eminent saints in this world, is truly very little in comparison of what it ought to be. Because the highest love, that ever any attain to in this life, is poor, cold, exceeding low, and not worthy to be named in comparison of what our obligations appear to be.' Even the most fervent love for God is far below what it ought to be. He then gives two reasons for this:

1. The reason God has given us to love him, in the manifestations he has made of his infinite glory, in his Word, and in his works; and particularly in the gospel of his Son, and what he has done for sinful man by him.

---

[1] Jonathan Edwards, *The Works of Jonathan Edwards*, vol. 2, *Religious Affections*, ed. John E. Smith (New Haven: Yale University Press, 1959), 95.

2. The capacity there is in the soul of man, by those intellectual faculties which God has given it, of seeing and understanding these reasons, which God has given us to love him. How small indeed is the love of the most eminent saint on earth, in comparison of what these things jointly considered do require![2]

According to Edwards, the regenerate have more than enough 1) reason to love God and 2) capacity to love God. Edwards' point here, as he labors to show that 'humiliation' is one of the signs of true regeneration, is to communicate that though believers have much reason and much capacity to love God, they do not. The point we note here pertaining to Christian motivation is simply that there is abundant reason to love God due to 'the manifestations he has made of his infinite glory, in his word and works; and particularly in the gospel of his Son, and what he has done for sinful man by him.' This is the motivation of gratitude. We ought to love and obey God because of the great saving work offered to us all.

THE PRIMACY OF AWAKENED TASTE BUDS

Yet this is not the critical point of *Religious Affections*. Rather, behind and beneath these more logically communicated reasons to obey is the foundation for obedience: unless the Holy Spirit is working in the heart, energizing obedience by giving a new spiritual taste, none of the motivations of chapter one will provide an effectual impetus toward obedience. Let us go to Edwards for his own words before returning to explain in what way he goes underneath these motivations.

The second of the twelve signs of truly gracious affections is that one is drawn to 'the transcendently excellent and amiable nature of divine things, as they are in themselves;

---

[2] Ibid, 325.

and not any conceived relation they bear to self, or self-interest.' In the context Edwards is pointing out that while one may have true affections for God which are a result of the benefit that one receives by them, yet authentic affections are those which are primarily based on the intrinsic beauty of God – the 'supremely excellent nature of divine things.'[3] In other words, *gratitude is not enough*. The love a person feels for God is an immediate experience. The believer does not first calculate all that God has done in the past and then act in response to careful consideration of such things, despite the quite real power of such truths. While believers must certainly make a regular habit out of preaching the gospel to themselves and reviewing God's mercies, and supremely the cross of Christ, the very ability to do this effectively is a fruit of something deeper. Fundamentally, obedience is the fruit of seeing God. Affections and obedience naturally follow a divinely-given vision of the moral beauty of God.

The point is that there is no such thing as any kind of true affection for God which has not first experienced the breathtaking reality of the love and glory of God in Christ. After one has been forgiven and regenerated and united with Christ, *then* one sees the power of gratitude, the incentive of adoption, the motivation of profit. Notice Edwards' order of events:

> Something else, entirely distinct from self-love, might be the cause of [love to God], viz. a change made in the views of his mind, and relish of his heart; whereby he apprehends a beauty, glory, and supreme good, in God's nature, as it is in itself. This may be the thing that first draws his heart to him, and causes his heart to be united to him, prior to all considerations of his own interest or happiness, although after this, and as a fruit of it, he necessarily seeks his interest and happiness in God.[4]

---

[3] Ibid, 240.
[4] Ibid, 241.

What Edwards is saying here is critical for rightly understanding saving faith, yet we rarely hear it among Christian leaders today. His point is that saving love for God is not the result of seeing the benefits of the gospel: moral acquittal before God, freedom from hell, and so on. Saving love for God is the result of seeing *God*. It follows from seeing God's majesty 'as it is in itself.' Certainly seeing the vested interest in the gospel will follow! But this is not ultimate.

Also, underlying Edwards' statements here is the implicit belief in the utter sovereignty of God in bringing a human soul to faith in Christ. Humans have a role to play (repentance), and God has a role to play (regeneration). Yet for Edwards it is fundamentally all one supernatural act of God. This is important to keep before us as we pursue Edwards' theology of motivation in *Religious Affections*, because the sovereignty of God is the hinge on which the whole discussion turns. The reason a believer is motivated in a pure and holy manner toward greater godliness is because of divine initiative. It is a short step, then, to note the residual effect for the topic at hand: all motivation to obey God is a direct result of his sovereign hand at work in a human heart that is thoroughly self-absorbed apart from imported grace.

In other words, in regeneration God fundamentally changes the human heart. He turns a light on. He flips a permanent switch. He gives a new set of taste buds by which to taste that which is delicious, a pair of glasses by which to see that which is truly beautiful. In short, he unites us to Christ in such a radically life-altering way that we are instinctively drawn toward something different than that to which we were drawn before. We now have a divinely-implanted distaste for sin, which once held us captive by its beauty; we are now repelled by such sin and drawn to the things of God. This is the miracle of conversion. We, as Christians, did not convert ourselves. Even less can we view conversion as a mere alteration in the set of religious beliefs to which we mentally assent. Rather, though we actively exercise our minds in choosing Christ, fundamentally it was God who converted us. The result? We now have totally different motivations. The sun rises on a horizon hitherto captivated only by self and a new day dawns, a day lived in the light of the interests and goals of God. The soul has been reworked so that life is no longer a perpetual scramble for self-assertion. A new figure has arisen on the scene: Jesus Christ, the Creator-Redeemer. The saint, who has been called out of sin and self-absorption into God's glorious light, suddenly – though it gradually increases throughout this life and never happens perfectly until glorification – finds himself driven by a new desire and motivation: the resplendent glory of God.

THE INSUFFICIENCY OF RATIONAL DEDUCTION

Returning once more to Edwards, the third sign of authentic religious experience is that 'those affections that are truly holy, are primarily founded on the loveliness of the moral excellency of divine things.' Here Edwards is arguing that true grace is a love of the *moral* perfections of 'divine things' and not their *natural* beauty. In a single sentence Edwards writes:

> Such a difference is there between true saints and natural men: natural men have no sense of the goodness and excellency of holy things; at least for their holiness; they have no taste of that kind of good; and so may be said not to know that divine good, or not to see it; it is wholly hid from them: but the saints, by the mighty power of God, have it discovered to them: they have that supernatural, most noble and divine sense given them, by which they perceive it: and it is this that captivates their hearts, and delights them above all things; 'tis the most amiable and

sweet thing to the heart of a true saint, that is to be found in heaven or earth; that which above all others attracts and engages his soul; and that wherein, above all things, he places his happiness, and which he lots upon for solace and entertainment to his mind, in this world, and full satisfaction and blessedness in another.[5]

In other words, 'natural' (unsaved) people might see and wonder at God's power or other natural perfections, but only true saints go beyond this to revel in His moral perfection. By the grace of God, only Christians can love the holiness of God, and indeed it is imperative that they do so lest they prove their alleged faith false. One editor goes so far as to deny that a person who has caught a sight of God is obeying primarily out of the desire for personal benefit: 'the underlying principle of the third sign is thus made to stand out most clearly; those affections are not spiritual that are determined by the individual's concern for his welfare; the proper determining ground is the apprehension of the divine holiness as something good in itself.'[6]

Once God effectually works the saving miracle in a human heart, that person is 'captivated' and subsequently 'delights' in holiness. Obedience, to the soul savingly wrought upon, is not a matter of applying a logical series of deductions to the mind; rather, the true saint delights in obeying God as it is naturally 'that which ... attracts and engages his soul.'

The fourth sign sheds particular insight on motivation: 'Gracious affections do arise from the mind's being enlightened, rightly and spiritually to understand or apprehend divine things.' Edwards explains that this 'spiritual understanding does not consist in any new doctrinal knowledge, or in having suggested to the mind any new proposition, not

---

[5] Ibid, 253, 262.
[6] Editor's introduction to *Religious Affections*, 30.

before read or heard of: for 'tis plain that this suggesting of new propositions, is a thing entirely diverse from giving the mind a new taste or relish of beauty and sweetness.' This fourth sign suggests true Christianity is an engagement not only of the head but of the heart. This is why he goes on to explain that the Spirit leads in two ways: on the one hand, by 'instructing' (the head); on the other hand, by 'inducing' (the heart). In his words, 'as to a gracious leading of the Spirit, it consists in two things; partly in *instructing* a person in his duty by the Spirit, and partly in powerfully *inducing* him to comply with that instruction.'[7] By compliance with instruction Edwards is referring to Christian obedience. And he is saying that while the Spirit does indeed teach us rock-solid, objective truth, He also acts upon the will by fueling the heart. The former objective kind of knowledge is achievable by anyone. The latter heart-knowledge is only experienced by those who have been born again of God's Spirit; indeed, it is what it means to be saved.

GOING TO THE ROOT: 'A RECTIFIED PALATE'
Obedience comes not only by knowing what to do but by being enabled (by wanting) to do it. The solution to motivational lethargy is not the accrual of more facts but having one's heart sensitized to the beauty to be seen and delight to be felt in holiness. Edwards explains that 'spiritual knowledge primarily consists in a taste or relish of the amiableness and beauty of that which is truly good and holy: this holy relish is a thing that discerns and distinguishes between good and evil, between holy and unholy, without being at the trouble of a train of reasoning.' The wonder-filled awe one feels when standing before Niagara Falls for the first time is not the fruit of rational deduction. It is simply the due response. '[H]e who has a true relish of

---

[7] Ibid, 266, 278, 281. Emphasis original. See also Nichols, *Absolute Sort of Certainty*, 60.

external beauty, knows what is beautiful by looking upon it: he stands in no need of a train of reasoning about the proportion of the features, in order to determine whether that which he sees be a beautiful countenance or no: he needs nothing, but only the glance of his eye.'

Edwards gives examples of this principle in other areas of life, such as music or food. 'He who has a rectified musical ear, knows whether the sound he hears be true harmony: he doesn't need first to be at the trouble of the reasonings of a mathematician, about the proportion of the notes. He that has a rectified palate, knows what is good food, as soon as he tastes it, without the reasoning of a physician about it.' He then makes the connection to spiritual life.

> When a holy and amiable action is suggested to the thoughts of a holy soul; that soul, if in the lively exercise of its spiritual taste, at once sees a beauty in it, and so inclines to it, and closes with it. On the contrary, if an unworthy unholy action be suggested to it, its sanctified eye sees no beauty in it, and is not pleased with it; its sanctified taste relishes no sweetness in it, but on the contrary, it is nauseous to it.[8]

Regeneration is the gift of 'a rectified palate' – what a picture! Taste buds are transformed. That which is good and holy becomes beautiful and attractive. At this point Edwards applies his illustrations involving beautiful music and delicious food to the spiritual reality of obedience:

> Thus a holy person is led by the Spirit, as he is instructed and led by his holy taste, and disposition of heart; whereby, in the lively exercise of grace, he easily distinguishes good and evil, and knows at once, what is a suitable amiable behavior towards God, and towards man, in this case and the other; and judges what is

---

[8] *Religious Affections*, 281-282.

right, as it were spontaneously, and of himself, without a particular deduction, by any other arguments than the beauty that is seen, and goodness that is tasted.[9]

I cannot tell you why I love my wife's chocolate chip cookies. I can tell you the recipe (if she'll let me), but that gives you a very different kind of knowledge of the cookies than if you were to take one, fresh out of the oven, and pop it in your mouth. To be told is different than to taste.

Not New Rules but a New Demeanor

This taste helps explain how a Christian can honor God without finding every decision explicitly laid out in Scripture. 'The saints in ... judging of actions by a spiritual taste, have not a particular recourse to the express rules of God's Word, with respect to every word and action that is before them, the good or evil of which they thus judge of: but yet their taste itself in general, is subject to the rule of God's Word.'[10] When the time comes to choose between a poodle and a retriever, believers are not meant to look up the term 'puppies' in their Bible concordance to find a specific verse of guidance. Rather, God has brought the spirit of Scripture to mesh with the spirit of the saint. The divine law has been written on the heart (Jer. 31:33-34). It is not fundamentally new rules to which a believer looks when making a choice of obeying or disobeying God. A new heart short-circuits this process and shows immediately what it is that God wants – and therefore what the believer himself wants to do.

This in no way demeans the Bible's worth or its value for guidance. Scripture is the main vehicle by which believers hone and cultivate their relish for God, for it is there that God stands out clearest. Nor is this to say that drawing to

---

[9] Ibid, 282.
[10] Ibid, 284.

mind particular Scripture verses when facing temptation is not helpful to fight the temptation. Any Bible-memorizing believer can testify to the effectiveness of deflecting the arrows of the enemy not only with the 'shield of faith' but also the 'sword of the Spirit, which is the word of God' (Eph. 6:16-17). Nevertheless, Edwards is saying here that a particular verse of Scripture will not be able to guide every decision in life with a direct and specific answer. The Bible is not a road atlas. Rather, it teaches us how to drive, saturating us with wisdom for which roads to take. We must have our whole demeanor fueled by a biblical mindset.

For this reason Edwards gives the following explanation of what he means by 'supernatural' as used in the first of the twelve signs.[11] Those who have experienced the invasion of the Spirit find a startling new motivational impulse within them: 'the mind has an entirely new kind of perception or sensation; and here is, as it were, a new spiritual sense that the mind has, or a principle of new kind of perception or spiritual sensation, which is in its whole nature different from any former kinds of sensation of the mind, as tasting is diverse from any of the other senses.' A totally new category of existence has been introduced, unexplainable to those who have not experienced it. The result is that 'something is perceived by a true saint, in the exercise of this new sense of mind, in spiritual and divine things, as entirely diverse from any thing that is perceived in them, by natural men' – and here we find the same word picture as used above in 'A Divine and Supernatural Light' – 'as the sweet taste of honey is diverse from the ideas men get of honey by only looking on it, and feeling of it.'

---

[11] The first sign is: 'Affections that are truly spiritual and gracious, do arise from those influences and operations on the heart, which are *spiritual*, *supernatural*, and *divine*' (Ibid, 197).

Edwards fleshes out the principle behind his illustration:

> So that the spiritual perceptions which a sanctified
> and spiritual person has, are not only diverse from all
> that natural men have, as after the manner that ideas
> or perceptions of the same sense may differ from
> one another, but rather as the ideas and sensations of
> different senses do differ.[12] Hence the work of the Spirit
> of God in regeneration is often in Scripture compared to
> the giving of a new sense, giving eyes to see, and ears
> to hear, unstopping the ears of the deaf, opening the
> eyes of them that were born blind, and turning from
> darkness unto light.

To put it differently, 'this new spiritual sense is not a new
faculty of understanding, but it is a new foundation laid in
the nature of the soul, for a new kind of exercises of the
same faculty of understanding.'[13] The new birth gives a new
sense, in which one's former delights (sin) no longer hold
appeal, and what one once abhorred (holiness) no longer
appears ugly but beautiful. This is the 'new foundation
laid in the nature of the soul.' Hughes Oliphant Old is
right: 'The religious affections are what really motivate
our spiritual lives. This was the great insight of Jonathan
Edwards.'[14]

INSIDE-OUT LIVING

Toward the end of *Religious Affections*, the author sums
up the twelve signs and shows how they lead directly to
Christian practice. Here Edwards returns to the central
thrust of the book: obedience is a natural outflow of God's
saving, energizing, metamorphosizing grace. The tendency

---

[12] In other words, it is a difference not only of degree but of kind. See also
'Concerning Faith,' in *The Works of Jonathan Edwards*, vol. 2, ed. Edward Hickman
(London, 1834), 592. Edinburgh: Banner of Truth Trust, 1974. Reprint.

[13] *Religious Affections*, 206.

[14] Old, *Reading and Preaching of the Scriptures*, 5:258.

of grace in the heart to holy practice, is very direct, and the connection most natural close and necessary. True grace is not an inactive thing; there is nothing in heaven or earth of a more active nature; for 'tis life itself, and the most active kind of life, even spiritual and divine life.' The result is necessarily a fruit-bearing life. "Tis no barren thing; there is nothing in the universe that in its nature has a greater tendency to fruit."[15]

We note well: the relationship between 'grace in the heart' (regeneration) and 'holy practice' (obedience) is 'very direct.' The intimacy between saving grace and obedience could not be closer. For Edwards, a tree is known by its fruit. As he so often does, Edwards uses analogies to explain this vital connection between regeneration and obedience: 'Godliness in the heart has as direct a relation to practice, as a fountain has to a stream, or as the luminous nature of the sun has to beams sent forth, or as life has to breathing, or the beating of the pulse....'[16] One can no more separate obedience from salvation than beams of light from the sun.

Edwards had earlier explained that the Holy Spirit enters the human heart in regeneration such that obedience is now experienced *from the inside out.* 'The Spirit of God is given to the true saints to dwell in them, as his proper lasting abode; and to influence their hearts, as a principle of new nature, or as a divine supernatural spring of life and action. The Scriptures represent the Holy Spirit, not only as moving,

---

[15] *Religious Affections*, 398. Edwards proceeds to reference and quote at length the following passages, each demonstrating the necessary relation between inner grace and outer actions: Eph. 2:10; Titus 2:14; 2 Cor. 5:15; Heb. 9:14; Col. 1:21-22; 1 Pet. 1:18; Luke 1:74-75; Exod. 4:23; John 15:16; Eph. 1:4. He also lists the following passages (without quoting): Exod. 7:16; 8:1, 20; 9:1,13; 10:3; Matt. 3:10; 8:8, 23-30, 38; 21:19, 33-34; Luke 8:6; John 15:1-6, 8; 1 Cor. 3:9; Heb. 6:7-8; Isa. 5:1-8; Cant. (Song of Solomon) 8:11-12; Isa. 27:2-3.

[16] Ibid. To these sentences we will return when discussing the relationship between faith and obedience (see below).

and occasionally influencing the saints, but as dwelling in them as His temple, His proper abode, and everlasting dwelling place.' But the Spirit does not set up residence in a human heart only to take a nap – 'he becomes there a principle or spring of new nature and life.'

> So the saints are said to live by Christ living in them (Gal. 2:20). Christ by his Spirit not only is in them, but lives in them; and so that they live by his life; so is his Spirit united to them, as a principle of life in them; they don't only drink living water, but this living water becomes a well or fountain of water, in the soul, springing up into spiritual and everlasting life (John 4:14), and thus becomes a principle of life in them.[17]

The difference between a mountain village which needs to journey every morning to the stream on the other side of the valley, and the village that has its own well in the town square, is that the first is outside-in and the second is inside-out. One imports water; the other has a never-ending source right in its own midst. Christianity is not a religion of importing obedience in the hope of cultivating a life pleasing to God. It is the living out of something already inside us. It is inside-out, not outside-in. 'Without a change of nature, men's practice will not be thoroughly changed. Until the tree be made good, the fruit will not be good. Men do not gather grapes of thorns, nor figs of thistles.' Rotten trees don't produce healthy fruit. Moving from plants to pigs, Edwards says, 'The swine may be washed, and appear clean for a little while, but yet, without a change of nature, he will still wallow in the mire.'[18]

Washed swine still wallow. They must be changed from the inside out.

---

[17] Ibid, 200.
[18] Ibid, 395.

A TREATISE ON GRACE

In the 1860s the Scotsman Alexander Grossart traveled to Northampton and then Yale University, where Edwards' writings were being held. Here, among several unpublished manuscripts, he discovered one which was neatly stacked and encircled with ribbon – presumably to be sent to the printer for publishing. Edwards had entitled it *A Treatise on Grace*.[19] This thirty-five-page book is in many ways a summary of *Religious Affections* – and according to Harold Simonson, 'Few things that Edwards wrote surpass it in intellectual and rhetorical brilliance.'[20] *A Treatise on Grace* attempts to show that a Christianity which divorces the mind from the heart is no Christianity at all. Salvation is an issue not only of the head but of the heart, and this heart 'taste' is solely a gift of God. After a brief review of this short treatise, we will draw our findings to a conclusion.

The treatise is divided into three chapters. The first is devoted to showing that the common grace which is given to all is different from the saving grace which is given to some, and that this difference lies not only in the degree of grace, but in the very nature of the grace. Second, 'divine love' is the sum of all that is required of us as Christians. What is this divine love? 'As to a definition of Divine Love, things of this nature are not properly capable of a definition. They are better felt than defined.' Edwards, however, does not totally disappoint. Though he calls it indefinable, he makes an attempt at describing it: 'Divine love, as it has God for its subject, may be thus described. 'Tis the soul's relish of the supreme excellency of the Divine nature, inclining

---

[19] This treatise can be found in Alexander B. Grossart, ed., *Selections from the Unpublished Writings of Jonathan Edwards of America* (Ligonier, PA: Soli Deo Gloria, 1992; reprint from 1865), 19-56. Hereafter *Treatise on Grace*.

[20] *Theologian of the Heart*, 142. See Simonson's pertinent comments on this treatise on pp. 142-43.

the heart to God as the chief good.'[21] To this description we will shortly return.

Edwards then goes on in the third chapter to argue that this divine love can only be enjoyed as a benevolent and sovereign gift of God in the person of the indwelling Spirit. All our obedience, says Edwards, can be summed up in the Great Commandment of Luke 10:25-28, and this will only happen if God takes our old nature and replaces it with a new one. In other words, motivation flows out of us because of the love that we have for God and (therefore) for mankind, and this love, 'the soul's relish ... inclining the heart to God,' comes to us as a result of God fundamentally changing us. And so Christian obedience is 'the prime and most natural breathing and acting of the Spirit in the soul.'[22]

REFORMATION THROUGH TRANSFORMATION

Let us zero in more closely on this work as it pertains to our study of motivation. *A Treatise on Grace* argues as clearly as any of Edwards' writings that saints are governed by a new principle of delight in which holiness no longer appears ugly but beautiful. This new delight is a direct gift of God by way of the third person of the Trinity: 'those that have not a saving interest in Christ have no degree of that relish and sense of spiritual things or things of the Spirit, of their Divine truth and excellency, which a true saint has.... The reason why natural men have no knowledge of spiritual things is, because they have nothing of the Spirit of God dwelling in them.'[23]

Again, 'ungodly men never had any degree of that holy oil poured upon them, and therefore have no discerning of spiritual things ... they are totally blind.' The godly, however, possess a predisposition toward 'holy inclinations

---

[21] *Treatise on Grace*, 36.
[22] Ibid, 46.
[23] Ibid, 22.

and affections ... from the indwelling of the Spirit of Christ.'[24] True Christianity is not an analysis of reasonable motivations to obey God. It is, rather, the natural outflow of the regenerative work of God in the soul – though this does not ignore, but implements and empowers such reasonable motivations.

Edwards later states that 'saving grace in man is said to be the new man or a new creature, and corrupt nature the old man.' This certainly sounds like the present-looking motivation of identity: the Christian is one who has been made 'a new creature.' Yet his point in this statement is that the work of sanctification – and the motivation and obedience subsumed therein – is wholly a divine work. This is because

> nothing can be produced in the soul by only its internal principles.... Nothing will be produced but only an improvement and new modification of those principles that are exercised. Therefore it follows that saving grace in the heart, can't be produced in man by mere exercise of what perfections he has in him already ... unless there be something more than all this, viz., an immediate infusion or operation of the Divine Being upon the soul.[25]

Moral reformation takes place only through divine transformation.

'THE SWEETNESS OF THE SUPREME EXCELLENCY'
At the heart of *A Treatise on Grace* we come to a portion of Edwards' writings that has been crucial to me in grasping Edwards' theology of motivation. Divine love, he says, can be defined as 'the soul's relish of the supreme excellency of the Divine nature, inclining the heart to God as the chief

---

[24] Ibid, 23.
[25] Ibid, 25, 29.

good. The first thing in Divine love, and that from which everything that appertains to it arises, is a relish of the excellency of the Divine nature; which the soul of man by nature has nothing of.' This gift from above changes everything. 'When once the soul is brought to relish the excellency of the Divine nature, then it will naturally, and of course, incline to God every way. It will incline to be with Him and to enjoy Him. It will have benevolence to God. It will be glad that He is happy. It will incline that He should be glorified, and that His will should be done in all things.'[26]

He continues on in what I believe is the single clearest statement in Edwards' writings of the nature of moral motivation for Christians.

> [T]he first effect of the power of God in the heart in regeneration, is to give the heart a Divine taste or sense; to cause it to have a relish of the loveliness and sweetness of the supreme excellency of the Divine nature; and indeed this is all the immediate effect of the Divine Power that there is, this is all the Spirit of God needs to do, in order to a production of all good effects in the soul. If God, by an immediate act of His, gives the soul a relish of the excellency of His own nature, other things will follow of themselves without any further act of the Divine power than only what is necessary to uphold the nature of the faculties of the soul. He that is once brought to see, or rather to taste, the superlative loveliness of the Divine Being, will need no more to make him long after the enjoyment of God, to make him rejoice in the happiness of God, and to desire that this supremely excellent Being may be pleased and glorified.[27]

---

[26] Ibid, 37.
[27] Ibid.

OBJECTIVE MOTIVATIONS FINALLY IMPOTENT

What then of such rational motivations as we have mentioned elsewhere in this book, such as profit or gratitude? 'And if this be true,' says Edwards, echoing a point we saw in *Religious Affections*, 'then the main ground of true love to God is the excellency of His own nature, and not any benefit we have received, or hope to receive, by His goodness to us.' Yet this does not mean such motivations as gratitude serve no purpose in the life of the Christian – 'there is such a thing as a gracious gratitude to God for mercies bestowed upon us; and the acts and fruits of His goodness to us may be, and very often are, occasions and incitements of the exercise of true love to God.' Acts of obedience may indeed by traced to feelings of thankfulness to God. 'But,' says Edwards,

> love or affection to God, that has no other good than only some benefit received or hoped for from God, is not true love. If it be without any sense of a delight in the absolute excellency of the Divine nature, it has nothing Divine in it. Such gratitude towards God requires no more to be in the soul than that human nature that all men are born with, or at least that human nature well cultivated and improved, or indeed not further vitiated and depraved than it naturally is.[28]

It takes no special grace from God to feel thankful that one is spared from hell. Gratitude for God's gifts is not in itself motivationally sufficient. The benefits of Christian faith are not ultimately enough to stoke the fires of the human heart to obey God. 'It is possible that natural men, without the addition of any further principle than they have by nature, may be affected with gratitude by some remarkable kindness of God to them, as that they should be so affected with some great act of kindness of a neighbor.' In other

---

[28] Ibid, 37-38.

words, 'A principle of self-love is all that is necessary to both. But Divine Love is a principle distinct from self-love.[29]

A vision of the 'excellency' of God calms the need to scramble for incentive to obey God. It is the natural response. This is not to say gratitude plays no role in our obedience. But it is not the fundamental impulse driving us. Personal benefits – and gratitude for them – are certainly 'occasions and incitements of the exercise of true love to God.' However, they are not the core of why one obeys God. If they were, one's fundamental motivation as a Christian would reside in oneself – what Edwards calls 'self-love.'

THE INDWELLING SPIRIT

Rather, one's foundational motivation resides in God Himself in all His beauty. The response of a child's obedience to a father is most authentic when it is driven by who the father is – namely, the child's own loving and magnanimous father! – rather than by the promise of dinner.

As always, Edwards underscores in *A Treatise on Grace* the essential truth that a Christian's relish for God is of the Spirit. Edwards writes that 'grace in the heart ... is no other than the Spirit of God itself dwelling and acting in the heart of a saint.' Because of one's Spirit-wrought union with Christ, one is able to experience the blessings of obedience and the motivation which drives it. 'Herein lies the mystery of the vital union that is between Christ and the soul of a believer, which orthodox Divines speak so much of, Christ's love – that is, His Spirit is actually united to the faculties of their souls.' Edwards concludes on the same note of dependence upon the Holy Spirit for obedient living: obedience in the lives of the saints is only attributable to the 'indwelling and acting of the Spirit of God in their habits.'[30]

---

[29] Ibid, 38.
[30] Ibid, 52, 54, 56.

I find my delight in your commandments which I love.
Psalm 119:47

God, who said, 'Let light shine out of darkness,'
has shone in our hearts to give the light of the knowledge
of the glory of God in the face of Jesus Christ.
The Apostle Paul, 2 Corinthians 4:6

No one who is born of God makes a practice of sinning,
for God's seed abides in him, and he cannot keep on
sinning because he has been born of God.
The Apostle John, 1 John 3:9

Our pleasure and our duty, though opposite before;
Since we have seen his beauty, are joined to part no more:
It is our highest pleasure, no less than duty's call
To love him beyond measure, and serve him with our all.
John Newton
'We Were Once As You Are'

4

SYNTHESIS:
EXPLORING THE KEY INGREDIENT

Gratitude for past mercies, wonder at current adoption, and consideration of future profit all have their motivational place in Jonathan Edwards' writings. Each is implemented. And all are biblical. Yet while we acknowledge the rightfully important place of each of these categories of motivation, none of them successfully motivates heartfelt holiness *apart from the grace of God*. Only by sovereignly imported power does true obedience – obedience from the heart – blossom. This was central to Edwards' theology, and he is right.

THE HEART OF EDWARDS' THEOLOGY OF MOTIVATION

We have seen in Edwards' sermons and works the necessity of divine initiative in human holiness. The point now is to engage this truth with past, present and future categories of motivation to crystallize our findings by recognizing that none of these effectually motivate if God does not fire them with holy energy. No strictly objective incentive, however true and beautiful in its own right, is sufficient if divorced from this vital ingredient.

It is not enough to say God's Spirit is a component of true obedience; obedience is in fact impossible apart from Him. The conclusion to which we have come is this: no moral act, if done in such a way that one relies for motivation *merely* on gratitude, newfound identity, or future blessing, will bring authentic, Spirit-fueled obedience. Conversely, every attempt at obedience guided by the influence of God's Spirit will indubitably succeed, whether or not one consciously looks to gratitude, identity, or future joy and other personal blessings. It matters not what logical motivation is implemented for motivational propulsion. The house will fall at the first storm if the foundation is not laid. Impeccable logic is not enough to overcome human sinfulness. Only God's Spirit is. 'The great kindness and generosity of another,' says Edwards in *Freedom of the Will*, 'may be a motive insufficient to excite gratitude in the person that receives the kindness, through his vile and ungrateful temper: in this case, the insufficiency of the motive arises from the state of the will or inclination of the heart, and don't at all excuse.'[1] Rational deduction cannot be a substitute for God's empowering grace.

The foundational impetus for any true act of obedience lies not in where one looks for motivation, but in whether or not we look – *wherever* we look – with spiritually enlightened eyes. God must 'produce a whole new dimension in human consciousness.'[2] This is not to say God resists rationality in motivation; the Scriptures discussed at the beginning of this book show that all three categories are commended by the writers of Scripture. God does indeed lay before us reasonable, sensible reasons for obeying Him, a point with which Edwards has been seen to agree. Such reasons include what God has done at the cross, our new identity as God's children, and the blessings that await us as we walk faithfully with Him. But glorious as these are they remain essentially hollow – in themselves, they provide no power

---

[1] Jonathan Edwards, *The Works of Jonathan Edwards*, vol. 1, *Freedom of the Will*, ed. Paul Ramsey (New Haven: Yale University Press, 1957), 310.

[2] Clyde A. Holbrook, *The Ethics of Jonathan Edwards: Morality and Aesthetics* (Ann Arbor, MI: University of Michigan Press, 1973), 23.

to be 'obedient *from the heart*' (Rom. 6:17). There is no power inherent in these truths to stimulate righteous living. God must give 'a new ability and disposition.'[3] Reflecting on the Northampton revival of 1734–5, Edwards states that 'conversion is a great change, wherein old things are done away, and all things become new.'[4]

In his treatise defending the historic orthodox understanding of original sin, one of the central arguments Edwards offers as proof of universal human depravity is just this. Throughout history even the Jews, God's privileged people, have persistently rejected holiness despite abundant objective motivation: 'the Jews, though so vastly distinguished with advantages, means and motives to holiness, yet are represented as coming, from time to time, to that degree of corruption and guilt, that they were more wicked, in the sight of God, than the very worst of the heathen.' In the face of such profuse 'motives to virtue and obedience' presented to the Jews, 'the generality of that people ... were men of a wicked character.'[5] Original sin is evidenced in that despite abundance of objective motivation to trust and obey God, we all still require divine renovation of the heart. We need a new, God-given relish.

MOTIVATED FROM FIRST TO LAST
For Edwards, moreover, what is true in conversion remains true throughout sanctification – we are utterly

---

[3] From the 1740 sermon 'They Sing a New Song,' based on Rev. 14:3, (*The Works of Jonathan Edwards*, vol. 22, *Sermons and Discourses, 1739–1742*, ed. Harry S. Stout and Nathan O. Hatch with Kyle P. Farley [New Haven: Yale University Press, 2003], 232).

[4] From *A Narrative of Surprising Conversions*, in *The Works of Jonathan Edwards*, vol. 4, *The Great Awakening*, ed. C. C. Goen (New Haven: Yale University Press, 1972), 178.

[5] *The Works of Jonathan Edwards*, vol. 3, *Original Sin*, ed. Clyde A. Holbrook (New Haven: Yale University Press, 1970), 181, 177. See also Simonson, *Theologian of the Heart*, 119.

dependent on the grace of God. A 'divine taste' is 'given *and maintained* by the Spirit of God, in the hearts of the saints.'[6] The Christian gospel is no soteriological Deism, in which God regenerates and then leaves us to fend for ourselves. The Spirit is perpetually active in the regenerate heart. No one can snatch a regenerate person out of Jesus' hand (John 10:28-29). For this reason one writer says that for Edwards, 'the progressive state of sanctification is no less dependent upon the full and immediate operation and will of God than in regeneration.'[7] Grace comes first (negatively) as forgiveness for sin, but continues in the life of the believer (positively) as fuel for sanctification (Rom. 5:20–6:23). Grace provides both pardon and power. Just as the heart transplant will not occur without the Divine Surgeon at work (Ezek. 36:26-27[8]), so too obedience comes

---

[6] *Religious Affections*, 283. Emphasis mine. What I refer to as (here and in what follows) as *conversion* I regard as the same instantaneous event as regeneration, the latter speaking of this great event from God's perspective, the former from the human's perspective. What I refer to as sanctification is the holiness that is progressive throughout life (2 Cor. 7:1; 1 Thess. 4:7; 1 Tim. 2:15; Heb. 12:14), not that which is ours instantaneously at the moment of regeneration (1 Cor. 1:30; 6:11; Col. 3:12; 2 Tim. 1:9; 1 Pet. 2:9; Rev. 20:6). Nevertheless, while these two aspects of sanctification are distinct they are inseparable; Rev. 22:11, e.g. joins them explicitly: 'Let ... the holy [those who have been definitively sanctified] still be holy [work out that sanctification].'

[7] John J. Bombaro, 'Jonathan Edwards's Vision of Salvation,' *Westminster Theological Journal* 65 (2003): 55. Spurgeon told the students in his Pastor's College that it must never 'be forgotten that the flesh is weak and naturally inclined to slumber. We need a constant renewal of the divine impulse which first started us in the way of service. We are not as arrows, which find their way to the target by the sole agency of the force with which they started from the bow; nor as birds, which bear within themselves their own motive power: we must be borne onward, like ships at sea, by the constant power of the heavenly wind, or we shall make no headway' (C. H. Spurgeon, *Lectures to My Students* [Grand Rapids: Zondervan, 1954], 312).

[8] On these verses and their connection with new motivation see Francis Turretin, *Institutes of Elenctic Theology, Vol. 2: Eleventh Through Seventeenth Topics*, trans. George Musgrave Giger, ed. James T. Dennison, Jr. (Phillipsburg, NJ: Presbyterian & Reformed, 1994), 551.

wholly by God's active enabling. Regeneration is a divine gift; so is motivation. And this gift of regeneration *is itself* the granting of a new[9] inner relish.

DEAD PEOPLE CANNOT RESURRECT THEMSELVES

We should not be surprised at the remarkable change inherent in conversion in light of Scripture's statements describing the human condition apart from God's grace. Paul reminded the Ephesian believers of their former state by describing them as

> you who were dead in the trespasses and sins in which you once walked, following the course of this world, following the prince of the power of the air, the spirit that is now at work in the sons of disobedience – among whom we all once lived in the passions of our flesh, carrying out the desires of the body and the mind, and were by nature children of wrath, like the rest of mankind (Eph. 2:1-3).

The change wrought in the granting of a new inner relish is so thorough and drastic that it is here described as being brought from death to life. To the Romans the Apostle wrote that 'the mind that is set on the flesh is hostile to God, for it does not submit to God's law; indeed, it cannot. Those who are in the flesh cannot please God' (Rom. 8:7-8). This is why regeneration, for Edwards, is

---

[9] The adjective 'new' is central to Edwards' theology and to the purpose of this book. A Christian is one who is, at the core, *new*. Here is a typical statement on Christian newness, drawn from Edwards' *Narrative of Surprising Conversions*, describing converts in the wake of the local revival of 1734–5: 'Persons after their conversion often speak of things of religion as seeming new to them; that preaching is a new thing ... that the Bible is a new book: they find there new chapters, new psalms, new histories, because they see them in a new light' (*The Great Awakening*, 181). In 'They Sing a New Song,' Edwards uses the word 'new' 141 times in the body of the sermon (*Sermons and Discourses, 1739–1742*, 227-44).

the point at which God awakens one's spiritual taste buds such that the mind lays down its hostility to God. God does not (1) justify, (2) begin progressive sanctification, and then (3) develop the new inner relish as some subsequent element of progressive sanctification. Rather, the moment of regeneration is naturally accompanied with a new inclination. This is not to deny growth and the cultivation of this inclination. Nonetheless, new desires are what it *means* to be regenerated. David Clyde Jones describes the human problem and the divine solution by explaining that the 'radical disinclination to godliness must be overcome for moral goodness to ensue. The good news is that God's grace in salvation uproots the hostility of the heart toward God and implants a new disposition of affection for him.'[10]

THE HEART OF THE MATTER

Jonathan Edwards will not fall neatly into one of the three categories of motivation outlined at the beginning of this book. He refuses to do so.

Edwards has gone beneath the problem of motivational dearth to the root. And he has there discovered that nothing external to a human being will invigorate obedience. Only a divinely initiated – though humanly sought! – internal change will effect heartfelt obedience. And this change is the furnishing of a new taste, a new sense, a new inclination, a new relish. It is not the cultivation of something already latent in the heart. This is contrary to the teaching of the famous nineteenth-century evangelist Charles Finney, who wrote of regeneration that 'the sinner has all the faculties and natural attributes requisite to render perfect obedience to God. All he needs is to be induced to use these powers and attributes as he ought.'[11] In the new birth, according to

---

[10] *Biblical Christian Ethics* (Grand Rapids: Baker, 1994), 38. Hafemann writes that 'having had their eyes opened to God's glory, believers have had the desires of their hearts changed' (*God of Promise*, 170).

Edwards' quite different view, God imports a new impulse for holiness that is foreign to anything naturally present. We sinners do not need to be straightened out. We need to be made new.

Nor is this new taste the warm fuzzy feelings that are experienced by both regenerate and unregenerate people – 'animal spirits.' A spiritually dead man may be emotionally moved by the story of a Jewish carpenter unjustly executed, but this is not the new inner relish. Though Edwards' new inner relish includes the emotions, 'the new sense is not simply an emotional reaction. Rather ... it is the overpowering of the self by the divine reality.'[12] *We are in need of motivational metamorphosis.*

The conclusion, then, is yes, motivate yourself by viewing the great price God paid on Calvary and obey the Lord out of loving gratitude – yes, motivate yourself by seeing the overwhelming victory won for you which has changed your fundamental identity, making you a son or a daughter of God – yes, motivate yourself by pursuing your greatest joy in the promises of God! May we never belittle such glorious truths. But we must do all of these in the God-honoring knowledge that if that motivation successfully prevents sin or fuels righteousness, this is attributable only to the active mercy of God. God's grace is wholly responsible, since 'holiness, both in principle and fruit, is from God.'[13] It was

---

[11] Charles Grandison Finney, *Lectures on Systematic Theology* (2 vols.; Longwood, FL: Xulon, 2003), 1:546. Reprint. For a solid engagement with Finney from an Edwardsean perspective see Iain H. Murray, *Pentecost – Today? The Biblical Basis for Understanding Revival* (Edinburgh: Banner of Truth Trust, 1998), 33-53; also, Murray's *Revival and Revivalism: The Making and Marring of American Evangelicalism: 1750–1858* (Edinburgh: Banner of Truth Trust, 1994), 223-98.

[12] Nichols, *Absolute Sort of Certainty*, 53. See also J. I. Packer, *A Quest for Godliness: The Puritan Vision of the Christian Life* (Wheaton: Crossway, 1990), 310-12.

[13] *Works*, ed. Hickman, 2:553. 'All moral good is from God,' Edwards later reiterates (557).

not conjured up by one's own logic or careful analysis or self-wrought emotion (though these be vehicles God employs). It was the gift of a new inner relish. The three categories of motivation outlined in this book are powerful but ultimately impotent in themselves apart from grace. Edwards wrote in his *Miscellanies*:

> The soul of man is determined [...] by an object without, and a quality within: the object is propounded with all its qualifications, that the understanding may be informed and convinced, and the will and affections persuaded in a potent and high way of reasoning: but this is not enough to determine man's heart without an internal quality or grace infused, which is his physical work upon the soul. There is not only a propounding of reasons and arguments, but a powerful inclination of heart.'[14]

The three categories of gratitude, identity, and benefit, therefore, are candles not yet lit. The materials are all present – wick, wax, and oxygen – but the candle remains both dark and cold until something other than the candle acts to light it. A flame must be given, a flame that the candle is incapable of producing on its own. Unless a relish for holiness ignites these three (or any other) motivations, none of them will produce authentic obedience. Twentieth-century Dutch theologian Louis Berkhof explains that only the Holy Spirit, and not doctrinal truth in itself (such as the objective motivations discussed in this book), is the efficient cause of regeneration and the desires which accompany it: 'The truth can be a motive to holiness only if it is loved, while the natural man does not love the truth, but hates it' (Rom. 1:18, 25). Consequently, the truth, presented

---

[14] Jonathan Edwards, *The Works of Jonathan Edwards*, vol. 23, *The 'Miscellanies' Entry Nos. 1153-1360*, ed. Douglas A. Sweeney (New Haven: Yale University Press, 2004), 71-72.

externally, cannot be the efficient cause of regeneration.'[15] In 'The Way of Holiness' in 1722, a nineteen-year-old Edwards preaches that to be a Christian is necessarily concomitant with the pursuit of holiness. 'Holiness is the image of God, his likeness, in him that is holy.' It is 'a doing as he doth: in acting holily and justly and wisely and mercifully, like him. It must become natural thus to be, and thus to act; it must be the constant inclination and new nature of the soul.'[16]

OBJECTIVE MOTIVATION NEGATED?

Here we run up against a problem, however. For is not (for example) gratitude a legitimate motivation? Does not the Bible call believers to be grateful? Of course! But a thankful heart is itself the effect of the new inner relish. It is not itself able to stimulate obedience. Gratitude is not a cause but an effect. 'True gratitude or thankfulness to God for his kindness to us,' says Edwards in *Religious Affections*, 'arises from a foundation laid before, of love to God for what he is in himself.' He goes on to say that the 'gracious stirrings of grateful affection to God, for kindness received, always are from a stock of love already in the heart, established in the first place on other grounds, viz., God's own excellency.'[17]

Thankfulness that we are avoiding hell is not the deepest spring of obedience. 'Self-love is not excluded from a gracious gratitude,' says Edwards. 'The saints love God for his kindness to them: Ps. 116:1, 'I love the LORD, because he hath heard the voice of my supplication.' But something else is included; and another love prepares the way, and lays the foundation for these grateful affections.'[18] Gratitude is absolutely critical to healthy Christian living. A thankless

---

[15] Louis Berkhof, *Systematic Theology* (Edinburgh: Banner of Truth Trust, 1958), 473.

[16] Kimnach, et al, *Sermons Reader*, 5.

[17] *Religious Affections*, 247. See also Nichols, *Absolute Sort of Certainty*, 29.

[18] *Religious Affections*, 248.

Christian is a contradiction in terms. But gratitude is itself the result of something deeper: 'another love prepares the way, and lays the foundation' for such gratitude. This is a relish for God himself wrought in regeneration.

CHRISTIANITY = MOTIVATION

For Edwards, then, to *be* a Christian is to *be* motivated. Duty and delight are not separate avenues of motivation for the Christian, because in regeneration one's duty *becomes* one's delight. In his hymn 'Love Constrained to Obedience,' John Newton writes:

> To see the law by Christ fulfilled,
> And hear his pard'ning voice,
> Changes a slave into a child,
> And duty into choice.[19]

This is why the Bible says 'everyone who practices righteousness has been born of him' and that 'his commandments are not burdensome' (1 John 2:29; 5:3). And it is why Edwards believes that for the regenerate, 'Nothing short of perfect holiness will satisfy the appetite and craving of their souls.'[20] Part of the package of God showing mercy to a hapless human soul by breathing new life into him, removing the heart of stone and replacing it with a heart of flesh, and giving the Holy Spirit as a permanent gift, is the presence of new desires. Motivation is necessarily implied in becoming a Christian. Edwards calls it a new 'inclination,' a new 'taste,' a new 'relish.' All refer to one thing: a regenerate heart is attracted to holiness rather than repelled by it. John wrote, 'We know that everyone who has been born of God does not keep on sinning' (1 John 5:18).[21]

---

[19] *The Works of The Rev. John Newton, Vol. 2* (New Haven: Nathan Whiting, 1826), 590.

[20] *Sermons and Discourses, 1734–1738*, 684.

[21] George Eldon Ladd comments that 'by the new birth and the implanting of the divine seed, John clearly means something more than a

And so it is not so much that God grants 'a sixth sense,'[22] but rather, as Stephen Nichols puts it, 'Edwards' notion of the new sense ... is not a sixth sense, but a complete overhaul of the self, resulting in a new creation.'[23] In his treatise on *Original Sin*, Edwards argues for universal human depravity by citing the pictures the Bible uses to describe redemption. He says that a person 'can never have any interest in Christ, or see the kingdom of God, unless he be the subject of that change in the temper and disposition of his heart, which is made in repentance, and conversion.' Edwards then lists some of the biblical pictures of this great change: 'circumcision of heart, spiritual baptism, dying to sin and rising to a new and holy life; ... he has the old heart taken away, and a new heart and spirit given.'[24]

We noted earlier how Edwards describes two kinds of knowing God, an external knowledge and an internal knowledge.[25] He reiterates the point in *Charity and Its Fruits*, here connecting this distinction explicitly to obedience, or 'practical knowledge' of 'the excellency of holiness':

A true knowledge of God and divine things is a practical knowledge. As to a speculative knowledge of things of religion, there are some wicked men who have attained to great measures of it. Men may be men of vast learning, and their learning may consist very much in their knowledge in divinity, their knowledge of the Scripture,

---

new relationship. It means that a new dynamic, a new power, has entered the human personality, which is reflected in a change of conduct' (*A Theology of the New Testament*, rev. ed, Donald A. Hagner, ed. [Grand Rapids: Eerdmans, 1993], 664). He had earlier stated (specifically regarding 1 John 3:9) that 'one who is born again cannot continue to live in sin because a new principle of life has been implanted in him or her. There *must* be an obvious change in conduct' (663). Edwards would concur.

[22] Marsden, *Edwards*, 96.
[23] Nichols, *Guided Tour*, 120. Cf. Gal. 6:15.
[24] *Original Sin*, 370.
[25] See discussion of 'A Divine and Supernatural Light' above.

and other things appertaining to religion, and they may
be able to reason very strongly about the attributes and
works of God, and doctrines of Christianity; but herein
their knowledge fails of being a saving knowledge, that
it is only a speculative and not a practical knowledge.
He who has a right and saving acquaintance with divine
things sees the excellency of holiness, and of all the
ways of holiness, for he sees the beauty and excellency
of God which consist in his holiness.[26]

Notice the recurring metaphor of 'seeing.' God gives new
eyes to see true 'beauty and excellency.' This sight is the
supernatural light that accompanies regeneration, and
is the same reality Edwards elsewhere describes as the
implantation of new desires within the heart.

THREE KINDS OF MEN

Such new desires are precisely what C. S. Lewis is talking
about in two of the most profound pages I have ever read,
pages dealing directly with motivation. In a short essay
called 'Three Kinds of Men,' Lewis writes this:

There are three kinds of people in the world. The first
class is of those who live simply for their own sake and
pleasure, regarding Man and Nature as so much raw
material to be cut up into whatever shape may serve
them. In the second class are those who acknowledge
some other claim upon them – the will of God, the
categorical imperative, or the good of society – and

---

[26] *The Works of Jonathan Edwards*, vol. 8, *Ethical Writings*, ed. Paul Ramsey
(New Haven: Yale University Press, 1989), 296. Nichols notes in *Religious
Affections* the same distinction between the logical knowledge of the head
and the motivating knowledge of the heart: '[I]f one has notional knowledge,
then one knows the propositions of the gospel or has a knowledge of God and
Christ's work and sin, much as one knows a phone number or today's date. If,
however, one has a spiritual knowledge of the gospel, then one is inclined to
it, relishes it, and sees it in all of its beauty, harmony, and excellency' (*Guided
Tour*, 113-114).

honestly try to pursue their own interests no further than this claim will allow. They try to surrender to the higher claim as much as it demands, like men paying a tax, but hope, like other taxpayers, that what is left over will be enough for them to live on. Their life is divided, like a soldier's or a schoolboy's life, into time 'on parade' and 'off parade', 'in school' and 'out of school'.

So far, then, we have two groups of people, both of whom regard obedience as contrary to what will truly make them happy, despite the fact that outwardly they look vastly different, as they each respond to this conviction in opposite ways – the first by disobeying, the second by obeying. Yet both find God's will at odds with their own. And neither achieves the kind of life offered in Christ. Neither describes someone 'obedient from the heart' (Rom. 6:17). Lewis continues:

> But the third class is of those who can say like St Paul that for them 'to live is Christ'. These people have got rid of the tiresome business of adjusting the rival claims of Self and God by the simple expedient of rejecting the claims of Self altogether. The old egoistic will has been turned round, reconditioned, and made into a new thing. The will of Christ no longer limits theirs; it is theirs. All their time, in belonging to Him, belongs also to them, for they are His.

> And because there are three classes, any merely twofold division of the world into good and bad is disastrous. It overlooks the fact that the members of the second class (to which most of us belong) are always and necessarily unhappy. The tax which moral conscience levies on our desires does not in fact leave us enough to live on. As long as we are in this class we must either feel guilt because we have not paid the tax or penury because we have. The Christian doctrine that there is

no 'salvation' by works done to the moral law is a fact of daily experience. Back or on we must go. But there is no going on simply by our own efforts. If the new Self, the new Will, does not come at His own good pleasure to be born in us, we cannot produce Him synthetically.[27]

There are three kinds of people, not two, says Lewis, because there are two kinds of disobedience, not one. There is a disobedience that *disobeys* and there is a disobedience that *obeys*. Both dishonor God and rely on oneself for happiness. But while one is obvious, the other we are normally blind to. In other words, every human being is in one of three motivational camps:

1. Not wanting to obey, therefore disobeying
2. Not wanting to obey, yet usually obeying (most of us are here)
3. *Wanting* to obey

A truly motivated Christian is not one who pays his dues to God by attending church, tithing, and denouncing the cultural taboos of the day. A true Christian is one whose desires have been turned inside out in such a way that instead of self's desires fighting against God's, the two have become one. Hear Lewis again: 'The old egoistic will has been turned round, reconditioned, and made into a new thing. The will of Christ no longer limits theirs; *it is theirs*.' He therefore closes the essay by saying, 'The price of Christ is something, in a way, much easier than moral effort – it is to want Him.'[28]

The fundamental distinction among people is not between those who obey God and those who don't. The essential distinction is between those who *want* to obey and those who don't. Some do not want to obey, so they don't. Some do not want to obey, yet, driven by guilt, they do – knowing

[27] C. S. Lewis, *Present Concerns* (London: Fount, 1986), 21-22.
[28] Ibid.

they ought to. *Others, driven by delight, want to obey.* This is authentic obedience. Joy-driven service. It is to possess a new inner relish.

The Heidelberg Catechism, written in Germany in 1563, asks in its ninetieth question, 'What is the coming-to-life of the new self?' Lewis and Edwards would approve of the answer: 'It is wholehearted joy in God through Christ and a delight to do every kind of good as God wants us to.'[29]

ADDICTED TO GOD

In 1694 the Puritan John Howe (1630–1705), who died in England when Edwards was two years old, preached a series of thirteen sermons on regeneration. Howe explains that regeneration 'will diffuse a mighty and efficacious influence through the whole soul,' that it is 'a great vital spring in the heart, that sets all the wheels in motion, and acteth every faculty and power,' and that 'its great effect is, that the will is proportionably framed, inclined, bowed, made to comply, according to this discovery and revelation that is made of so great and glorious an object' as Christ. He then says:

> You see by this what a Christian is. And all will agree (no doubt) in the common notion, a Christian is one that believeth that Jesus is the Christ. But you see who are reckoned to believe to this purpose, such as are born thereupon another sort of creatures from what they were, and so continue as long as they live: and such as are heaven born, born of God by immediate divine operation and influence, a mighty power from God coming upon their souls, conforming them to God, addicting them to God, uniting them with God, making them to centre in God, taking them off from all this world.[30]

---

[29] *Ecumenical Creeds and Reformed Confessions* (Grand Rapids: CRC, 1988), 54.

[30] Edmund Calamy, ed., *The Works of the Rev. John Howe*, (London: William Ball, 1838), 891, 896. See the appendix for fuller statements by Howe on the new inner relish wrought in regeneration.

To come to believe in Christ, says Howe, is to be born of God. To believe 'that Jesus is the Christ' is not to be given a hell-avoiding fire insurance policy only to go on living as before. It is to be fundamentally changed at the core of one's being and will, a change so comprehensive that it is likened to physical birth. Does this involve rescue from Hell? Oh yes! – but it also involves experiencing the first glimmers of Heaven here on earth (Rom. 8:23). One's entire person is awakened to ultimate reality with the smelling salts of divine beauty. It is to be addicted, says Howe, to God.

PETRI DISH DOCTRINE?

This addiction to God, this relish for holiness, is precisely the difference between believers and unbelievers. Non-Christians may understand the gospel with their head to much the same degree as believers. The trouble is not inability to *understand* the concept that God came to earth and died in place of bad people. The trouble is inability to embrace and love and cherish this truth – indeed, to love the person of God himself. According to Scripture, in fact, we need not limit this to the human realm: demons, too, can understand divine things with penetrating insight. James 2:19 tells us that 'Even the demons believe – and shudder!' The devil and his minions would ace the exams given in our best seminaries. Their orthodoxy is impeccable. There is not one heretic among them. In the sermon 'True Grace Distinguished From the Experience of Devils,' Edwards provocatively writes: 'The devil is orthodox in his faith; he believes the true scheme of doctrine; he is no Deist, Socinian, Arian, Pelagian, or antinomian; the articles of his faith are all sound, and in them he is thoroughly established.'[31] International awards for 'Best Theologians'

---

[31] *Works*, vol. 2, ed. Hickman, 43. In this 1752 sermon Edwards preaches on the very verse under discussion here – James 2:19 – to explain that

ought to go to the inhabitants of Hell. And if Satan be their pope, infallible he most certainly is. If post-Enlightenment thought is right in attributing pre-eminence to the cognitive over the affective, let's sign up the demons to teach our next *Evangelism Explosion* seminar. Surely they understand the truth of the gospel better than anyone.

But another way exists. For what makes demons fundamentally different from saints? *Saints delight in God; demons gnash their teeth at Him.* Saints strive to promote holiness while demons strive to squelch it. Why? Because demons have not tasted the inner relish for true beauty in holiness that the Holy Spirit has imparted to the regenerate. They have not heeded David's summons to 'taste and see that the LORD is good!' (Ps. 34:8). The theology of the devils is immaculately orthodox, but their failure to *relish* God renders their right doctrine worthless and, ultimately, makes them all the more deserving of God's righteous wrath.[32]

'Nothing in the mind of man, that is of the same nature with what the devils experience, or are the subjects of, is any sure sign of saving grace' (41). He goes on to delineate several aspects of human experience which may seem to belong only to saints, yet which the devils also experience, and which therefore cannot be seen as signs of saving grace among people. See also 'Concerning Faith,' ibid, 594.

[32] Not only can Satan not experience this relish, he cannot grant it. In the 1735 sermon 'False Light and True' (echoing 'A Divine and Supernatural Light' from a year earlier), Edwards says: 'Satan can't give any spiritual discovery. He can't let in divine light into the soul, nor anything indeed like it. He can't give a discovery of the spiritual excellency of Christ and glory of God, and the glory of the way of salvation. The giving of such a discovery is the greatest and most excellent gift that God himself imparts to the minds of men; and therefore, without doubt, is far beyond Satan to give. Satan can't give the spiritual knowledge of God, for he han't it himself; and surely he can't give what he has not' (*Sermons and Discourses, 1734–1738*, 133). Likewise, Edwards points out in *Religious Affections*, 'This [inward witness of the Spirit] the devil cannot imitate' (*Religious Affections*, 233).

The same is true for unbelievers. An unregenerate person, according to Edwards, may have many right ideas about God, and may even be able to explain certain aspects of theology with more penetrating erudition than many of the saints. Nevertheless, it is only the saints of God who long to be more like the object of those theological queries. 'Regeneration,' writes Marsden, 'changed the whole person by changing the love at the heart of the person's being.'[33] Unbelievers are repelled by holiness. Believers are attracted to it. Neither the unerring theology of demons nor the hollow orthodoxy of the unregenerate alleviates their deserved condemnation, because

> there is a difference between having a right speculative notion of the doctrines contained in the Word of God, and having a due sense of them in the heart. In the former consists speculative or natural knowledge of the things of divinity; in the latter consists the spiritual or practical knowledge of them.
>
> Neither of these is intended ... exclusively of the other: but it is intended that we should seek the former in order to the latter. The latter, even a spiritual and practical knowledge of divinity, is of the greatest importance; for a speculative knowledge of it, without a spiritual knowledge, is in vain and to no purpose, but to make our condemnation the greater.[34]

Note that right doctrine is never an end in itself. It is a means. Doxology takes flight on the wings of theology. Knowledge is not the final goal, but an avenue to deeper depths of enjoyment of God. Who ever baked a chocolate cake in order to scrutinize its contents in the laboratory? Cake is not meant for the Petri dish. It exists to be tasted

---

[33] Marsden, *Edwards*, 286.
[34] From 'The Importance and Advantage of a Thorough Knowledge of Divine Truth' (Kimnach, et al, *Sermons Reader*, 30).

and enjoyed – relished! Glorious truth about God that enters the human mind is never meant to stay there. Its appointed destination is the heart, where such truth, where God Himself, is tasted and loved. This emphasis on enjoying God leads one biographer to mistakenly conclude, 'Edwards gave people new ways to approach their spirituality in their everyday lives, a practice based in a subjective, intuitive interpretation of religious experience.'[35] This is mistaken because Edwards did not see doctrinal truth as something to be discarded and replaced with subjective experience. He saw doctrine as what ignites and sustains Christian experience. 'We should seek the former in order to the latter,' says Edwards, not 'we should skip the former to get to the latter.' Christianity, while *thoroughly affective*, is not *exclusively subjective*. Clearly defined theology is foundational to, not smothering of, felt experience.

MOTIVATIONAL METAMORPHOSIS

The difference, then, between authentic Christian obedience and the experience of non-believers takes place at the most fundamental level of the human will. This is why I use the phrase *motivational metamorphosis*, for, as Mark Valeri has rightly put it in explaining Edwards' thought, 'the faculty of moral affection or taste shaped understanding and constituted, in effect, the will.'[36] Truly born-again people do not obey God against their will, summoning themselves to duty against all their desires – though fleshly struggles still plague us: see below – because the very definition of a Christian is one who finds one's will essentially changed such that the desires of the heart delight in, not compete against, the commands of God.[37] Adolf Schlatter (1852–

---

[35] Gura, *Edwards*, 90.

[36] *Sermons and Discourses, 1730–733*, 42.

[37] This is, of course, qualified by the reality of *progressive sanctification*: as the Holy Spirit works in the life of the believer over time, he is brought more

1938), long-time professor of New Testament at Tübingen University in southern Germany, describes conversion in terms of this change of the will:

> Conversion does not merely alter individual thoughts and aspirations; if so, it would reveal itself only as long as the sole focus were the performance of the repentant person. It produces an effect that transcends this, since God accepts and forgives the repentant person and makes him his own son. Jesus did not base this on the repentant person's performance according to a doctrine of merit, *nor did he conceive of a change of human nature by a person's own willpower.* He rather invested repentance with the effect of granting salvation and life, since God's gracious act upon man answered it and gave him a share in the divine sonship and eternal life. This occurred by the Spirit.[38]

The conclusion with which we are confronted is that to hear a believer ask, 'Why should I obey God?' is not so much a difficult question to answer as the wrong question to ask. It is like a young man recently fallen in love asking

---

and more into conformity with the likeness of God's Son (2 Cor. 3:18). What we are saying above, however, is that there is an essential change that has taken place in the believer's heart by which he is drawn toward obedience rather than repelled by it. See Ps. 19:7-11 and all of Ps. 119, e.g., for a picture of what it means for a regenerate person to delight in God's commands. See also the discussion under 'Moral Struggling Neglected?' below.

[38] *The History of the Christ*, trans. Andreas J. Köstenberger (Grand Rapids: Baker, 1997), 338. Emphasis added. In our time, Bryan Chapell has written similarly of the Spirit-wrought change of will necessary to authentic Christian obedience: 'Hearts formerly cold toward God do not become warm toward his people and purposes by a mere act of willpower. While we can will a change in behavior, we do not by an act of will change what we find attractive, appealing, and lovely. The Spirit accomplishes what willpower cannot in reconstructing the affections of our hearts. This is a supernatural work that is facilitated by the means of grace, but that cannot be accomplished by them apart from the Spirit' (*Holiness by Grace: Delighting in the Joy That Is Our Strength* [Wheaton: Crossway, 2001], 152).

why he should telephone the object of his affection to ask about her well-being; the internal impulse of his heart precludes such absurd reticence. The question is not 'Why should I obey God?' but 'How can I not? In light of what God has done in me by His Spirit such that I long for greater faithfulness to Him, how can I continue to pursue sin instead of holiness?' Dwelling in sin and being indwelt by God are mutually exclusive. Yes, Christians still sin. Fleshly struggles will plague us our whole lives long, often resulting in discouraging moral failure. But have we taken the Bible seriously when we are told, 'No one who abides in him keeps on sinning. No one who keeps on sinning has either seen him or known him.... No one born of God makes a practice of sinning, for God's seed abides in him, and he cannot keep on sinning because he has been born of God' (1 John 3:6, 9; see 5:4)? The connection between the new birth and sin's demise is plain. And herein sanctification finds its energy. Edwards says of 1 John 3:9, 'As 'tis said of him that is born of God, that his seed abideth in him ... so may it be said of that holy fire from heaven put into his soul in conversion, that it abides in him and doubtless will be felt in the effects of it in the heart from time to time.'[39]

---

[39] From 'Zeal an Essential Virtue of a Christian' (*Sermons and Discourses, 1739–1742*, 153; this sermon was preached in 1740 and based on Titus 2:14). Edwards also quotes 1 John 3:9 in his *Treatise on Grace* (see above). In another place Edwards comments on 1 John 3:9 thus: 'A wicked man has none of that principle of nature that a godly man has.... The natural import of the metaphor shows, that by a seed is meant a principle of action: it may be small as a grain of mustard seed. A seed is a small thing; it may be buried up and lie hid as the seed sown in the earth; it may seem to be dead, as seeds for a while do, till quickened by the sun and rain. But any degree of such a principle, or a principle of such a nature, is what is called the seed; it need not be to such a degree, or have such a prevalency, in order to be called a seed. And it is further evident that this seed, or this inward principle of nature, is peculiar to the saints; for he that has that seed, cannot sin; and therefore he that sins, or is a wicked man, has it not' (From 'Concerning Efficacious Grace,' in *Works*, vol. 2, ed. Hickman, 563).

And so the question for one who has been born of God is: In light of what Almighty God has done to fundamentally change me from the inside out, what else would happen but that I follow in obedience? I say this is the question, because in regeneration God invades the human heart such that one desires holiness in a way never before possible. The Apostle Paul explains conversion in terms of God bringing light and love where there once dwelt only darkness and hatred. In 2 Corinthians 4:3-6, Paul explains regeneration in just these terms, speaking of the light of faith versus the darkness and blindness of unbelief. Verse 6, here italicized, is key.

Even if our gospel is veiled, it is veiled only to those who are perishing. In their case the god of this world has

---

From these statements and others we learn that while Edwards certainly was interested in and drew from the philosophical frameworks of the time, his primary influence in theological formation of the new inner relish is not Platonic categories but Scripture (whether Scripture itself is influenced by these categories is another question). Philip Gura, for example, notes the theme of regeneration and the resulting new inclination of the will, labeling this 'the new simple idea' and attributing it to Lockean empiricism (see pp. 66-69, 227-238). He writes: 'Scholars have long recognized that the language in which Edwards spoke of consciousness and cognition derived from his wide reading in contemporary philosophy, particularly in the works of the Cambridge Platonists John Smith, Anthony Ashley Cooper (the third Earl of Shaftesbury), and Francis Hutcheson among the 'Moral Sense' philosophers; and John Locke and other empiricists.... Edwards applied [Locke's] propositions to his own spirituality. If grace was, in Locke's terms, 'a new simple idea' and best described as spiritual effulgence or a 'divine and supernatural light,' then its effect on a human soul was incalculable as well as irresistible' (*Edwards*, 66). It seems to me, however, that Edwards utilized philosophical frameworks only as they served the truth of Scripture, and not the other way round. It is commonplace, in most of his treatises, to find a proposition followed by a litany of Scripture texts apparently brought to mind from memory in those pre-concordance and pre-computer days; but I have yet to discover a proposition supported by a list of quotes from contemporary philosophers – to say nothing of the fact that the main labor of his life – preaching – was devoted to being immersed in, and drawing meaning from, the Bible. While Scripture and modern philosophical categories are not necessarily mutually exclusive, then, the former always trumped the latter for Edwards.

blinded the minds of unbelievers, to keep them from seeing the light of the gospel of the glory of Christ, who is the image of God. For what we proclaim is not ourselves, but Jesus Christ as Lord, with ourselves as your servants for Jesus' sake. *For God, who said, 'Let light shine out of darkness,' has shone in our hearts to give the light of the knowledge of the glory of God in the face of Jesus Christ.*

At the beginning of time, God created the universe. He then made light shine in it. A similar immediate illumination takes place in human hearts when He breathes His living breath into them. God Himself 'has shone in our hearts.' And what glorious light it is! That which the Apostle here refers to as being unveiled is what Edwards labels a new inner 'relish.' Our eyes are opened; the veil is lifted. God is seen and loved. How can we continue in sin now that God has shown us what it means to enjoy life by glorifying Him as we pursue holiness?

NEW BIRTH, IMPERISHABLE SEED, AND FRESH WATER SPRINGS
We have mentioned Paul and John; other New Testament voices join to affirm the need for a new relish for holiness. Jesus told Nicodemus, 'Truly, truly, I say to you, unless one is born again he cannot see the kingdom of God.' After Nicodemus mistakenly takes him to be referring to physical birth, Jesus explains: 'Truly, truly, I say to you, unless one is born of water and the Spirit, he cannot enter the kingdom of God. That which is born of the flesh is flesh, and that which is born of the Spirit is spirit. Do not marvel then that I said to you, "You must be born again"' (John 3:3, 5-7). There is only one path to the kingdom of God: new birth from above. 'Human nature is capable of propagating or producing only human nature,' writes Sam Storms in commenting on these verses. 'It is unable to produce anything that transcends its character as human.

Simply put, like produces like.'[40] One must therefore be utterly renovated from the inside out, a change so radical it may be likened to exiting the womb all over again. In the prologue to his Gospel account, John writes that 'to all who did receive him, who believed in his name, he gave the right to become children of God, who were born, not of blood nor of the will of the flesh nor of the will of man, but of God' (John 1:12-13).

Likewise, Peter exhorts his readers to 'love one another earnestly from a pure heart, since you have been born again, not of perishable seed but of imperishable, through the living and abiding word of God' (1 Pet. 1:22-23; cf. Eph. 2:1-6). The reason given for the obedience of love is the reality of a new birth. God had done something definitive in the souls of the elect to whom Peter wrote (1:1-2), and it is only in light of this that they would be able to pursue the holiness earlier called for: 'As he who called you is holy, you also be holy in all your conduct, since it is written, "You shall be holy, for I am holy" ' (1:15-16).

James says no less. 'Does a spring,' he asks, 'pour forth from the same opening both fresh and salt water? Can a fig tree, my brothers, bear olives, or a grapevine produce figs? Neither can a salt pond yield fresh water' (James 3:11-12). One's actions – in this context, one's words – do not lie. They show the state of one's heart in a way no X-ray ever can. A morally upright, law-abiding, family-loving, maritally faithful, church-attending person – if God has not taken out the stony heart and replaced it with a new one with like desires – is able to produce authentic obedience no more than a salt water spring is able to produce fresh water. He who possesses living water (John 4:10-14) must grant the fresh water spring of a new inclination. And the implantation of this spring, affirms James, is attributable only to sheer grace – 'Of his own will he brought us forth by the word of truth' (James 1:18).

---

[40] *Chosen for Life*, 153.

As I write, I am sipping a cup of hot chocolate to keep warm (I'm not a coffee drinker). The reason I am drinking it instead of pouring it onto my skin (aside from the mess it would make and the pain I would feel) is that I warm up most effectively from the inside out, not outside in. The same is true in motivation. It is an internal to external dynamic, not external to internal. Regeneration is (permanent) transformation, not (temporary) reformation.[41]

Motivation is a mark of divine presence. It is holy desire for God which is divinely initiated and sustained.

Is this Hyper-Calvinism?

All this raises an important question. In the portrait of motivation painted here, what role is left for me to play? For the Bible teaches not only that God alone gives salvation (Rom. 9:10-21) but also that humans are culpable for rejecting it (Rom. 2:6-11). Indeed, the difficulty with which these two truths are reconciled has always led some to abort one side of the equation or the other. Hyper-Calvinism and Arminianism both agree that God's sovereignty is ultimately incompatible with human responsibility. Yet the two views respond to this alleged difficulty in opposite ways; hyper-Calvinism by neglecting human responsibility in the name of God's unswerving sovereignty and Arminianism by neglecting the sovereignty of God in the name of human responsibility. Both are rationalistic errors, trumping the mystery of biblical truth with the authority of human reason.

---

[41] See 2 Cor. 3:18. Hugo Odeberg suggests that the difference between one who has been born again and one who has not is the difference between a human being and an animal dressed up as a human being (*Pharisaism and Christianity*, trans. J. M. Moe [St. Louis: Concordia Publishing House, 1964], 104-12).

The question for us is: Does the picture of Christianity here presented fall into the error of hyper-Calvinism? Is human responsibility obscured or even wiped clean away by this picture of a divinely-implanted relish for holiness? This is an understandable question. For it is true that I am pre-eminently focusing on the action of God. Nevertheless three things must be said.

THE WITNESS OF SCRIPTURE
First, the Bible teaches that the necessity of divinely imported energy does not *eradicate* but *encourages* Christian action. If obedience is finally up to us, our efforts are ultimately hopeless. No one naturally possesses the resources to live a life pleasing to God. But if we can be confident that God has determined to carry us through, we are encouraged in our attempts at greater degrees of holiness. God has undertaken to stimulate our spiritual apathy with divine energy. Authentic obedience is indeed possible – no, promised!

Scripture happily weds human striving with divine activity in sanctification; more than this, the former is not only co-existent with, but rooted in, the latter. Paul tells Christians at Philippi to 'work out your own salvation.' Why? 'For it is God who works in you, both to will and to work for his good pleasure' (Phil. 2:12-13). We 'toil,' Paul elsewhere says, yet we labor not in our own energy; we are 'struggling with all his energy that he powerfully works within' us (Col. 1:29). The Apostle proclaims that he worked 'harder than any of them; though it was not I but the grace of God that is with me' (1 Cor. 15:10). Isaiah declares, 'All that we have accomplished you have done for us' (Isa. 26:12, NIV).[42] So Christians work as hard as possible, yet at the end of the

---

[42] For other affirmations of divine sovereignty and human responsibility in Christian living see also Jos. 11:20; 21:44; 23:3-5; 1 Sam. 12:1,13; 23:3-5; 2 Cor. 9:8; 2 Tim. 1:6; 2:1; 1 Pet. 1:5; 2 Pet. 1:10; and Jude 21.

SYNTHESIS: EXPLORING THE KEY INGREDIENT

day look back and humbly praise God for any fruit borne. Such fruit grows only under the providential hand of the Divine Gardener – 'God gives the growth' (1 Cor. 3:7).

THE RECOVERY OF THE DIVINE PREROGATIVE

Second, God's utter sovereignty is the side of the equation that most needs to be underscored in the church today. Incipient Arminianism is the air twenty-first-century Western believers breathe. We are human-centered to the core. The total prerogative of God in all things – including the free actions of moral human agents – is a suffocating concept to many today instead of the freeing, peace-bringing, hope-giving, life-sustaining, God-exalting concept it is meant to be. This was true in Edwards' day (hence his *Freedom of the Will*, a philosophically-reasoned argument against Arminianism) as it is in ours. Therefore, if I am accused of imbalance, I confess it freely and welcome it. At times imbalance is needed in order to regain balance.

'GOD DOES ALL, AND WE DO ALL'

Third, Jonathan Edwards was a balanced thinker himself. The 'conjoining of theological objectivism with his call to human effort is one of the most baffling of Edwards' concepts,' writes Clyde Holbrook. 'It has been called the Edwardsean paradox, although its origin is rooted in Paul's advice to the Philippians to work out their own salvation with fear and trembling, 'for God is at work in you, both to will and to work for his good pleasure' (2:13).'[43] Edwards exhorts his hearers in one sermon to 'labor that you may have Christ's mark set upon you.'[44] We *labor* – yet Christ is the one who sets his mark upon us. In 'The Reality of Conversion' Edwards applies his message this way: 'Let me

---

[43] Holbrook, *Ethics of Jonathan Edwards*, 19.
[44] From 'The Spiritual Blessings of the Gospel Represented By a Feast,' *Sermons and Discourses, 1723–1729*, 294.

now earnestly exhort you to seek deliverance from your present state by being the subjects of a true and saving conversion to God.'[45] We are to 'seek' to 'be the subject' of conversion! Perhaps his clearest statement of the marriage of divine and human working is a remarkable statement in *Remarks on Important Theological Controversies*: 'in efficacious grace we are not merely passive, nor yet does God do some, and we do the rest. But God does all, and we do all. God produces all, and we act all.' How can both be true? 'For that is what he produces, viz. our own acts. God is the only proper author and fountain; we only are the proper actors. We are, in different respects, wholly passive and wholly active.'[46]

In numerous places Edwards lofts high human responsibility alongside divine sovereignty. Another example is from the sermon 'Glorying in the Savior,' in which he describes Christians as those who 'have subjected themselves to him and chosen him for their king; such as have indeed given themselves to him; such as have admitted Christ into the heart and placed him upon the throne there; such as have been begotten by the Spirit of Christ, been born of God, and been made partakers of Christ's nature and temper.' Though he begins by using active verbs to indicate the human role in conversion ('subjected themselves ... chosen him ... given themselves ... admitted Christ,'), he concludes by using passive verbs to indicate God's ultimacy ('been begotten ... been born of God ... been made

---

[45] Kimnach, et al, *Sermons Reader*, 92.

[46] *Works*, vol. 2, ed. Hickman, 557.

[47] *Sermons and Discourses, 1723–1729*, 462-63. Interestingly, Edwards changed an earlier description of believers in a way that shows his commitment to the ultimacy of divine action in conversion. The sermon initially labeled Christians as those who 'have been so convinced of the reality and sufficiency and excellency of Christ as a savior, and have entirely inclined and drawn the heart to him, to choose and acquiesce in him.' He later revised this to speak of those who (with changes italicized) 'have been so convinced of the reality

partakers').[47] The paradoxical logic is consistent with Paul's words in 2 Timothy 2:1: 'Be strengthened by the grace that is in Christ Jesus.' Paul is calling Timothy to do something; namely, be strengthened. But how? By the grace of Christ. Spiritual strength is found in God's grace, not (ultimately) our effort. Hence the passive: 'be strengthened.'

OBEDIENCE FUELED, NOT ERASED, BY GRACE

Yet we must be careful to do justice both to Scripture and to Edwards. For the nature of the relationship between human obligation and divine action is that such spiritual strength is discovered *not by God's grace trumping and erasing our effort but by fueling it*. Divine determinacy does not ignore but invigorates human striving. In this way Edwards was not hyper-Calvinistic. He left a staggering role for the individual to play. He urged his people to 'earnestly seek'[48] salvation. While salvation and the ensuing obedience are thoroughly dependent on God, this is not to the exclusion of human striving. He explains:

> When I say that the acts and influences of the Spirit determine the effects, it is not meant that man has nothing to do to determine in the affair. The soul of man undoubtedly, in every instance, does voluntarily

and sufficiency and excellency of Christ as a savior *as to have their hearts inclined and drawn to him*, to choose and acquiesce in him.' The editors of this sermon add the following explanation: 'In thus rewording the sentence, he removed the implication that believers are able to incline their own hearts to God' (462, n. 1). This work of revision is telling.

[48] From 'They Sing a New Song' (*Sermons and Discourses, 1739–1742*, 239). See also his 1740 sermon 'Seeking After Christ' (Ibid, 287-97). By frequently including in his sermonic 'application' exhortations to strive eagerly for greater holiness in various aspects of living, Edwards prevented his strong Calvinism from sliding into antinomianism. An example of explicit rejection of hyper-Calvinism and antinomianism is found in the sermon 'The Curse of Meroz,' the doctrine of which is: 'When God remarkably appears in a great work for his church and against his enemies, it is a most dangerous thing for any of his professing people to lie still and not to put to an helping hand' (Ibid, 494).

determine with respect to his own consequent
actions. But this determination of the will of man, or
voluntary determination of the soul of man, is the effect
determined. This determining act of the soul is not
denied, but supposed, as it is the effect we are speaking
of, that the influence of God's Spirit determines.[49]

In other words, human choices are real; but the choice itself,
not only the outcome, is decreed by God. Human striving does
not *compete* with but *completes* the sovereign will of God.

Jonathan Edwards would agree with Henry Scougal,
professor at Aberdeen in the century before Edwards lived:

It is true, religion in the souls of men is the immediate
work of God, and all our natural endeavors can neither
produce it alone, nor merit those supernatural aids by
which it must be wrought: the Holy Ghost must come
upon us, and the power of the Highest must overshadow
us, before that holy thing can be begotten, and Christ be
formed in us: but yet we must not expect that this whole
work should be done without any concurring endeavors
of our own: we must not lie loitering in the ditch, and
wait till Omnipotence pulls us from thence; no, no! we
must bestir ourselves, and actuate those powers which
we have already received: we must put forth ourselves to
our utmost capacities, and then we may hope that, 'our
labour shall not be in vain in the Lord' (1 Cor. 15:58).[50]

In our own time J. I. Packer has said it well: 'God's method
of sanctification is neither activism (self-reliant activity) nor
apathy (God-reliant passivity), but God-dependent effort.'[51]

---

[49] *Works*, vol. 2, ed. Hickman, 559. For a helpful discussion of the balance
in Edwards' preaching between divine sovereignty and human responsibility,
and a description of some of his sermons emphasizing the latter, see *Sermons
and Discourses, 1730–1733*, 8-13.

[50] Henry Scougal, *The Life of God in the Soul of Man* (Fearn, Scotland:
Christian Heritage/Christian Focus, 2001), 94-95.

So Edwards liberally called his people to strive as furiously as they were humanly able. A favorite citation was Matthew 11:12: 'From the days of John the Baptist until now the kingdom of heaven has suffered violence, and the violent take it by force.'[52] The Northampton congregation were encouraged to strive as hard as they could to be shown mercy. Yet their attitude must always be, on the one hand, 'I labor ...' and on the other hand, '... struggling with all his energy' (Col. 1:29). When all is said and done, our striving is itself a gift of God from beginning to end. So strive! Seek! In the final exhortation of 'A Divine and Supernatural Light' Edwards urges just this: 'earnestly ... seek this spiritual light.'[53] Although it is wholly a divine gift, God is eager to meet our feeble requests for more exquisite delight in Him (2 Chron. 16:9).

Edwards refused therefore to allow the necessity of divine action in regeneration and sanctification to disparage human effort as mere illusion. 'That true faith, by which persons rely on the righteousness of Christ, and the work that he hath done for them, and do truly feed and live upon him, is evermore accompanied with such a spirit of earnestness in the Christian work and course.'[54] The one who has been made into a new creation will experience not laziness but 'earnestness.' Edwards uses the same word, 'earnestness,' in another sermon: 'Pressing into the kingdom of heaven denotes earnestness and firmness of resolution.'[55] This is because God's gift of a new inner relish is a direct act upon the human will. In 'Glorying in

---

[51] J. I. Packer, *Concise Theology: A Guide to Historic Christian Beliefs* (Wheaton: Tyndale House, 1993), 170.

[52] See, for example, his sermon on Luke 16:16 entitled 'Pressing into the Kingdom of God' (*Sermons and Discourses, 1734–1738*, 274-304).

[53] Kimnach, et al, *Sermons Reader*, 139. See also Gerstner and Gerstner, 'Edwardsean Preparation,' 46.

[54] *Religious Affections*, 388.

[55] *Sermons and Discourses, 1734–1738*, 277.

the Savior,' Edwards calls God 'exceeding glorious in the manner of his ruling his people by sweetly and powerfully influencing their hearts by his grace: not governing them against their wills, but by powerfully inclining their wills.'[56] God changes our inclinations, our desires, our very will. This is why we can say that it is both God who does all and we who do all in sanctification. 'Regeneration,' writes George Marsden of Edwards' theology, 'changed the whole person by changing the love at the heart of the person's being.'[57]

ENERGIZING GRACE

God transforms the will. Therefore obedience will indeed be sought. It will be pursued with the utmost endeavors. And this itself is a gift of God's grace as He grants a new attraction to and thirst for holiness. The true believer will work vigorously; but at the end of the day, as we look back and see fruit borne and obedience exercised, we give all thanks to God for performing this miracle in us. And so to endorse God's sovereign grace as reason for laxity is not to make too much of grace but too little, for grace comes to us not only as pardon (to counteract sin's penalty), but as power (to counteract its pollution). Grace is not only escaping (judgment), but enabling (righteousness). God has made provision not only *after* we sin but also *before*. 'Sincere grace is a powerful principle in the soul, and the power of it appears partly in the nature of its actings. It is no dull, inactive, ineffectual thing. There is an holy ardency and vigor in the actings of grace.'[58] Grace is not

[56] *Sermons and Discourses, 1723–1729*, 465-466.

[57] Marsden, *Edwards*, 286. In context, Marsden is discussing the first sign of authentic religious experience, which is: 'affections that are truly spiritual and gracious, do arise from those influences and operations on the heart, which are *spiritual*, *supernatural*, and *divine*' (*Religious Affections*, 197).

[58] From 'Zeal an Essential Virtue of a Christian' (*Sermons and Discourses, 1739–1742*, 144).

only passive but active; it not only forgives but fuels. 'What is grace but a principle of holiness? or a holy principle in the heart?'[59]

So no, Edwards is not commending hyper-Calvinism.[60] Believers are to seek and strive after God with all that is in them. But the deeper reality from which this spawns is a divinely revolutionized will: 'The Spirit of God is given to the true saints to dwell in them, as his proper lasting abode; and to influence their hearts, as a principle of new nature, or as a divine supernatural spring of life and action.'[61] In the 1730 sermon 'Born Again,' Edwards is crystal clear about what it means to be a saint:

> There is a new principle of will and inclination. The man now loves God, and loves Christ, which he could not love before. He relishes holiness and holy and heavenly things, which he could not relish before. He could not find these things in his heart before, so that 'tis as if God gives man a new heart; Ezek. 36:26, 'A new heart will I give unto you, and a new spirit will I put within you.'[62]

---

[59] From *Charity and Its Fruits*, in *Ethical Writings*, 298.

[60] For a similar defense of Calvinism against hyper-Calvinism, this time in the thought not of Edwards but of C. H. Spurgeon, see Iain H. Murray, *Spurgeon v. Hyper-Calvinism: The Battle for Gospel Preaching* (Edinburgh: Banner of Truth Trust, 1995).

[61] *Religious Affections*, 200.

[62] *Sermons and Discourses, 1730–1733*, 188. Similarly, 'Striving After Perfection' asks the question, 'Why are God's laws more to be desired than gold, than much fine gold? Why are they sweeter than honey?' Edwards' answer is that 'the new nature that is in the saints is of God, and is a divine nature, and therefore must be an enemy to every degree of that which is against God. Every saint has a new nature in him.... This new nature is from God, and is something of God; and therefore it tends to God again, and is contented with nothing short of God.... This nature, as 'tis from God, so it is a divine or godlike nature.... [H]ence it will necessarily follow that every degree of sin, even the least degree, must be burdensome to the new nature' (*Sermons and Discourses, 1734–1738*, 691-92). One is reminded of 2 Pet. 1:3 – 'His divine power has granted to us all things that pertain to life and godliness ...'

Christian motivation is rooted in a gracious act of God's Spirit resulting in a new impulse of the heart. This impulse renders holiness sweet instead of sour, beautiful instead of ugly.[63]

Moral Struggling Neglected?

A related difficulty is the role of the struggle to obey in the Christian life. What does one do when one believes one is regenerate and yet still struggles to defeat sin? We have just finished discussing whether the need for a new heart and inclination minimizes human striving, concluding that it fuels rather than eradicates striving. Now we are asking if it minimizes remaining indwelling sin. The first asks, If regeneration is up to God, why should I exert any effort? The second asks, If sanctification is up to God, how am I to understand remaining sin in my life? It might be objected, in other words, that Edwards' view of the new motivational relish in regeneration overlooks the power of sin which, though dealt a death blow, continues to wage war on the soul after conversion.

And so, the mere (though glorious) fact of regeneration does not suddenly cause all temptations and struggles with sin to vanish away. Christ's work on the cross completely eliminates the *penalty* of sin, progressively eliminates the *power* of sin, and does not eliminate at all the *presence* of sin. Sin continues to dwell in believers just as good continues to be done by unbelievers. *We will avoid much confusion and simplistic overstatement if we remember both the remaining presence of sin in the regenerate and the remaining presence of the image of God in the unregenerate.* Unbelievers are not as

---

[63] See also Wilson H. Kimnach's discussion of 'Light and the Heart' (*The Works of Jonathan Edwards*, vol. 10, *Sermons and Discourses, 1720–1723* [New Haven: Yale University Press, 1992], 199-207), in which Kimnach discusses the importance of these two concepts in Edwards' theology and helpfully connects divine bestowal with human striving.

bad as they might possibly be; believers are not as good as they might possibly be. We must forget neither the doctrine of Creation (when tempted to see unbelievers as capable of no good) nor the doctrine of the Fall (when tempted to see believers as capable of no bad). Regarding the latter, then, we must admit that we are acutely aware that the new birth does not have the same immediate effect on the presence and influence of sin as does the rising sun on last night's nightmares, putting them immediately and completely to flight as a fading memory of the past. Rather the influence of sin lingers.

Let the weight of this difficulty sober us. For we must be realists, not triumphalists. It is a mistake to neglect the 'not yet' while emphasizing the 'already' of biblical thought. No living Christian is yet sinless, and we never will be until we see the Lord 'face to face' (1 Cor. 13:12).[64] The Christian life is one of tremendous struggle. There is no point in Paul urging the Ephesians to strap on their spiritual armor (Eph. 6:10-17) and Timothy to 'fight the good fight of the faith' (1 Tim. 6:12) unless we are in a war.

How then does one understand these temptations and our repeated succumbing to them? What does one do when simply not motivated to obey, despite believing oneself to have been born again?

WESLEY CLOSER TO THE TRUTH?
John Wesley, the founder of Methodism and three months Edwards' elder, saw this difficulty. But he came to the opposite conclusion than did Edwards. Wesley decided that to tell people God was wholly responsible for their salvation crippled human striving and motivation to seek God. Mark Noll writes:

---

[64] I have found no text to be more consistently and helpfully faithful to the already/not yet tension of biblical eschatology than George Eldon Ladd's *Theology of the New Testament*.

For Wesley the Calvinist insistence that God's electing power was the basic element in the sinner's conversion verged dangerously close to antinomianism: in emphasizing God's actions in bringing the sinner to himself, 'it wholly takes away those first motives to follow after [holiness], so frequently proposed in Scripture, the hope of future reward and punishment, the hope of heaven and fear of hell.'[65]

For Wesley (here emphasizing the future aspect of motivation), the preeminence of divine energy in Christian living is incompatible with the Bible's rational appeals to obey God. The two are mutually exclusive: if one exists, the other cannot.

Edwards too recognizes the tension. He knows that 'the godly, after they have grace in their hearts, many times do gradually sink down into very ill frames through their unwatchfulness: they insensibly get into carnal frames; their hearts are overcharged with the cares of this life; their lusts prevail and get ground more and more, and their grace is buried up. The good seed is overgrown with weeds.'[66] Edwards understood the complexities of the human (even the regenerate) soul. He is not simplistic, teaching Christian victory while ignoring Christian struggle. 'A man is brought, when converted, wholly to

[65] *The Rise of Evangelicalism: The Age of Edwards, Whitefield, and the Wesleys* (Downers Grove, IL: InterVarsity Press, 2003), 122, quoting John Wesley, 'Free Grace' (1740), in *The Works of John Wesley*, ed. Thomas Jackson, 14 vol. (London: Wesleyan Conference Office, 1872), 7:376. Nevertheless see the statements by Wesley in the appendix. For a helpful discussion of Edwards' theological differences with Wesley, see Murray, *Edwards*, 256-67. See also Murray's treatment of Wesley's 'Collision with Calvinism' in his *Wesley and Men Who Followed* (Edinburgh: Banner of Truth Trust, 2003), 56-79.

[66] From 'The Subjects of a First Work of Grace May Need a New Conversion' (*Sermons and Discourses, 1739-1742*, 189). See John H. Gerstner, *The Rational Biblical Theology of Jonathan Edwards* (Orlando: Ligonier Ministries, 1993), 3:230-32.

renounce all his sins.... But that don't argue that he is wholly freed from all remains of sin.'[67] Even in regenerate people obedience is mixed. The human heart, despite having been softened by God, remains complex and mysterious, and it is often difficult to ascertain the motives of even our own hearts.[68] Moreover, it is simplistic to level out the effects of regeneration by assuming that everyone who is given this relish is given it to the same degree or in a static way that never waxes or wanes. Those who have been given a new relish for God are 'led and guided in discerning and distinguishing the true spiritual and holy beauty of actions; and that more easily, readily, and accurately, as they have more or less of the Spirit of God dwelling in them.'[69] For this reason Marsden describes the realism of Edwards' theology of sanctification: 'For the Christian who was to be united to Christ, life remained a struggle of the deepest contrasts. Edwards resolved the highs and lows of his own spiritual experiences into the lessons of this tough-minded theological heritage that did not flinch at the discomforts of a lifetime of struggles, even for the regenerate.'[70]

THE IMPORTANCE OF RATIONAL MOTIVATIONS

All this helps us see why Edwards often includes objective motivations (such as gratitude, new identity, and personal benefit) right alongside a proclamation of the truth that to be regenerate is to be motivated. For example, we saw in 'Heaven Is a World of Love' that Edwards preached the

---

[67] From 'Bringing the Ark to Zion a Second Time' (*Sermons and Discourses, 1739–1742*, 257).

[68] C. S. Lewis wrote a letter to an (anonymous) American correspondent in which he wisely commented: 'Humans are very seldom either totally sincere or totally hypocritical. Their moods change, their motives are mixed, and they are often themselves quite mistaken as to what their motives are' (C. S. Lewis, *Letters to an American Lady* [Grand Rapids, MI: Eerdmans, 1967], 95).

[69] *Religious Affections*, 283.

[70] Marsden, *Edwards*, 137.

necessity of a gracious work of the Spirit in order to be motivated unto good works. Yet Edwards also motivated his people by painting a picture of holiness and heaven – that is, by providing rational grounds for virtue. So we return to this sermon to see that Edwards does indeed employ practical 'motives.' Both supernatural motivational necessity (the divine aspect of Christian motivation) and objective motivational aid (the human aspect of Christian motivation) must be held together. Consider the words with which Edwards closes this sermon, as he exhorts his beloved flock to 'live a life of love':

Here let several things be considered as motives ...

1. This will be the way to make you like [the inhabitants of heaven] in happiness and comfort. For this happiness and joy and rest lies in loving the inhabitants of that world. And by living in love in this world the saints partake of a like sort of inward peace and sweetness. It is in this way that you are to have the foretastes of heavenly pleasures and delights.

2. This is the way to have a sense of glory of heavenly things, as of God and Christ, and holiness, and heavenly enjoyments ...

3. This is the way to have clear evidences of a title to heaven ...

4. By living a life of love, you will be in the way to heaven...[71]

With that the sermon ends. We reproduce these final four points because while they are clearly motivations that appeal to reason, they come at the end of a sermon in which Edwards shows that the desire for this kind of love and

---

[71] Kimnach, et al, *Sermons Reader*, 271-72.

holiness is only possible if God acts in the human heart. In other words, we saw in our earlier analysis of this sermon that the Spirit must bring new desires; here at the end of the message Edwards demonstrates that this does not therefore exclude objectifiable reasoning.

EVEN WORKING RUDDERS NEED WIND

The premise of this book has consistently relegated the objective incentives of Scripture (past, present and future) to a secondary role. Yet I must make clear that I wholeheartedly affirm such motivations as *glorious and powerful truths in the Christian life.* Eternity will not be too long to ponder the work God has done for us in Christ at the cross, nor the staggering truth that the God of the universe and Judge of mankind has adopted us as his own children, nor the lavish blessings God has promised those who seek to honor him. These truths are indeed powerful incentives to a holy life. Consider these words of Edwards' on the motivating strength of (as an example) gratitude:

> If a neighbor does another a remarkable kindness, and he be really suitably thankful to him for it, he will be ready when occasion presents to do him as good a kindness. And though we cannot requite God's kindness by doing anything which shall be any profit to God, yet a spirit of thankfulness will dispose men to do what they can. Though they cannot profit God, yet, as far as in them lies, to do what shall be well pleasing and acceptable to God, and shall tend to his declarative glory.[72]

My aim is not to suffocate the power of the sensible motivations laid out for us in the Bible. They are the rocks on which I stand; without them I flounder like a rudderless

---

[72] From *Charity and Its Fruits*, in *Ethical Writings*, 305. On the question of whether one can 'requite' God, see *The Nature of True Virtue*, in *Ethical Writings*, 552.

ship. My desire in this book is not to drown out the voice of the incentives God has given us. I aim rather to show that any such rational motivations are hollow and powerless if the eyes that view them have not been transformed to behold them as worthy of consecrated living. Even ships with working rudders are useless without wind.

SPIRIT OR REASON? YES!

The question, however, remains: who is responsible for this new heavenly taste Edwards so often placarded before his people? The Holy Spirit or the preacher's reasoning and persuasion? The answer is a resounding yes: in that order. The preacher must labor and preach and persuade and work as if it is up to him to convince his flock of the beauty and delights to be found in obedience. Ultimately, however, only the Spirit can motivate effectually to this end, though he uses the preacher's diligent labors to do so. So yes, motivation is fundamental to simply being a Christian, and will only exist (and will always exist) if one is a true saint, but it is also true that the vehicle God uses to motivate believers is primarily those means laid out in Scripture: gratitude, a newfound identity, and personal benefit, for example. 'Heaven Is a World of Love' is a clear example of these two truths existing side by side.

So the two realities of the necessity of the Spirit and objective categories of motivation are happy neighbors in Edwards. Wesley failed to reconcile the twin biblical truths of divine causality and human earnestness, emphasizing the latter to the exclusion of the former. In *Charity and Its Fruits*, Edwards explains that regeneration does not equal perfection. Rather, 'persons who try themselves by their practice, may find that they greatly fail every day, and are in many instances often wandering out of the way, and yet not see just cause to condemn themselves.' Moral failing is not a sign of condemnation.

For when we speak of a life of Christian practice, and when the Scripture speaks of holiness of life in Christians, that is not the meaning of it, that it should be a perfect life. Yea, a Christian's life may be attended with many and exceedingly great imperfections, and yet be a holy life, or a truly Christian life. It may be such a life as does manifestly show that the grace which he has is of that kind which has a tendency to practice.'[73]

Note Edwards' word 'tendency.' Regeneration grants a new *direction*, not a new *perfection*.

'A LOVELINESS IMMENSELY ABOVE ALL'

Let us go to one more place to see Edwards' understanding of how the two truths of regeneration and continued moral struggling can co-exist. In 'Zeal an Essential Virtue of a Christian,' Edwards takes up the question of how Christians are supposed to obey God when, though regenerate, there is still so much sin and temptation to be dealt with. I have found no greater resolution in the writings of Jonathan Edwards than this sermon to the objection that the presence of remaining temptation, and succumbing to sin, in the regenerate disproves the sufficiency and permanence of a divinely-granted relish for obedience.

Having declared that true saints cannot remain spiritually tepid and that unless our affections for God are greater than our affections for the things of the world we are not truly saved, Edwards says this:

A question or objection may arise, which I will now take occasion to speak something to. The objection is this: viz. How can it be necessary that men, in order to be true Christians, should love God above all things else in the world, when we are so often taught that true Christians have so little grace and so much corruption?

---

[73] *Ethical Writings*, 309-10.

We are often taught that grace in this life is but an infant state, that grace is but as a spark, faith but as a grain of mustard seed, but that men carry about with them a load of sin, a body of sin and death. His corruption, which is so great, inclines him to love the world and make that his happiness, and, if there be so much of it and so little grace, how can it be that all truly godly men should love God more than the world?[74]

In other words, how can believers obey God if they are still as sinful as we say they are? Every Christian knows what it is to lapse into sin and to be constantly aware of its powerful sway. How then do we pursue holiness in light of the remaining strongholds of sin that seem so immovable? Edwards explains: "Tis from the nature of the Object loved rather than the degree of the principle in the lover. The Object beloved is of supreme excellency, of a loveliness immensely above all.' Look at God, not yourself, says Edwards. 'Worthy he is to be chosen, pursued, and cleaved to, and delighted in, far above all. And he that truly loves him, loves him as seeing this superlative, seeing of it as superlative, and as being convinced that it is far above all.'[75] The reason saints are able to overcome sin is because their eyes have been opened and they now see *God*.

But what if we cannot seem to grasp the gloriousness of this 'Object?' Will it not then be insufficient to truly motivate us to alter our behavior at all, though we be regenerate? No –

Though a man has but a faint discovery of the glory of God, yet if he has any true discovery of him, so far as he is discovered he sees this; he is sensible that he is worthy to be loved far above all. The Spirit of God is a Spirit of truth, and if he makes any true discovery of God it must be a discovery of him as lovely above

---

[74] *Sermons and Discourses, 1739–1742*, 145.
[75] Ibid.

all. If such an excellency is not discovered, there is no divine excellency discovered, for the notion of divine excellency is superlative, supreme excellency.

Now that wherein a godly man may be said to love God above all seems to be no more than what immediately and necessarily follows from a sight of this supreme excellency. Though it may be a comparatively faint discovery, yet 'tis a convincing discovery. Hence God must be above all in his esteem: for to be convinced that he is more excellent than all, is in fact to esteem him above all.

And so He must be above all in his choice, for the choice follows the esteem. And hence also it will follow that God is above all in his purpose and resolutions. He cleaves to the Lord with purpose of heart and so, in the sense of the scripture, with his whole heart.

Though there may be but little of the principle of love, yet the principle that there is, being built on such a conviction, will be of this nature, viz. to prize God above all. There may be an endless variety of degrees of the principle, but the nature of the object is unalterable. Therefore if there be a discovery of the object, whether in a greater or a lesser degree, if that discovery be true and agreeable to the nature of the object, the nature of the principle that is the effect of the discovery will answer the nature of the object. And so it will evermore be the nature of it to prize God above all, though there may be but little of such a principle.[76]

So how is Edwards answering the objection that one may be a regenerate soul and yet still struggle with temptation and being motivated to obey? If one truly has had a sight of the 'divine excellency,' there is no such thing as not

---

[76] Ibid, 146.

seeing enough of this to effectually propel one to 'cleave to the Lord with purpose of heart' in glad obedience. Seeing God to a mediocre degree is an impossibility – if one sees Him at all, there is nothing mediocre about it! The vision of the goodness and consequent greatness of God made immediately sensible to the saint in regeneration cannot fail to make a difference that flows out into how that person lives. Yes, sin remains. But something superior has been introduced. A little of God conquers a lot of sin.

THE SMALLEST DEGREES OF A HOLY DISPOSITION

In *A Treatise on Grace*, Edwards quotes 1 John 3:9 ('No one born of God makes a practice of sinning, for God's seed abides in him, and he cannot keep on sinning because he has been born of God') and comments, 'If by the seed is meant the word of God, yet when it is spoken of as abiding in him that is born again, it must be intended, with respect to its effect, as a holy principle in the heart.' In other words, 'the word of God abides in the heart of a regenerate person as a holy seed, a Divine principle there, though it may be but as a seed, a small thing.... The smallest degrees and first principles of a Divine and holy nature and disposition are inconsistent with a state of sin.' Even 'the smallest degrees' of grace in the soul is enough for the Apostle John to boldly assert that those born of God no longer sin.

But what if one still feels that the saving grace imparted will not fuel cherishing God above all else? God will see that it does. 'Where God infuses grace, he will give it a predominance by his upholding of it and time after time giving it the victory, when it seemed for a time to be overborne and ready to be swallowed.' Such victory, though from one angle certainly the fruit of human labor, is fundamentally a gift. 'This is not owing to our strength but the strength of God, who won't forsake the work of his hands, and will carry on his work when he has begun it, and always causeth us to triumph in Christ Jesus, who is the author and has undertaken to be the finisher of our faith.'[77] God will see us through.

In order to be truly motivated to serve God faithfully, all that is needed is the smallest measure of holy grace. Jesus taught the same principle when he told his disciples, 'If you had faith like a grain of mustard seed, you could say to this mulberry tree, "Be uprooted and planted in the sea," and it would obey you' (Luke 17:6).[78] It is a question not of degree but of kind. The disciples were not in need of an increase of already existing faith. They were in need of the presence of an imported spring of life. They were in need of a new inner relish.

SUCCULENT SAINTLINESS FROM ON HIGH

The point to which we return, then, is that God Himself, even in small doses, is our motivation. Our only hope to obey God is if He intervenes and reverses the savoring tendencies of our spiritual taste buds. Saintliness becomes succulent while sin loses its savor. The theme runs all through Edwards' writings. God himself must convince us of the true 'pleasantness of religion.' He whom the psalmist called 'a sun' (Ps. 84:11) and who later declared himself to be 'the light of the world' (John 8:12) must awaken us by 'a divine and supernatural light' leading to

---

[77] *Treatise on Grace*, 25. Again we are confronted with the mystery of man's responsibility as a morally culpable being and God's ultimate determination as the only one truly able to save. Just as this mystery is allowed in soteriology, so in the subject of Christian motivation we must hold together man's prerogative to look to reasonable, objective motivations (human responsibility) as well as the reality that only God can ultimately motivate (divine sovereignty). And he does so, according to Edwards, by granting a new relish.

[78] This statement by Jesus is remarkably relevant to the present discussion as it comes in the context of a discussion of 'temptations to sin' (Luke 17:1-6). Jesus knows struggles still will exist in the lives of his people. And the answer was not better living of the same kind but a different kind of living.

delight-filled obedience. We must be born again. Only God-given 'religious affections' will bring about the necessary incentive to keep the commands of God. Even Edwards' titles point us in the right direction.

This is why Christians defeat sin. 'When God gives men true grace and rightly disposes their hearts with respect to divine things, he will give 'em such kind of dispositions and affections towards them as do in some measure become their nature and importance.'[79] In 'Striving After Perfection,' having demonstrated the value of pursuing Christ-likeness, Edwards hastens to add:

> The new nature that is in the saints is of God, and is a divine nature, and therefore must be an enemy to every degree of that which is against God. Every saint has a new nature in him that is quite diverse [from] that old nature, the nature that he was born with, and is above it; and differs from it, as that which is heavenly differs from that which is earthly, or as that which is angelical does from that which is brutish, or as that which [is] divine does from that which is devilish.

> This new nature is from God, and is something of God; and therefore it tends to God again, and is contented with nothing short of God, and a perfect conformity to Him. As long as there is any separation or alienation remaining, it will not be easy; because as long as it is thus, the soul is kept off in some measure from God, whence its new nature is.[80]

Edwards is teaching biblical truth. As a result of the believer's union with Christ (Rom. 6:1-14), God has replaced the old with the new (2 Cor. 5:17). He has exchanged the heart of stone for a heart of flesh (Ezek. 36:26-27). The law has been

---

[79] From 'Zeal an Essential Virtue of a Christian,' *Sermons and Discourses, 1739–1742*, 145.

[80] *Sermons and Discourses, 1734–738*, 691.

etched indelibly on our hearts (Jer. 31:31-34). God's Spirit energizes us (Rom. 8:2-11). Do we still struggle? Of course (Rom. 7:7-25). But these struggles themselves are evidence that God has savingly revolutionized us.[81] Regeneration is not the elimination but the inauguration of true moral struggle.[82] And the hope for victory in these wrestlings lies in this: God has resurrected us.

Do you trust Christ and desire holiness above all else? Take heart. Grace comes to you both as forgiveness for past sins and fuel for future battles. If you long to know and love God, be not discouraged by your moral failures. He knows all about it. A day is coming soon when sin will become a forgotten nightmare, a fleeting memory never to be dealt with again. Press on. God will see you through.

> [T]hough you may fall, through God's mercy you shall rise again. He that hath begun a good work in you will carry it on until the day of Jesus Christ. Though you may be, at times, faint, yet if pursuing, you shall be borne on from strength to strength, and kept by the power of God, through faith, unto salvation.[83]

PERSONALITY OVERLOOKED?

Perhaps a thought has been nagging you: But aren't we all different? And if so, does this not play into a discussion

---

[81] See the tenth sermon of *Charity and Its Fruits*, in which Edwards lists seven signs that one is saved despite the presence of remaining sin (*Ethical Writings*, 310-12). 'Blessed Struggle,' a 1735 sermon based on Jacob's wrestling with God in Gen. 32, is another instance in which Edwards maintains and explains the role of Christian ethical struggling (*Sermons and Discourses, 1734–1738*, 418-34).

[82] Scott Hafemann is therefore right that 'we must resist downsizing repentance and faith into a change of mind and mental assent concerning the truth of data from the past. Repentance and faith are not "decisions" we make once and for all. The Holy Spirit's invasion of our lives is the *beginning* of our transformation into the character of God, not its end (2 Cor. 3:18)' (*God of Promise*, 215).

[83] From *Charity and Its Fruits*, in *Ethical Writings*, 312.

of what motivates us to obey God? In short, what is the role of personality in motivation? Surely different people are driven by different temperaments and individual make-up. Perhaps Mike is helped to fight the greed that plagues him by reflecting on what God has done for him in the past, invoking a sense of gratitude that makes him virtually unable to idolize material wealth. Bill, on the other hand, is most effectively motivated to reject the same vice by contemplating the fact that he is a child of the King of the universe and has a newfound identity. Tom is yet again different in that he finds help in the truth that there is a greater pleasure to be had in godliness than in money. Is the strength of a particular motivation, then, located (at least to a degree) in the personality of the individual?[84]

We can be even more specific by narrowing down to a single individual. In the various transgressions one is tempted to commit (or acts of righteousness from which one is tempted to abstain), are different motivations more helpfully applied to some sins than to others? In other words, could it be possible that the sin of lust is generally more effectively defeated by focusing on the personal benefit to be gleaned by obeying God and rejecting the lustful thought, while the sin of worry is more effectively battled by reflecting on one's identity as a child of God? Here we are asking if even within one person, different temptations might be defeated by different kinds of motivation.

TRANSCENDING PERSONALITY

Both questions – that of different personalities and that of different temptations within one personality – are legitimate. And yet both questions betray a misappropriation of Jonathan

---

[84] Archibald Alexander explores the ways different 'temperaments' lead to varieties of spiritual experience (*Thoughts on Religious Experience* [Philadelphia: Presbyterian Board of Publication, 1844; reprint], 48-69).

Edwards' understanding of Christian motivation. While it is true that different personalities may be more helped by reflecting on one of the three categories of motivations than on others, and that even the nature of the particular sin itself may determine how best a believer is to be motivated to defeat it, *no personality and no specific temptation is beyond the need for a divinely-given inclination toward holiness* to defeat it. We must remind ourselves, in other words, that past-, present-, and future-looking motivations, glorious and powerful as they are, remain inadequate apart from a spiritual work of God whereby one is given a new spiritual taste, no matter who we are. Any motivation to obey that is based on gratitude, identity, or personal benefit to the exclusion of a work of God's Spirit will never effectually bring lasting obedience.

If this is true, it makes sense why Edwards does not address head-on this issue of the role of personality in any thorough manner. As we have seen, Edwards most often goes underneath these three categories of motivation to provide the foundation for making any of them effective in the first place. Sereno E. Dwight, Edwards' great-grandson and first biographer, asserts that those newer to the faith may find gratitude to be a stronger motive than those who have been saved for a longer period of time. Dwight believes that in *Religious Affections* Edwards 'lays too little emphasis on gratitude, and those kindred emotions, which undoubtedly hold an ascendant influence in the bosom of a *young* convert.'[85] But Edwards shows us that such is

---

[85] Says Dwight: 'We might illustrate the progress of religion in the soul, by the feelings of a criminal who has unexpectedly received pardon from a magnanimous and merciful sovereign. A transport of gratitude to his benefactor is the first impulse; he is lost in amazement at his *unhoped-for* escape. His first emotions, therefore, naturally have a reference chiefly to the *benefits* he has received. After a while, and as his mind reverts again and again to the character of his sovereign, admiration of his moral worth and excellence begins gradually to attain the ascendancy: as such feelings slowly

the nature of regeneration – and the moral motivation that accompanies it – that gratitude is not necessarily a stronger motive for those young in the faith. While there may be an element of truth here, the deeper reality is that the regenerate soul is so taken with the beauty and excellencies of God in Christ that motivation is the natural outflow of the working of the Spirit in the human heart, giving a new apprehension of and delight in holiness.

Personal Benefit Pre-eminent

Yet we cannot quite end here without an added concession, for Edwards often does employ with partiality one of the objective motivations to convince his people that obedience is worth it. A careful reading of Edwards makes it impossible to miss. Only the Spirit can effectually motivate, and the result of this motivation is the gift of a new inclination. Yet Edwards consistently exhorts by showing the greater pleasure to be had in pursuing obedience rather than sin. He is hardly impartial in implementing most often the future-looking motivation of personal benefit. In his words, 'the Scripture from one end of the Bible to the other is full of things which are there held forth to work upon a principle of self-love. Such are all the promises and threatenings of the Word of God, and all its calls and invitations; its counsels to seek our own good, and its warnings to beware of misery.'[86]

---

strengthen into habits, he at length becomes enamored of these excellencies for their own sake, and thinks less of them in relation to the happiness they have conferred upon *him* than in relation to their intrinsic beauty. It is just thus, in our opinion, with the Christian convert. The approximation to a pure and disinterested love of God, (and whether such love can be *ever* attained, may well become a question,) must at all events be the last and most exalted attainment of piety' (*Works*, ed. Hickman, 1:xlix, xlviii).

[86] From *Charity and Its Fruits*, in *Ethical Writings*, 254-55.

'WE WILL FIGHT THEM WITH THEIR OWN WEAPONS'

Perhaps the best example of this is the 1723 sermon 'The Pleasantness of Religion', in which a nineteen-year-old Edwards explains that 'it would be worth the while to be religious, if it were only for the pleasantness of it.'[87] Here we find a beautiful and lucid picture of Edwards motivating his hearers to holiness by the sheer personal benefit – the 'pleasantness' – to be found in doing so. Edwards not only says that religion (i.e. Christianity) is, like honey, pleasant, but that even if this life's pleasures were the only thing profitable in religion, it would still be worth it. *'The Pleasantness of Religion* evinces Edwards' attempt to allure his audience with the sensuous delights of faith.'[88]

Edwards gives five reasons why religion is worthwhile if only for the pleasantness of it in this life. He is not constrained to argue for Christianity's appeal based on the pleasantness that our faith will usher in when we die and are with the Lord – even now Christianity is worth it. These reasons are: 1) Religion does not take away a person's senses but enables one to truly enjoy them; 2) Religion sweetens the pleasures of this life; 3) Sin brings more unpleasantness than pleasantness; 4) Religion brings more pleasure than new trouble; and 5) The pleasures of religion 'are much better and sweeter than any others.' As Edwards comes to his application at the end of the sermon, he begins by emphasizing that 'sinners are left without any manner of objection against religion.' He then lists the various ways in which sinners object to religion based on its supposed unpleasantness and shows his hearers that none of these

---

[87] Kimnach, et al, *Sermons Reader*, 15.

[88] Kimnach, et al, *Sermons Reader*, xl. For an explanation of how this fits with 1 Cor. 15:19 ('If in this life only we have hoped in Christ, we are of all people most to be pitied'), the reader is directed to the last two pages of the sermon (Kimnach, et al, *Sermons Reader*, 24-25), where Edwards deals with this verse.

objections holds water. He then makes one of his most memorable and powerful statements:

> We come with double forces against the wicked, to persuade them to a godly life. The most common argument that is used to urge men to godliness is the pleasures of the life to come; but this has not its effect for the sinner [who] is in pursuit of the pleasures of this life. Now, therefore, we urge to you the pleasures of this [life]: therefore you can have nothing to say. The common argument is the profitableness of religion, but alas, the wicked man is not in pursuit of profit; 'tis pleasure he seeks. Now, then, we will fight them with their own weapons, for religion does not deny us outward delights and pleasures.[89]

Here then is the thrust of what Edwards is saying and why it is relevant to a discussion of his theology of motivation.[90] It makes overwhelming sense to embrace Christianity. True, heaven alone supplies abundant reason to choose Christ. The Christian faith will profit us eternally in heaven, where we will be forever in Paradise, making this life on earth a mere dot of blemish in a mosaic of beauty. Yet one need not look beyond this life to heaven to see that the Christian religion is worthy of pursuit. The avenue Edwards takes to prove this is the pleasure Christianity offers *in this life*, commonly labeled simply 'pleasantness' or 'sweetness.'

---

[89] Ibid, 23-24.

[90] While it is true that this is a study of *Christian* motivation, and Edwards is here exhorting 'sinners' (unbelievers) to come to Christ, we note three things: 1) Edwards has just finished, before the section above quoted, using a very similar argument to exhort *saints* on to greater holiness; 2) Edwards was speaking to a congregation which presumably comprised many saints, and so his words needed to be of at least some relevance to those who had already been saved; and 3) there is enough of sin left even in those who have become a 'new creation' (2 Cor. 5:17; cf. Rom. 6:2 and Rom. 8:13) that his words are pertinent to all (though believers are no longer categorically 'sinners' as both Jesus and Paul use the term).

Christianity is to be pursued for the joy to be had therein: in this way he battles worldly hedonists 'with their own weapons.' He is defeating pleasure-seekers (is this not everyone?) on their own ground by showing that the very thing they are pursuing is found in that which they are rejecting. The greatest degree of pleasure is to be found in the Christian religion, the life for which every soul has been created. Sinners who refuse to repent and embrace Christ are like the unfortunate person bitten by a deadly viper who refuses to swallow the counteracting antivenin on account of its taste. True healing and joy can only be discovered by drinking the fluid.

At the same time, Edwards makes crystal clear that his objective is not to create self-centered individuals. This is lucidly affirmed in the nine different ways he gives in which religion provides spiritual pleasures which far outweigh worldly ones (part of his fifth and final main point, in which he shows that the pleasures to be experienced by the soul are greater and more solid than the pleasures to be had by the body[91]). The second of these nine types of spiritual pleasures is the pleasure to be experienced by a human being in knowing that he is an 'excellent' creature. So is this human-centeredness? No. It is 'not (that) the godly are pleased with proud and haughty thoughts of their own excellency, for they know they have nothing but what they received and that their excellency is wholly communicated to them by God. But the believer may rejoice, and does rejoice, to see the image of God upon their souls, to see the likeness of his dear Jesus.' It is the divine image that is so excellent in humanity, and it is the enjoying of this that is one of the pleasures of Christianity. Finding pleasure in religion is opposed to self-centeredness because 'there is very great delight the Christian enjoys in the sight he has

---

[91] Though both are legitimately enjoyed by Christians! (1 Tim. 4:1-5)

of the glory and excellency of God.'[92] The delight of the saint consists in the enjoyment and exaltation (for Edwards the two cannot be separated) of a Being outside of himself; namely, God. The joy of the regenerate heart is the Creator. This is not self-centeredness.

To find pleasure in religion, then, is the principal motivation Edwards uses to draw his listeners into the Kingdom. But it is not strictly self-satisfying pleasure. Rather, it is a pleasantness that finds its source and culmination in the God who bestows it on those who seek it by seeking him. We are motivated, says Edwards, by the benefit of the sweetness of religion to the soul.

EVEN PERSONAL BENEFIT ULTIMATELY IMPOTENT

For Edwards, the power of sin is not broken by trying to stomp it out and dutifully march on in obedience. The power of sin is broken by lifting one's eyes above the sin and seeing that the crumb of sin cannot compare to the feast of joy to be enjoyed in lovingly obeying the Lord who has wired human beings to run on him. The 'profit motive'[93] is the hue with which much of Edwards' work is tinted.

Nevertheless, while Edwards emphasized this category of rational motivation over others, he understood that none of these incentives are sufficient to compel obedience apart from the gracious implanting by the Spirit of a new relish. *The very ability to lift one's eyes and see that greater joy resides in obedience than in sin is itself a direct gift of God.* Recall these words from *Religious Affections*:

> Something else, entirely distinct from self-love, might be the cause of [love to God], viz. a change made in the views of his mind, and relish of his heart; whereby he apprehends a beauty, glory, and supreme good, in

---

[92] Kimnach, et al, *Sermons Reader*, 20-21.
[93] Holbrook, *Ethics of Jonathan Edwards*, 1.

God's nature, as it is in itself. This may be the thing that first draws his heart to him, and causes his heart to be united to him, prior to all considerations of his own interest or happiness, although after this, and as a fruit of it, he necessarily seeks his interest and happiness in God.[94]

The new inner relish is what brings love for God and takes place 'prior to all considerations of his own interest or happiness.' And so while Edwards does employ future benefits more than other motivations, there is something more foundational yet. A new inclination is what fuels rational motivation, including future benefit.

Edwards makes similar statements elsewhere. In Miscellany 631 Edwards explains that the profit motive is not all that is involved in authentic obedience, despite our concession that he does indeed use such incentive in his preaching: 'Unless men would love God from some real respect to God or sense of duty, that is, of the goodness of their duty, or disposition to their duty, as in itself good and lovely, and not merely from an aversion to pain and desire of pleasure, it is in no wise from any good principle.'[95] Though personal benefit is involved in virtue, there is something even more fundamental that must set virtue on fire if authentic obedience is to follow. 'Concerning Efficacious Grace' explains that even God's promises, which show us the bountiful benefits of Christianity, are kept only by his grace: 'the sovereign grace and will of God must determine the existence of condition of the promises, and so still the whole must depend on God's determining grace.'[96] So while it is true that Edwards utilized the future benefit element of objective motivation more than any other, this still was not

---

[94] *Religious Affections*, 241.

[95] *The 'Miscellanies' 501-832*, 158-59.

[96] *The Works of Jonathan Edwards*, vol. 21, *Writings on the Trinity, Grace, and Faith*, ed. Sang Hyun Lee (New Haven: Yale University Press, 2003), 306.

the determining factor for him as he understood obedience: beneath any objective motive lies the ultimate determinant of divine action.

A MISSIONARY'S TESTIMONY

Perhaps David Brainerd, the New England missionary who stayed in the Edwards home for a season and of whom Edwards wrote a biography, sums it up best. In his last year of life at age twenty-nine, Brainerd wrote in his diary that while he was convinced holiness contained 'the only happiness of my soul,' he pursued it primarily to 'please God ... and glorify him.' Moreover, writes Brainerd, this vision of the 'beauty of holiness' was 'discovered' to him. He did not discover it himself. God granted Brainerd a new inner relish.

> [O]ne morning, in secret meditation and prayer, the excellency and beauty of holiness, as a likeness to the glorious God, was so discovered to me, that I began to long earnestly to be in that world where holiness dwells in perfection: And I seemed to long for this perfect holiness, not so much for the sake of my own happiness (although I saw clearly that this was the greatest, yea, the only happiness of the soul) as that I might please God, live entirely to him, and glorify him to the utmost stretch of my rational powers and capacities.[97]

Brainerd did not long for holiness mainly for his own happiness, though he knew this would be included. He wanted simply to 'please God, live entirely to him.' Even the powerful motivation of personal benefit must be fueled by something deeper.

------

[97] *The Works of Jonathan Edwards*, vol. 7, *The Life of David Brainerd*, ed. Norman Pettit (New Haven: Yale University Press, 1985), 444-45.

Let us motivate ourselves by the joys to be gained in godliness, while reverently resting in the truth that the human heart only responds to such incentives if the living God is at work, graciously giving new eyes to see the all-surpassing worth of the pleasures of Christ. This is the gift of a new inner relish.

When we are drawn to duties out of wrong motives or fear or custom, and not from a new nature, this is not from the Spirit, and their performance is not from the true liberty of the Spirit. For under the liberty of the Spirit, actions come off naturally, not forced by fear or hope or any extra motives.... [T]here is a new nature in those who have the Spirit of God to stir them up to duty, though God's motives of sweet encouragement and rewards may help. But the principal is to do things naturally, not out of fear or to appease other people.

Richard Sibbes,
Glorious Freedom

The heart has its reasons of which reason knows nothing.

Blaise Pascal,
Pensées

I cannot, by direct moral effort, give myself new motives. After the first few steps in the Christian life we realize that everything which really needs to be done in our souls can be done only by God.

C. S. Lewis,
Mere Christianity

5

IMPLICATIONS

Tepid acknowledgment is not an optional response to Jonathan Edwards' perspective on motivation. His teaching must be either rejected outright or embraced as the all-transforming foundation for one's life. We cannot halfheartedly accept the truth of the need for an inner relish.

If heartfelt gladness in God is *definitive* of authentic Christianity, every sphere of human existence becomes increasingly colored with the 'delight to draw near to God' (Isa. 58:2) in a way never before feasible. Reading the Bible, for example, is done neither to appease some demand from God nor even primarily to gather new doctrinal data, but to cultivate enjoyment of Him. Prayer is not undertaken mainly to prevent illness and ensure safe travel – legitimate and necessary as these requests are! – but to indulge the insatiable universal human impulse to worship something beyond ourselves. Attending church is not a three-hour interruption into an otherwise relaxing weekend; it is an opportunity to taste the sweetness of Christ *together* in the nurturing fellowship without which even the most earnest believer will sputter along and eventually languish.[1] And what

---

[1] 'When Jesus called for taking up the cross and following him,' writes Robert W. Yarbrough, 'he probably had something more radical in mind than motoring to an air-conditioned sanctuary, amen-ing the show, and returning to the real life of Sunday TV and family fun (after sumptuous repast at the

about the more mundane daily activities in which we are all engaged – driving to work in thick traffic, taking a coffee break, doing a load of laundry, devouring a good burger, changing a diaper (with the birth of our son Zachary, I was recently initiated into this aromatic responsibility)? These too are opportunities not for Christians to have a break from bothering with God, but to see and rejoice in Him, the God who 'satisfies your hearts with food and gladness' (Acts 14:17). Mundane many days will be; Christians are not magically exempt from the strife of a fallen world and the 'vanity' of which the Preacher speaks (Eccles. 1:2ff.). But even he, in the end, concludes with an exhortation to 'Go, eat your bread in joy, and drink your wine with a merry heart, for God has already approved what you do' (9:7). A Christian is one who has been given a new set of glasses. Nothing looks the same again.

So what difference exactly does this make in your life and mine? If it is true that obedience in all the various avenues of life comes only as God gives a new taste for holiness, how do our lives look any different tomorrow as we continue to roll out of bed, slap the alarm, and brace ourselves for another day of emotional storms and moral temptations and difficult relationships?

Five main implications arise out of Jonathan Edwards' understanding of Christian motivation: the necessity of the new birth, the importance of prayer, the centrality of joy, the marriage of faith with works, and the pre-eminence of the glory of God.

The New Birth

Anyone with a hope of authentic obedience must be born again, or regenerated.[2] Nothing is more fundamental to

---

crowded new restaurant that everyone is dying to try)' ('Biblical Authority and the Ethics Gap: The Call to Faith in James and Schlatter,' *Presbyterion* 22/2 [1996]: 74).

Christianity. It is 'absolutely necessary for every one,' says Edwards, 'that he be regenerated, or born again.'[3] If conversion is defined solely as mental adherence to the most persuasive creed on the market, motivation will not follow, because nothing can impel a person to honor God with a pure life apart from the foreign importation of new desires. Naturally corrupt human beings do not stand in need of behavioral improvement. Graceless people cannot cultivate some moral principle latent in the soul. We all find ourselves in need of nothing less than total renewal. We apply band-aids to cancer in our attempts to please God by outward conformity not energized by an 'internal governing principle'[4] which finds its root in regeneration. Each of us leaves the womb in need not of reformation but of transformation. 'Attempted reformation' for those who have not been born again, says Edwards, is 'merely transitory and external'[5].

---

[2] Though the Greek word for *regeneration* occurs only twice in the New Testament (Titus 3:5; see also Matt. 19:28, where it refers to creation), the concept is found more broadly. Mark R. Talbot notes that 'the idea of spiritual renewal or rebirth or regeneration is often found in passages like John 3:1-8; Ephesians 2:1-5; Colossians 2:13; 1 Peter 1:3, 23; and throughout 1 John.' Though it is mysterious, he says, 'we know that it is entirely God's work and that it involves his making a radical, instantaneous change in us that rescues us from spiritual death by making us spiritually alive. This change then manifests itself over time in the regenerated person's daily life' ('Godly Emotions (*Religious Affections*),' in Piper and Taylor, *Legacy of Jonathan Edwards*, 229 n22). The Old Testament, too, spoke of the need for a new heart (Deut. 30:6; Jer. 24:7; 31:31-34; 32:39-40; Ezek. 11:19-20; 36:26-27). See also Sam Storms' helpful discussion of the biblical words used to speak of the new birth in *Chosen for Life*, 156-57. See Gerstner's thorough review of Edwards' theology of regeneration in his *Rational Biblical Theology*, 3:137-90. The doctrine of regeneration has been sidelined in recent New Testament scholarship; see the analysis of why this is so in Guy Prentiss Waters, *Justification and the New Perspectives on Paul: A Review and Response* (Phillipsburg, NJ: Presbyterian & Reformed, 2004), 196-97, 206-09.

[3] *Original Sin*, 361.

[4] From 'Efficacious Grace' in *Writings on the Trinity, Grace, and Faith*, 301.

[5] *Sermons and Discourses, 1730–1733*, 43.

C. S. Lewis displays characteristic insight in delineating the connection between new desires and the new birth. In a letter to a friend he writes:

> Here is the paradox of Christianity. As practical imperatives for here and now the two great commandments[6] have to be translated 'Behave as *if you* loved God and man.' For no man can love because he is told to. Yet obedience on this practical level is not really obedience at all. And if a man really loved God and man, once again this would hardly be obedience; for if he did, he would be unable to help it. Thus the command really says to us, 'Ye must be born again.'[7]

According to Lewis, even the moral commands of Jesus point to the need for a radical internal change. Edwards would agree. Like a suffocating animal that finally stops struggling, the naturally rebellious human heart must 'die.' But unlike that animal, this dying is not the end but the beginning of life. There is a death that ushers in new life. Jesus was explicit about this on several occasions. 'Unless a grain of wheat falls into the earth and dies,' he told his disciples the week before his own death, 'it remains alone; but if it dies, it bears much fruit. Whoever loves his life loses it, and whoever hates his life in this world will keep it for eternal life' (John 12:24-25).[8] Life comes through death. Have you died?

---

[6] 'You shall love the Lord your God with all your heart and with all your soul and with all your strength and with all your mind, and your neighbor as yourself' (Luke 10:27).

[7] C. S. Lewis, *Letters to Malcolm: Chiefly on Prayer* (London: Harcourt Brace & Company, 1964), 115.

[8] Other passages affirming the counter-intuitive paradox in Christianity that a certain death must precede authentic life – or, to become less will actually result in becoming somehow more – are 1 Sam. 2:4; Job 5:11; Prov. 11:24-25; 21:25-26; 29:23; Ezek. 21:26; Matt. 10:39; 18:1-4; 19:30; 20:16, 26-28; Mark 9:35; Luke 9:23-24; 9:48; 13:30; 14:11; 17:33; 18:14; John 3:30; 13:14-16; 1 Cor. 1:26-29; 2 Cor. 1:9; 4:7-12; 12:7-10; James 4:10.

The grace of God is the sole source of such transformational death-unto-life. Regeneration is utterly beyond the innate abilities of any of us. It is not mustered up by humans but transported in by God. He alone can 'cause us to be born again to a living hope' (1 Pet. 1:3). And though the effects of such a radical change are worked out over a lifetime, the change itself is instantaneous. In his battle against Arminianism, Edwards declares: 'everything in the Christian scheme argues, that man's title to, and fitness for heaven, depends on some great divine influence, at once causing a vast change, and not any such gradual change as is supposed to be brought to pass by men themselves in the exercise of their own power.'[9] Let us not neglect the truth of progressive sanctification. Certainly there is gradual growth in holiness throughout the Christian life (2 Cor. 7:1; 1 Thess. 4:7; 1 Tim. 2:15; Heb. 12:14). Triumphant victory is certainly not the immediate possession of the young Christian. Yet something decisive and irreversible happens when God confronts a rebellious soul and with sovereign softening, brings it to love him. Regeneration and progressive sanctification are not at odds with one another. Just the opposite. Regeneration presents not a *dilution of,* but the *foundation for* progressive sanctification, because the new birth is the seed from which sanctification sprouts. Unless we have been born again, our spiritual appetite will never incline to press after holiness. Dead people don't get hungry.

---

[9] From 'Concerning Efficacious Grace,' *Works*, vol. 2, ed. Hickman, 557. He had earlier stated that 'the power, and grace, and operation of the Holy Spirit, in, or towards, the conversion of a sinner, is immediate: ... the habit of true virtue or holiness is immediately implanted or infused; ... the operation goes so far, that a man has habitual holiness given him instantly, wholly by the operation of the Spirit of God, and not gradually by assistance concurring with our endeavors' (552). Simonson is wrong, then, when he attempts to explain Edwards' conversion by saying, 'Edwards' conversion was not an instantaneous happening but rather a succession of deepening disturbances' (*Theologian of the Heart,* 21). For Edwards, this is a false dichotomy.

Nor does this deny common grace, as if unless one is born again one will never act uprightly in any form or fashion. Unregenerate people are not as evil as they possibly might be. There is a measure of God's grace that extends to the whole creation, not just the redeemed (Matt. 5:45; Acts 14:17). Even so, there remains a 'universal need for supernatural grace.'[10] Only this supernatural grace introduces the irreversible process experienced by those born again. Unbelievers remain slaves to sin (Rom. 6:15-23). As the doctrine of one Edwardsean sermon puts it, 'We are all in ourselves utterly without any strength or power to help ourselves.'[11]

Archibald Alexander, the founder of Princeton Seminary, reminds us of the importance of the new birth. 'There is no more important event,' he writes, 'which occurs in our world, than the new birth of an immortal soul. Heirs to titles and estates, to kingdoms and empires, are frequently born, and such events are blazoned with imposing pomp, and celebrated by poets and orators; but what are all these honours and possessions but the gewgaws of children, when compared with the inheritance and glory to which every child of God is born an heir!'[12] Let us then examine our hearts and ask if we are truly born again. Dear friend, have you perceived God by way of 'a divine and supernatural light'? While allowing that you and I will never attain perfection before standing face to face with Jesus (1 Cor. 13:12) and knowing that sinful urges will plague us throughout our Christian journey, the question remains as unavoidable as tomorrow: *do you relish God?* Is he more than an object of 'speculative' knowledge – do you not only consider loving God, but love considering him? Do you ache

---

[10] *Sermons and Discourses, 1730–1733*, 7.

[11] *Sermons and Discourses, 1734–1738*, 380. From the 1735 sermon 'Our Weakness, Christ's Strength,' based on Rom. 5:6.

[12] *Thoughts on Religious Experience*, 35.

for his glory to be spread across the sky, or does ruthless honesty reveal a deeper longing for your own name to be known and loved and cherished? Such questions expose our hearts. To use Edwards' words, then: 'Let this put all who think themselves gracious upon examining themselves, whether they find that their grace is [real and sincere].'[13] Let us seek God with all our heart (Jer. 29:13-14), knowing he is quick to shower his rebellious creatures with mercy, for the question confronting us all at this moment is: Have I been born again?

PRAYER

And let us pray. Though we are utterly unable to quicken our own spirits to love him, God has not left us without avenues for soliciting divine aid. The need for an internal relish brightly illumines the awesome importance of prayer, for unbelievers as well as for believers. For unbelievers, prayer is the means God has appointed for them to seek him. God stands ready to hear the cries of those who are being awakened to an awareness of the weight of their sin.

But my focus in this book has been on those who are already children of God (*Christian* motivation), so let us consider the Christian first. To you I say that prayer is the resource by which every saint must cling to God for obedience, because, as we have seen, it is only by divine action that we will be motivated unto the bearing of fruit in our lives (John 15:1-8).

It is impossible to overstate this truth. If Edwards is right, and the importance of human striving is exceeded only by the importance of divine invigoration, what could be more crucial than prayer? If David Brainerd was speaking of a common Christian experience when he cried out in 1744,

---

[13] From *Charity and Its Fruits*, in *Ethical Writings*, 309. By 'gracious' Edwards refers not to those who are kind in personality but those who have been the subjects of the saving grace of God.

'Oh, my soul, what death it is, to have the affections unable to center in God, by reason of darkness,'[14] then nothing could be more vital to walking faithfully with God than calling on Him who is alone able to bring energy and light where there persists lethargy and darkness. It is God whom we ask for conversions; ought we not to ask Him also for motivation? If He alone grants a new relish in regeneration, must we not reverently and earnestly plead with him to sustain this miracle in us in sanctification?

Perhaps it will be objected that this is not consistent with the whole point of this book. After all, have we not seen that conversion *is* the gift of a new inner relish? In other words, if God changes us to the radical degree that I have been asserting throughout this book, then what remains for Christians to pray for? Two truths help give clarity here.

First, we must remember the way the Bible holds these two truths together: God changes us internally in a permanent way, *and* we must strive in the Christian course to show ourselves to be truly born again. To divorce the two is to create a false dichotomy. Scripture exhorts us to be 'diligent to make your calling and election sure' (2 Pet. 1:10). While God grants a new inclination in salvation, this does not eradicate the value of and need for prayer to sustain desire in the Christian life. We have addressed several of these Scriptures already (1 Cor. 15:10; Phil. 2:12-13; Col. 1:29; Isa. 26:12; 2 Tim. 1:6; 2:1). To these we could add passages such as Psalm 63:8, 'My soul clings to you; your right hand upholds me.' God's upholding hand does not mean we need not pursue Him with all our might. Jude, too, challenges Christians to 'keep yourselves in the love of God, waiting for the mercy of our LORD Jesus Christ that leads to eternal life' (v. 21). Notice how Jude holds both God's sovereignty and our responsibility in tension without explaining away either.

---

[14] *The Life of David Brainerd*, 268-69.

While it is Christ's mercy that leads to eternal life, we have a very real and awesome responsibility to keep ourselves in that love. So regeneration does not preclude Christian earnestness. The many warnings against apostasy in the letter to the Hebrews confirm that professing Christians do not have a license to be lackadaisical in the Christian life (Heb. 2:1-4; 3:7-4:13; 5:11-6:12; 10:19-39; 12:1-29).

Second, the radical change wrought in regeneration is logically consistent with striving in the wake of this change, because regeneration includes God's act of turning the human heart to him *in prayer*. When God breathes new life into us, one of the results of this transformation is a new impulse to pray. A natural result of the new birth is the presence of God's Spirit within us, prompting us to cry out to God (Rom. 8:14-17). Rather than regeneration ending the need for prayer, then, it inaugurates a life of prayer, just as physical birth inaugurates for children a life of dependence upon and communication with their earthly father. Therefore, let us cry out with the psalmist, 'Incline my heart to your testimonies!' (Ps. 119:36)[15]

Did Jonathan Edwards himself believe all this on a practical level? Did he call his people to pray? Repeatedly. In late 1740, for example, he preached 'Praying for the Spirit.' The doctrine of the sermon was: 'Of the more excellent nature any blessing is that we stand in need of, the more ready God is to bestow it in answer to prayer.' He went on to 'exhort God's people in this town earnestly to cry to God for the renewed pouring out of his Holy Spirit upon us.'[16] Humans are utterly dependent on God for everything, from working lungs and a beating heart to holy thirstings after godliness. Edwards knew prayer was crucial to the

---

[15] Earlier the psalmist had connected obedience with divine influence on the heart, as we have been seeing throughout this book: 'I will run in the way of your commandments when you enlarge my heart!' (v. 32)

[16] *Sermons and Discourses, 1739–1742*, 215.

presence of a new relish, and he called his people to pray for the Spirit as a result.

This means that when tempted to sin, we must both *pray* and *think* about why we ought not to indulge in that sinful action. We *pray* in light of the reality that the only sure defense against that temptation is the direct work of the Spirit of God, and we *think* in light of the fact that there are sound logical reasons for us to obey God. Yet Edwards reminds us of the preponderance of the former. Prayer is ultimate; rational reflection, whether of gratitude for past divine work, a changed identity, or personal benefit, is penultimate. Such reasons are the vehicles used – yet even vehicles need someone else to fuel them. Prayer is primary and cognitive observation secondary. For while sensible rational thinking may be immediately responsible for defeating a temptation, such moral victory is ultimately the working of God's Spirit.

What then about the prayers of unbelievers? The objection may be raised, if it is prayer that brings the new inner relish, then is not this gift up to humans after all? In other words, does not the assertion of this book – namely, that motivation is ultimately a gift of God – snatch the gift of motivation out of God's hands just when we thought it was there to stay?

This question arises from a faulty conception of the sovereignty of God as it relates to prayer. God's sovereignty encompasses all things – including prayer. Our prayers are not somehow 'outside' God's sovereign plan but inside it. *The request itself is a gift of God's prompting grace.* As a Christian prays, the deepest reality is that God Himself is energizing that prayer. The string of contingencies in the asking and answering of prayer does not start with the prayer but the God who prompts it. 'Prayer,' according to one scholar's interpretation of Edwards, 'is a God-ordained means to carrying out his will.'[17] We must pray in the hope-giving conviction that God is ultimately behind not only the answering but also the asking of that prayer. Against those in Edwards' day who taught that humans are ultimately determinant in the course of their lives, Edwards argues that 'the determination of the will is the gift of God; otherwise virtue is not his gift, and it is an inconsistence to pray to God to give it to us. Why should we pray to God to give us such a determination of will, when that proceeds not from him but ourselves?'[18] Human dependence on God does not quench prayer but fuels it with hope and expectation that it will be answered (Rom. 8:26-27).

God stands prepared to lavish His blessing of a new inclination on the human heart. Will we ask for it for our friends? Will we ask for it for ourselves? He is more ready and eager to meet us than we are to meet Him. He is not reluctant. Just the opposite – the Lord 'will rejoice over you with gladness; he will quiet you by his love; he will exult over you with loud singing' (Zeph. 3:17). Is your God a singing God? 'Behold, I stand at the door and knock,' says Jesus. 'If anyone hears my voice and opens the door, I will come in to him and eat with him, and he with me' (Rev. 3:20). 'Draw near to God, and he will draw near to you' (James 4:8). Our utter dependence on God does not mean His mercy is murky or fleeting or slippery.

He runs to meet us (Luke 15:20). We have but to ask.

Seeing we have such a prayer-hearing God as we have heard, let us be much employed in the duty of prayer: let us pray with all prayer and supplication: let us live prayerful lives, continuing instant in prayer, watching there unto with all perseverance; praying always, without ceasing, earnestly, and not fainting.[19]

---

[17] Nichols, *Guided Tour*, 210.

[18] *Works*, vol. 2, ed. Hickman, 557.

[19] Ibid, 118. This quote is taken from the end of the sermon 'The Most High a Prayer-Hearing God.' For another sermon on the importance of prayer

JOY

'All men seek happiness,' reflected Pascal one hundred years before Edwards. 'There are no exceptions; however different the means used, they all tend towards this goal.... The will never makes the slightest move except in the direction of this object. It is the impulse behind all human actions, even those of men who go and hang themselves.'[20] Thomas Aquinas had noted even earlier that sin itself is chosen because of the joy it promises: 'That to which the will tends by sinning, although in reality it is evil and contrary to the rational nature, nevertheless is apprehended as something good and suitable to nature, in so far as it is suitable to man by reason of some pleasurable sensation or some vicious habit.'[21] Jonathan Edwards would agree. Every human is endowed from birth with a desire to be happy. And only in God is this desire satisfied. 'Delight yourself in the LORD,' sings the psalmist, 'and he will give you the desires of your heart' (Ps. 37:4).

The need for a new inner relish enthrones joy in its rightful place of centrality in the life of the Christian. While Christianity inaugurates a life of suffering (Acts 14:22; 2 Tim. 3:12) and while for many bouts of melancholy often persist, it more deeply inaugurates a life of joy. Depression is real and not to be treated lightly. Nevertheless, a perpetually unhappy Christian is an oxymoron.[22] In Christ one discovers 'the highest and most ravishing pleasures, the most solid and substantial delights that human nature is capable of,'

see 'Importunate Prayer for Millennial Glory' (*Sermons and Discourses, 1739–1742*, 365-77). Cf. Luke 11:5-13; 12:32; 18:1-8; James 1:5-6; 4:8.

[20] Blaise Pascal, *Pascal's Pensées*, trans. Martin Turnbull (London: Harvill Press, 1962), 187.

[21] *Summa Theologica*, 1:619.

[22] The reader is referred to John Piper's *Desiring God: Meditations of a Christian Hedonist, 3d ed.,* (Sisters, OR: Multnomah, 2006) and Sam Storms' *Pleasures Evermore: The Life-Changing Power of Enjoying God* (Colorado Springs: NavPress, 2000) and *One Thing: Developing a Passion for the Beauty*

wrote 26-year-old Henry Scougal to a friend in seventeenth-century Scotland.[23]

The will is bound to do what it loves. Ultimate neutrality of will is a myth, as Edwards shows in *Freedom of the Will*.[24] Real biblical freedom is not the American ideal of unimpeded individual autonomy, but the renovation of the will such that happiness is pursued in godliness rather than in 'the fleeting pleasures of sin' (Heb. 11:25). God changes us by giving us new capacities, and new reasons, for joy. And so when Maharishi Mahesh Yogi, founder of the 'Transcendental Meditation' program of the 1970s, confidently pronounces that 'the purpose of life is the expansion of happiness,' he says the right thing with the wrong foundation. For Yogi calls people to experience joy by discovering innate human energy.[25] Edwards calls us to experience an invasion of foreign energy, that of the Holy Spirit of God whose presence has been made copiously available through Christ's cross and resurrection.

From one perspective, then, the change we have spoken of all through this book is a God-given and God-centered *joy*. Thomas Aquinas was right: 'Final and perfect happiness can consist in nothing else than the vision of the

---

of God (Fearn, Scotland: Christian Focus, 2004) for book-length treatments of the central place of joy in the life of the Christian. Both writers draw extensively on Edwards.

[23] *The Life of God in the Soul of Man*, 71.

[24] '[T]he will is always, and in every individual act, necessarily determined by the strongest motive; and so is always unable to go against the motive, which all things considered, has now the greatest strength and advantage to move the will.... The will in the time of that diverse or opposite leading act or inclination, and when actually under the influence of it, is not able to exert itself to the contrary, to make an alteration, in order to a compliance. The inclination is unable to change itself; and that for this plain reason, that it is unable to incline to change itself' (*Freedom of the Will*, 305).

[25] Harold H. Bloomfield and Robert B. Kory, *Happiness: The TM Program, Psychiatry, and Enlightenment* (New York: Pocket, 1977), xxx. Bloomfield and Kory call TM 'a major breakthrough in psychiatry' (xxvi). I suspect Edwards would not sign on.

Divine Essence.... The very sight of God causes delight. Consequently, he who sees God cannot need delight.' And even this is a gift of grace: 'man cannot attain happiness by his rational powers.'[26] Pascal too concludes: 'Happiness is neither outside nor inside us; it is in God.'[27]

In Psalm 19, after declaring the glories of God in the revelation of creation, David exults in the glories of God in written revelation: 'reviving the soul' (v. 7) and 'rejoicing the heart' (v. 8). The psalm climaxes with the following celebration of the instructions of the Lord: 'More to be desired are they than gold, even much fine gold; sweeter also than honey and drippings of the honeycomb' (v. 10).[28] This is the expression of the inner relish for God. Nothing else compares – neither the worth of gold nor the sweetness of honey adequately does justice to the worth and sweetness of Him apart from whom our hearts are ceaselessly restless. It is interesting also to note the next verse of the psalm: 'Moreover, by them is your servant warned; in keeping them there is great reward' (v. 11). Here we see precisely the pattern established in Edwards' thought in this book: it is deeply true that one finds motivation in the personal benefit of obedience (v. 11), yet the ultimate key to Christian motivation is the newfound, God-given ability to delight in God Himself (v. 10). Only the latter fuels lasting, heartfelt, joy-energized obedience.

---

[26] *Summa Theologica*, 1:601-2, 612. The reader is referred to the whole of Aquinas' discussion of happiness and the human will in Questions 2-33 of Part II in Vol. I (pp. 589-735) of his *Summa Theologica*. Relying heavily both on Scripture and on Augustine, Aquinas anticipates much of what Edwards would say on these two subjects half a millennium later.

[27] *Pensées*, 185. He later reiterates the point: 'In order to make men happy religion must show him that there is a God; that we are bound to love him; that our true happiness lies in being in him, and that our only sorrow is to be separated from him' (190).

[28] This theme of joy in God and his Word is replete in Ps. 119, too: see e.g. vv. 14, 24, 47, 72, 111, 127, and 131.

'No one has ever spoken better of the joy of finding salvation than Jonathan Edwards,' judges Hughes Oliphant Old.[29] It is hard to disagree. What else, after all, do the words we have used throughout this book denote but newfound joy? We have called Christianity the gift of a new *relish*. What is it to relish but to enjoy? We have described it as a new *inclination*. But what is it to be inclined one way and not another but to find greater joy in one thing than another? We have reflected on Edwards' metaphor of a newfound *taste*, yet this too implies that we find God intrinsically pleasant. Our language all through reminds us that Christians are those whose eyes have been opened to a new and superior joy – the joy of holiness. 'Joy in God,' wrote the Scottish pastor William Anderson in 1871, 'is necessary as an evidence of the heart being regenerated.' He later concludes:

> Christian faith properly commences with persuasions of the Father's love in his essential paternal character; and, from the beginning to the end of its course, contemplates Christ as being His Gift; so that the more it sees of Christ's preciousness, the more does it discover of the love of the Father who gave Him. I, therefore, press the question, Does *your* heart delight itself in God?[30]

The whole Christian life hinges on one's capacity to find joy in God – not mainly in God's benefits, staggering as these are, but in God himself. Edwards relentlessly reminds us that joy is not a take-it-or-leave-it addendum to Christianity. It is neither optional nor peripheral. Rather, *authentic obedience comes when happiness and holiness meet such that holiness becomes the source of happiness rather than its alternative*. Holiness is meant to ignite, not eliminate, joy.

---

[29] Old, *Reading and Preaching of the Scriptures*, 5:278.
[30] William Anderson, *Treatise on Regeneration* (Philadelphia: Smith, English and Company, 1871), 289, 291.

Let us not squelch our yearning to be happy but cultivate it. God delights in giving new desires to His creatures and meeting those desires with overflowing abundance, spilling out to a world quenching its thirst with the sand of sin instead of the wine of the King. So let us enjoy the endlessly enjoyable God. 'In your presence there is fullness of joy; at your right hand are pleasures forevermore' (Ps. 16:11).

Faith and Obedience

[A]ll true Christian grace tends to holy practice.... If any have a notion of grace that it is something put into the heart there to be confined and lie dormant, and that its influence does not govern the man as an active being, or that the alteration of the heart which is made when grace is infused, though it indeed mends the heart, yet has no tendency to a proportionable emendation of life, they have a quite wrong notion of it.[31]

The need for a supernatural relish happily reunites faith and works. These two aspects of the Christian life – what we believe and how we behave – are often put in tension with one another, or one side is neglected and so they are put out of balance. When the sole saving sufficiency of faith is neglected while works are emphasized, moralism ensues. We believe the lie that our obedience earns God's favor, rather than flows out of divine favor. On the other hand, when salvation by faith alone is recovered to the exclusion of a changed life, antinomianism ensues. We believe the lie that God's grace is such that we are freed from moral obligation. Grace becomes a license to live any old way we want.

Yet we have learned from Edwards the vital connection between these two aspects of Christianity, for 'if men are changed in their hearts by God, all else will follow.'[32] The

---

[31] *Charity and Its Fruits*, in *Ethical Writings*, 294.

IMPLICATIONS

two cannot be divorced if regeneration involves a new inclination. For this reason, the New Testament teaches that a tree is known by its fruit (Matt. 7:17-18; 12:33; Luke 3:7-9; 6:43-44; James 3:11-12). Our actions display what is inside us better than any stethoscope. Real faith – faith that exists because God has put it there – is by its very nature clothed with changed behavior. Though the mind plays a central role, God does not save us fundamentally by convincing us of the intellectual veracity of the Christian creed. He saves us by total transformation, including not only the mind but also the will.

This helps us see why faith without good works is dead (James 2:14-26). Real faith comes by virtue of an inner change, a change that does not exist apart from a changed life. Butterflies no longer crawl along branches as if they were still caterpillars. Why not? They've been transformed. Metamorphosis has given a new capacity: the capacity to fly. Before the change, they never could have imagined flying; after the change, they cannot imagine life without it.

This is how Jonathan Edwards understands the nature of saving faith and its influence on the affections, or emotions. He reunites faith and works by showing that the two are part and parcel of a soul whose fundamental disposition has been reversed. *Religious Affections* explains the connection between divine grace and changed behavior:

> The tendency of grace in the heart to holy practice, is very direct, and the connection most natural close and necessary.... Godliness in the heart has as direct a relation to practice, as a fountain has to a stream, or as the luminous nature of the sun has to beams sent forth, or as life has to breathing, or the beating of the pulse,

---

[32] Holbrook, *Ethics of Jonathan Edwards*, 78. See also George Hunsinger, 'Dispositional Soteriology: Jonathan Edwards on Justification by Faith Alone,' *Westminster Theological Journal* 66 (2004): 107-20.

or any other vital act; or as a habit or principle of action
has to action: for 'tis the very nature and notion of grace,
that 'tis a principle of holy action or practice.[33]

In *Charity and Its Fruits* Edwards uses equally strong
metaphors: 'all grace has a direct relation to a holy practice,
as a root has to the plant which springs from it, and as
the head of a spring has to the stream, or as a light has to
shining, or as a principle of life has to living.'[34] It is no more
feasible to separate works from faith than it is to separate
light from the sun. The former inevitably follows from the
latter. The wedding in an individual of a profession of faith
in Christ with a corresponding change of life is as axiomatic
as a healthy young man simply *living*: breathing, thinking,
growing. How could it be otherwise? C. S. Lewis makes a
similar observation when he writes that Christian obedience
is 'not hoping to get to Heaven as a reward for your actions,
but inevitably wanting to act in a certain way because a first
faint gleam of Heaven is already inside you.'[35]

---

[33] *Religious Affections*, 398. See also Simonson, *Theologian of the Heart*,
58-60. Clyde Holbrook describes Edwards' understanding of obedience in
Religious Affections as affirming that 'nothing is more active than true grace,
so it follows as a matter of course that the heart truly moved will express
itself spontaneously in beneficent acts' (*Ethics of Jonathan Edwards*, 33).
Gerald McDermott provocatively suggests that 'Martin Luther's salvation by
faith *alone* becomes for Edwards salvation by faith *primarily*. While Luther
emphasizes that in justification sinners are *counted* as righteous, Edwards
insists that sinners are actually *made* holy in the act of regeneration' (Gerald
R. McDermott, *Jonathan Edwards Confronts the Gods: Christian Theology,
Enlightenment Religion, and Non-Christian Faiths* [Oxford: Oxford University
Press, 2000], 136).
[34] *Ethical Writings*, 308. See also Edwards' series of sermons together
labeled 'Justification by Faith Alone,' in which he responds extensively to
the objection that the doctrine of justification by faith renders obedience
irrelevant in the Christian life (*Sermons and Discourses, 1734–1738*, 201ff.).
This was the sermon series, according to Edwards, that God blessed to
inaugurate the first wave of revival at Northampton, in 1734.
[35] C. S. Lewis, *Mere Christianity* (New York: MacMillan, 1943), 131.

Here again is opportunity for self-examination. If our Christian faith consists of newly accepted information without accompanying transformation, let us hear with sobriety Edwards' closing words from his sermon 'Christ the Spiritual Sun': 'Let this put persons upon examining themselves whether or no they are not unbelievers. Though you have a standing in God's vineyard, yet are you not barren? Then if so, consider what Christ did to the barren fig tree. Are you not rooted in stony ground? Are you not dry and dead plants?'[36]

Furthermore, the inner relish, as well as the remarriage of faith and works which it illumines, resists the human impulse to earn one's own way to God with moral living. The imparting of a new relish demolishes legalism by affirming that grace always exists *before* truly God-honoring obedience. Holy living does not effect God's mercy; it is an effect *of* God's mercy. Grace is not caused by moral success, but itself causes moral success (2 Cor. 9:8; 1 Pet. 4:11). So to consider dutiful living as that which elicits God's favor (legalism) is to fall prey to a deformed view of grace. The truth is that grace prompts obedience as God grants and fuels a new desire for holy and consecrated living, and so to view our obedience as earning God's smile is in fact having the opposite effect we think it to be having: since God's grace is itself directly responsible for good deeds, to view such deeds as meritorious is to put us more in God's debt, not less. Therefore, the gift of a new relish for God helps us see legalism as an inverted view of God and his grace.

There is one sure way to know a volcano is active – it erupts. The inner reality invisible to an outside observer could not be contained. It had to spill out. So it is with a true Christian.

---

[36] *Sermons and Discourses, 1739–1742*, 62.

The Glory of God

A final implication of the truth that all obedience is the outflow of divinely-implanted taste buds points us to what Edwards believes to be the ultimate purpose of every event in the history of the universe. For if there is something Edwards believes drives God in all He does, we are wise to learn what this is as it will lay bare God's ultimate purpose in motivating His people.

Jonathan Edwards believed the driving force in all God does is to display, for the joy of His people, His own glory – 'the resplendent radiance of his power and personality.'[37] 'His greatest emphasis of all,' preached Martyn Lloyd-Jones of Edwards in 1976, was 'the glory of God.'[38] The manifestation of His own magnificence is God's driving motivation.

How does this tie in to Christian motivation? In two ways Edwards' teaching on the new inner relish highlights God's glory, one with reference to the *giver* of grace and one with reference to the *recipients* of grace.

First, with a view to the giver of grace, God is glorified by being the sole benefactor of saving and motivating grace. He alone is responsible for the inner relish. Edwards cites Acts 12 as he battles contemporaries seeking to attribute moral improvement to the cultivation of principles latent in natural man. In this passage (vv. 21-23) Herod is lauded for his skill in public speech, and when he does not give God the glory, he is struck down and eaten by worms. Edwards comments:

---

[37] Storms, *One Thing*, 34.

[38] Lloyd-Jones, 'Jonathan Edwards,' 120. For a book-length elucidation of Edwards' belief in the centrality of the glory of God see Stephen R. Holmes, *God of Grace and God of Glory: An Account of the Theology of Jonathan Edwards* (Grand Rapids, MI: Eerdmans, 2000). Holmes believes that at the heart of Edwards' message was the conviction that 'God creates for the promotion and display of His own glory' (31).

God was so angry with Herod for not giving God the glory of his eloquence, that the angel of the Lord smote him immediately, and he died a miserable death.... But if it be very sinful for a man to take to himself the glory of such a qualification as eloquence, how much more a man's taking to himself the glory of divine grace, God's own image, and that which is infinitely God's most excellent, gracious and glorious gift, and man's highest honor, excellency and happiness, whereby he is partaker of the divine nature, and becomes a Godlike creature?[39]

In other words, if, as Acts 12 shows, God is zealous for His glory to be recognized in the natural gifts of unbelievers, how much more zealous must He be for it in the supernatural gift of grace in believers?

Second, with a view to the recipients of grace, the gift of a new inner relish connects with the pre-eminence of God's glory because this new sense is in its very nature a longing *for God to be glorified*. In regeneration God turns upside-down the self-exalting inclinations of the soul. This conviction drove Edwards to preach sermons such as 'That it Is the Temper of the Truly Godly to Delight to Exalt God and to Lay Themselves Low,' in which he asserts of a regenerate person that 'since God has graciously enlightened him, how doth he immediately quit his seat, give place to God, and deliver up the scepter to him and with pleasure cast himself down to the footstool.'[40]

The new birth, in other words, is a Copernican revolution. For centuries the world had accepted that the sun and other planets revolved around the earth, but in the sixteenth century the Polish scientist Copernicus challenged this by

[39] From 'Efficacious Grace' in *Writings on the Trinity, Grace, and Faith*, 298-99.
[40] Michael D. McMullen, ed., *The Blessing of God: Previously Unpublished Sermons of Jonathan Edwards* (Nashville, TN: Broadman & Holman, 2003), 75.

presenting to the world his conviction that our planet is not the center around which the universe revolves; rather the earth revolves around the sun. Though this was the truth, it was not well-received (it took the telescopes of Galileo to later vindicate Copernicus' belief). But we now know that these early scientists were right. My point is that what they discovered astronomically, we discover spiritually: *we are not at the center of the universe*. At the heart of the new inner relish is the understanding that we are not the center. God is the center. God is the sun. Christians are those who have come to see and love the truth that the sun does not revolve around them, but they revolve around the sun.

God is honored, then, not only because He is the giver of grace, but because by its very nature this grace imparts a desire for Him to be seen more truly for who He is. Clyde Holbrook brings these two together when he says that 'the absolute primacy of God ... in Edwards's moral theology moves the emphasis in morality from the human subject and his capacities to a plane where the nature and purpose of deity are determinative of virtue.' Put another way, 'the deity is the originative power as he is also the supreme end.'[41] These are scholarly ways of saying simply that the Creator and the creation aspire together to magnify the unspeakable beauty and brilliance of the God of might and mercy. The immediate goal of motivation is greater holiness; but the ultimate goal of greater holiness is greater glorification of the Holy One. Holiness is an awesome goal, but it is not the ultimate goal of all things. A touchdown is nice, but it is not the ultimate goal of a football game. Winning the game is the goal. If the game is not won, touchdowns are meaningless. If God is not glorified, similarly, obedience is meaningless. The display of the splendor of God is the ultimate purpose of all things

---

[41] Holbrook, *Ethics of Jonathan Edwards*, 103.

– including holiness.[42] This leaves no room for boasting in obedience or greater holiness, because it is all a result of God and God alone (Exod. 31:13; Rom. 4:2, 20). 'Then what becomes of our boasting? It is excluded' (Rom. 3:27). 'Let him who boasts, boast in the Lord' (1 Cor. 1:31; 2 Cor. 10:17). 'From him and through him and to him are all things. To him be glory forever' (Rom. 11:36).

We could draw from countless writings of Edwards to demonstrate that 'fully exhibiting the divine glory, was the primary motive, which impelled the Creator to give existence to the universe';[43] that is, 'man was made to serve and glorify his Creator.'[44] We have already mentioned, for example, the remarkable resolutions to which Edwards committed himself. The first reads: 'Resolved, that I will do whatsoever I think to be most to God's glory, and my own good, profit, and pleasure, in the whole of my duration, without any consideration of the time, whether now, or never so many myriads of ages hence.' The fourth determination echoes this theme: 'Resolved, never to do any manner of thing, whether in soul or body, less or more, but what tends to the glory of God; nor be, nor suffer it, if I can avoid it.'[45] Such was the resolve of Jonathan Edwards.

---

[42] Consider Paul's words to the Philippians: 'This is my prayer: that your love may abound more and more in knowledge and depth of insight, so that you may be able to discern what is best and may be pure and blameless until the day of Christ, *filled with the fruit of righteousness that comes through Jesus Christ – to the glory and praise of God*' (1:9-11, italics added). Clyde Holbrook identifies 'the secret of Edwards' as 'theological objectivism,' as distinct from theological subjectivism (*Ethics of Jonathan Edwards*, 1-3). By this he means that the central hermeneutic for understanding Edwards is to understand that theology and life find meaning pre-eminently in God, not humanity. God and his glory are ultimate. 'At no point ... does the human subject become the chief aim of God's creation; he is completely subordinated to God's glory and contributes to it. Theological subjectivism has no place in this view of reality' (107).

[43] *Works*, vol. 1, ed. Hickman, xlix.

[44] Kimnach, et al, *Sermons Reader*, 136.

[45] *Letters and Personal Writings*, 753. See also resolution number 23.

The magnification of God – seeing God, and bringing others to see Him, more accurately for who He is – was Edwards' highest aim in life. All other goals are subsumed under this and find their consummation in it. Hence Sereno Dwight's comment that the preacher of Northampton was incessantly 'encouraging upon all occasions an earnest concern for the glory of God, the grand object for which he desired to live both upon earth and in heaven, an object compared with which all other things seemed in his view but trifles.'[46]

In his *Dissertation Concerning the End for Which God Created the World*, Edwards says that 'all that is ever spoken of in the Scripture as an ultimate end of God's works is included in that one phrase, "the glory of God." '[47] God created the world and redeemed the church to display himself in all His glory. Likewise his *History of the Work of Redemption* sets out to show the design by which God has set out to redeem a people for Himself from this fallen world. In the introduction Edwards gives five reasons for what were 'the design of this great work' of redemption. The fifth and final reason is this:

> In all this [creation and redemption] God designed to accomplish the glory of the blessed Trinity in an exceeding degree. God had a design of glorifying himself from eternity, to glorify each person in the Godhead.... And that the Son should thus be glorified and should glorify the Father by what should be accomplished by the Spirit to the glory of the Spirit, that the whole Trinity conjunctly and each person singly might be exceedingly glorified.[48]

---

[46] *Works*, vol. 1, ed. Hickman, lxv.

[47] *Ethical Writings*, 526. Marsden comments on this treatise well: 'It is as though the universe is an explosion of God's glory' (Marsden, *Edwards*, 463).

[48] *The Works of Jonathan Edwards*, vol. 9, *A History of the Work of Redemption*, ed. John F. Wilson (New Haven: Yale University Press, 1989), 125-26.

Concerning this important work, John Wilson says that 'God's self-glorification ... explained the significance Edwards attached to the project.'[49]

Everything that happens is either directly or indirectly one link in the chain of history leading to God being seen more accurately for what He is: unendingly glorious, beautiful, magnificent. This is God's great aim in all things, and the loving gift of grace to his saints is that he makes it their great and joy-giving aim in all things: 'a truly virtuous mind, being as it were under the sovereign dominion of *love to God*, does above all things seek the *glory of God*, and makes *this* his supreme, governing, and ultimate end.'[50]

A Christian heart is a motivated heart, and a motivated heart yearns to make known the magnificence of the God of grace.

---

[49] Ibid, 41. The display of God's own glory is a theme found not only in Edwards' works but in his sermons, such as the 1731 sermon 'God Glorified in Man's Dependence' (Kimnach, et al, *Sermons Reader*, 66-82).

[50] From *The Nature of True Virtue*, in *Ethical Writings*, 559. Italics original. Marsden writes, concerning this treatise: 'True virtue is ultimately distinguished from its imitators by motive or disposition. This crucial point needs to be underscored because it reflects Edwards' overall vision of a personal universe and affective religion. True virtue grows out of a disposition to true love' (Marsden, *Edwards*, 470).

Those former delights, never reached the heart;
and did not arise from any sight
of the divine excellency of the things of God;
or any taste of the soul-satisfying,
and life-giving good, there is in them.

Jonathan Edwards

6

CONCLUSION

The Bible provides several different kinds of motivation for believers to obey God, including a past emphasis on what God has done, a present emphasis on who one now is in Christ, and a future emphasis on the promises of God. Scripture employs all three and encourages the believer to implement them in one's battles with sin. Perhaps other categories could be added.

None of these, however, provides the motivational engine in the life of the Christian. While all three provide powerful incentives to walk in the path of God's will, none of them will effectively and lastingly fuel obedience *apart from a work of God's regenerating grace whereby He imparts a new inner relish for holiness*. At the heart of the ministry of Jonathan Edwards is the conviction that unless God gives this new taste, this new inclination of the heart, no amount of objective rationale will ignite authentic obedience – that which is from the heart and not hollow legalism. God must change us from the inside out. Conversion is not mental assent to a new creed – though the mind is of course active! Rather, it is the divine granting of a new love for God such that holiness appears beautiful instead of ugly, while sin becomes repulsive instead of attractive. As we saw in both Edwards and C. S. Lewis, immoral people don't want to obey, so they don't; moral people don't want to obey, but they do; Christians *want* to obey.

While God delights to use such logical motivations as gratitude, a new identity, and future profit, these are not the foundation for obedience. The fundamental ingredient is rather a new sense of and love for God. For Edwards, while believers will continue to struggle with sin until heaven, to be a Christian is to be motivated.

AUGUSTINE'S BREAKTHROUGH

At the beginning of this book we saw in Augustine a poignant portrait of the human heart's need for a radical change of heart. As a boy it was sin, he said, that he 'relished and enjoyed.' In his words, 'I was inwardly starved of that food which is yourself, O my God.' The famine turned to feast, however, with the heaven-sent gift of a new inner relish. Conversion for Augustine meant coming to cherish and enjoy God Himself. He described his deepest longing by telling the Lord that 'it is on you that I want to gaze with eyes that see purely.'[1] Such a gaze is possible only as the Divine Optometrist bestows a divine and supernatural light. God mercifully gave Augustine the gift of tasting the sweetness of divine flavor (Ps. 34:8).

Christian faith is not fundamentally a mental decision. Though not less than this, it is much more. It is the furnishing of holy esteem for God. It is being awakened to sacred beauty. Without this, obedience will remain half-hearted drudgery instead of whole-hearted delight. Authentic obedience, in distinction from both disobedience and cold, inauthentic obedience, is the cultivating and living out of a newfound love for God which is a result of one's heart being inclined to treasure God simply by virtue of who He is. Only in this way do we become 'obedient from the heart' (Rom. 6:17).

---

[1] Augustine, *Confessions*, 32, 37, 33.

Only one question remains. What about Edwards? We know what he taught. But did *he* know first-hand this relish for God? Or did he speak of a foreign experience when he spoke of the new sense of the heart? Was it as an abstract theologian that Jonathan Edwards explained the difference between true believers and stony-hearted, though morally upright, men and women? He speaks for himself as we close. God grant such grace in overflowing, happy abundance to Christ's Church in the twenty-first century.

> The first that I remember that ever I found anything of that sort of inward, sweet delight in God and divine things, that I have lived much in since, was on reading those words, 1 Tim. 1:17, 'Now unto the King eternal, immortal, invisible, the only wise God, be honor and glory for ever and ever, Amen.' As I read the words, there came into my soul, and was as it were diffused through it, a sense of the glory of the divine being; a new sense, quite different from any thing I ever experienced before....
>
> The delights which I now felt in things of religion, were of an exceeding different kind, from those ... that I had when I was a boy. They were totally of another kind; and what I then had no more notion of, than one born blind has of pleasant and beautiful colors. They were of a more inward, pure, soul-animating and refreshing nature. Those former delights, never reached the heart; and did not arise from any sight of the divine excellency of the things of God; or any taste of the soul-satisfying, and life-giving good, there is in them.[2]

---

[2] *Letters and Personal Writings*, 792, 794-95.

Appendix:

The Inner Relish Before and After Jonathan Edwards

In what follows I attempt to trace Edwards' understanding of the critical motivational need for a Spirit-ignited 'relish' for holiness through two thousand years of church history, stopping at important figures along the way. Though such an endeavor must of necessity be highly selective, my own eyes have been opened in the process to the widespread support of Edwards' teaching, though I feel more confirmed than ever that no one explained it as thoroughly and forcefully as Edwards.

While I have found it to be more pervasive than I expected among the old writers, however, this teaching on regeneration and the inner motivation necessarily concomitant with it is a truth largely absent in today's pulpits and Christian literature. In my generation this teaching must regain its crucial emphasis if we are to see authentic, sin-killing, culture-transforming Christianity revitalized in our pews.

I have tried to draw from various sectors of the church, though it is readily confessed (and will be painfully obvious) that significant movements have been neglected, the Patristic period and Roman Catholicism being the most notable examples. The Reformation, Puritanism, and American Calvinism have been my main sources. I have at times stepped outside the bounds of this stream of thought, appealing to medieval and post-Reformation Scholasticism (Aquinas and Turretin, respectively), Pietism (Francke), Wesleyanism (Wesley), German post-Enlightenment thought (Schlatter), and reflective thinkers who defy categorization (Lewis). I have also shamelessly neglected non-Western thinkers, as well as much of non-English-speaking Christendom. So be it; I have dealt with what I know. I leave the many gaps to be filled by those more competent than I.

In some of the writers cited, many more quotes could have been brought forth. In such cases I have culled what I take to be the statements most pertinent to the present study of regeneration-wrought motivation, keeping this appendix to a reasonable length.

The selections are presented in chronological order of birth. I include at the end a few of the formative historic creeds of the church in which regeneration-produced, joy-fueled obedience is plainly confessed as historic Christian orthodoxy.

Throughout, I am attempting to illumine in the thought of these pillars of the church the thesis of this book: rational, objective motivation is integral to healthy Christianity, but it is not foundational. It is itself fueled by something deeper. Only a divinely wrought change of the will at the center of the human heart renders obedience one's delight, providing effectual and truly God-honoring motivation.

* * *

Augustine (354–430), North African church father central to both Catholic and Protestant theology:[1]

> If that commandment is observed out of fear of punishment, not out of the love of righteousness, it is observed in the manner of a slave, not in the manner of someone free, and for that reason it is not observed. For there

---

[1] All italicized statements throughout this appendix are original.

is lacking the good fruit that springs up from the root of love. But if *faith that works through love* is present (Gal. 5:6), one begins to find delight in the law of God in the interior human being. This delight is a gift, not of the letter, but of the Spirit....

The Lord is the Spirit, but where the Spirit of the Lord is, there is freedom (2 Cor 3:17). This is the Spirit of God by whose gift we are justified; by his gift there comes to be in us a delight in not sinning so that we have freedom. So too, without this Spirit we find delight in sinning so that we are enslaved.[2]

Are we then doing away with free choice through grace? Heaven forbid! Rather, we make free choice stronger.... through faith we obtain grace to struggle against sin; through grace the soul is healed from the wound of sin; through the good health of the soul we have freedom of choice; through free choice we have the love of righteousness; through the love of righteousness we fulfill the law. The law is not done away with, but strengthened by faith, because faith obtains the grace by which we fulfill the law. In the same way, free choice is not done away with by grace, but strengthened, because grace heals the will by which we freely love righteousness.[3]

Everything is, of course, easy for love; for love alone Christ's burden is light, or rather it alone is the burden which is itself light. In this sense scripture says, *And his commandments are not burdensome* (1 John 5:3). Hence, people who find them burdensome should consider that God could only say that they are not burdensome, because there can be a disposition of the heart for which they are not a burden, and such persons should

---

[2] 'The Spirit and the Letter,' in *The Works of Saint Augustine, Vol. 23: Answer to the Pelagians*, trans. Roland J. Teske, ed. John E. Rotelle (New York: New City, 1997), 167, 168.

[3] Ibid, 185.

beg for what they lack so that they may fulfill what is commanded.[4]

God pours out ... an ineffable sweetness in the depths and interior of the soul, not merely through those who externally plant and water, but also through himself who gives the increase secretly. In that way he not merely reveals the truth, but also imparts love. After all, that is the way God teaches those who have been called according to his purpose (Rom 8:28); at the same time he grants them both to know what they should do and to do what they know.[5]

[T]hat righteousness is said to be from the law which is produced by the curse contained in the law, but that righteousness is said to be from God which is given through the benefit of grace so that his commandment does not bring terror, but sweetness. Thus we pray in the psalm, *You are sweet,* Lord, *and in your sweetness teach me your righteousness* (Ps. 119:68), that is, so that I am not forced to live under the law as a slave out of fear of punishment, but may find delight in the law with the love that makes me free. The person, of course, who gladly carries out the commandment does so in freedom. And those who learn in this sense do whatever they learn that they should do.[6]

Pelagius speaks about this ability in his first book in defense of free choice. He says, 'We have the ability for each alternative implanted in us by God as a sort of fruitful and fertile root, if I may use this comparison. It generates and brings forth diverse products from the human will and can at the choice of its gardener either be radiant with the flowers of virtues or bristle with the thorns of vices'. Here he does not see what he

---

[4] 'Nature and Grace,' in *Works of Augustine*, 23:269.
[5] 'The Grace of Christ and Original Sin,' in *Works of Augustine*, 23:410.
[6] Ibid, 411.

is saying; he makes one and the same root the source of both good and evil in opposition to the truth of the gospel and the teaching of the apostle. For the Lord said that a good tree cannot bear bad fruit, and a bad tree cannot bear good fruit. And when the apostle Paul said that covetousness is the root of all evils, he certainly indicated that we should understand that love is the root of all good. If, then, the two trees, the good one and the bad one, are two human beings, a good one and a bad one, what is the good human being but one with good will, that is, a tree with a good root? And what is a bad human being but one with a bad will, that is, a tree with a bad root? After all, the fruits of these roots and trees are thoughts, words, and deeds; the good ones come forth from a good will, the evil ones from an evil will.

But human beings become good trees, when they receive the grace of God. They do not, after all, by themselves change themselves from bad to good. Rather, they do this from him and through him and in him who is always good.[7]

Thomas Aquinas (1225–1274), Italian church doctor and philosopher-theologian:

As the intellect is moved by the object and by the Giver of the power of intelligence ... so is the will moved by its object, which is good, and by Him who creates the power of willing. Now the will can be moved by good as its object, but by God alone sufficiently and efficaciously. For nothing can move a movable thing sufficiently unless the active power of the mover surpasses or at least equals the potentiality of the thing movable. Now the potentiality of the will extends to the universal good; for its object is the universal good; just as the object of the intellect is universal being. But every created good

---

[7] Ibid, 413.

is some particular good; God alone is the universal good. Whereas He alone fills the capacity of the will, and moves it sufficiently as its object. In like manner the power of willing is caused by God alone. For to will is nothing but to be inclined towards the object of the will, which is universal good. But to incline towards the universal good belongs to the First Mover, to Whom the ultimate end is proportionate; just as in human affairs to him that presides over the community belongs the directing of his subjects to the common weal.[8] Wherefore in both ways it belongs to God to move the will; but especially in the second way by an interior inclination of the will.

A thing moved by another is forced if moved against its natural inclination; but if it is moved by another giving to it the proper natural inclination, it is not forced; as when a heavy body is made to move downwards by that which produced it, then it is not forced. In like manner God, while moving the will, does not force it, because He gives the will its own natural inclination....

Rectitude of the will is necessary for Happiness both antecedently and concomitantly. Antecedently, because rectitude of the will consists in being duly ordered to the last end. Now the end in comparison to what is ordained to the end is as form compared to matter. Wherefore, just as matter cannot receive a form, unless it be duly disposed thereto, so nothing gains an end, except it be duly ordained thereto. And therefore none can obtain Happiness, without rectitude of the will. Concomitantly, because ... final Happiness consists in the vision of the Divine Essence, Which is the very essence of goodness. So that the will of him who sees the Essence of God, of necessity, loves, whatever he loves, in subordination to God; just as the will of him who sees not God's Essence, of necessity, loves whatever he loves, under that common notion of good which he knows. And this

---

[8] 'Weal' is an Old English term for 'welfare.'

is precisely what makes the will right. Wherefore it is evident that Happiness cannot be without a right will.[9]

[T]he act of the will is nothing else than an inclination proceeding from the interior principle of knowledge: just as the natural appetite is an inclination proceeding from an interior principle without knowledge.

God Who is more powerful than the human will, can move the will of man, according to Prov. xxi. 1: *The heart of the king is in the hand of the* LORD; *withersoever He will He shall turn it.*

We speak of an end in a twofold sense: first, as being the thing itself; secondly, as the attainment thereof. These are not, of course, two ends, but one end, considered in itself, and in its relation to something else. Accordingly God is the last end, as that which is ultimately sought for: while the enjoyment is as the attainment of this last end. And so, just as God is not one end, and the enjoyment of God, another: so it is the same enjoyment whereby we enjoy God, and whereby we enjoy our enjoyment of God. And the same applies to created happiness which consists in enjoyment.[10]

Now it is evident that the act of the reason giving direction as to the means, and the act of the will tending to these means according to the reason's direction, are ordained to one another. Consequently there is to be found something of the reason, viz., order, in that act of the will, which is choice: and in counsel, which is an act of reason, something of the will, – both as matter (since counsel is of what man wills to do), – and as motive (because it is from willing the end, that man is moved to take counsel in regard to the means).[11]

---

[9] *Summa Theologica of St. Thomas Aquinas*, trans. Fathers of the English Dominican Province (3 vols.; New York: Benziger Brothers, 1947-48), 1:604.
[10] Ibid, 1:638-39.
[11] Ibid, 1:647.

Now grace is prior to virtue, and accordingly has a subject which is prior to the powers of the soul, such as the essence of the soul. Just as it is through the virtue of faith that a man partakes of the divine knowledge by means of the power of his intellect, and through the virtue of charity that he partakes of the divine love by means of the power of his will, so it is through regeneration or recreation of his soul's nature that he partakes of the divine nature by way of a certain likeness.[12]

Martin Luther (1483–1546), German sparkplug of the Reformation through his teaching, preaching, and writing:

At an earlier time there was no pleasure in the law for me. But now I find that the law is good and tasty, that it has been given to me so that I might live, and now I find my pleasure in it. Earlier, it told me what I ought to do. Now I begin to adapt myself to it. And for this I worship, praise, and serve God.[13]

'The law is spiritual.' What is that? If the law were for the body, it could be satisfied with works; but since it is spiritual, no one can satisfy it, unless all that you do is done from the bottom of the heart. But such a heart is given only by God's Spirit, who makes a man equal to the law, so that he acquires a desire for the law in his heart, and henceforth does nothing out of fear and compulsion, but everything out of a willing heart. That law, then, is spiritual which will be loved and fulfilled with such a spiritual heart, and requires such a spirit. Where that spirit is not in the heart, there sin remains,

---

[12] A. M. Fairweather, ed. and trans., *Nature and Grace: Selections from the Summa Theologica of Thomas Aquinas* (Philadelphia: Westminster Press, 1954), 163.

[13] Sermon on John 1:17, cited in Justo Gonzalez, *The Story of Christianity, Volume 2: The Reformation to the Present Day* (San Francisco: Harper, 1985), 32.

and displeasure with the law, and enmity toward it; though the law is good and just and holy....

How can a man prepare himself for good by means of works, if he does no good works without displeasure and unwillingness of heart? How shall a work please God, if it proceeds from a reluctant and resisting heart?

To fulfill the law, however, is to do its works with pleasure and love, and to live a godly and good life of one's own accord, without the compulsion of the law. This pleasure and love for the law is put into the heart by the Holy Ghost.[14]

Faith ... is a divine work in us. It changes us and makes us to be born anew of God (John 1); it kills the old Adam and powers, and it brings with it the Holy Ghost. Oh, it is a living, busy, active, mighty thing, this faith; and so it is impossible for it not to do good works incessantly. It does not ask whether there are good works to do, but before the question rises, it has already done them, and is always at the doing of them. He who does not these works is a faithless man.[15]

The inner man, who by faith is created in the image of God, is both joyful and happy because of Christ in whom so many benefits are conferred upon him; and therefore it is his one occupation to serve God joyfully and without thought of gain, in love that is not constrained....

Since by faith the soul is cleansed and made to love God, it desires that all things, and especially its own body, shall be purified so that all things may join with it

---

[14] Martin Luther, *Commentary on the Epistle to the Romans*, trans. J. Theodore Mueller (Grand Rapids: Kregel, 1954), xiv-xv. The reader is also referred to Bernhard Citron's very helpful dissertation, *New Birth: A Study of the Evangelical Doctrine of Conversion in the Protestant Fathers* (Edinburgh: Edinburgh University Press, 1951), especially his discussion of Luther, Calvin and Melanchthon on conversion (pp. 85-123) and his examination of 'The Marks of the New Birth' (145-160).

[15] Luther, *Romans*, xvii.

in loving and praising God. Hence a man cannot be idle, for the need of his body drives him and he is compelled to do many good works to reduce it to subjection. Nevertheless the works themselves do not justify him before God, but he does the works out of spontaneous love in obedience to God and considers nothing except the approval of God, whom he would most scrupulously obey in all things.[16]

John Calvin (1509–1564), French pastor and systematizer of Reformation theology:

Being born again. Here is ... reason for an exhortation, – that since they were new men and born again of God, it behooved them to form a life worthy of God and of their spiritual regeneration.[17]

[T]he beginning of obedience, as well as its source, foundation, and root, is love of God ... [T]his love cannot exist until we have tasted the goodness of our God.... [W]e must realize that he is our father and savior.... [O]nce we have tasted his mutual love which he reserves for us, then we will be motivated to love him as our father. For if this love is in us, then there will be no doubt that we will obey him and that his law will rule in our thoughts, our affections, and in all our members.[18]

God's grace, as this word is understood in discussing regeneration, is the rule of the Spirit to direct and regulate man's will. The Spirit cannot regulate without

---

[16] 'The Freedom of a Christian,' in *Martin Luther's Basic Theological Writings,* ed. Timothy F. Lull (Minneapolis: Fortress, 1989), 611.

[17] John Calvin, *Commentaries on the Catholic Epistles,* Owen, trans. and ed. John Owen (Grand Rapids: Baker Book House, 1999), 56. Reprint. Calvin is here commenting on 1 Peter 1:23 ('You have been born again, not of perishable seed, but of imperishable').

[18] John Calvin, *Sermons on the Ten Commandments*, ed. Benjamin Wirt Farley (Grand Rapids: Baker, 2001), 76.

correcting, without reforming, without renewing. For this reason we say that the beginning of our regeneration is to wipe out what is ours. Likewise, he cannot carry out these functions without moving, acting, impelling, bearing, keeping. Hence we are right in saying that all the actions that arise from grace are wholly his. Meanwhile, we do not deny that what Augustine teaches is very true: 'Grace does not destroy the will but rather restores it.' The two ideas are in substantial agreement: the will of man is said to be restored when, with its corruption and depravity corrected, it is directed to the true rule of righteousness. At the same time a new will is said to be created in man, because the natural will has become so vitiated and corrupted that he considers it necessary to put a new nature within.[19]

Motives for the Christian Life.

Now this Scriptural instruction of which we speak has two main aspects. The first is that the love of righteousness, to which we are otherwise not at all inclined by nature, may be instilled and established in our hearts; the second, that a rule be set forth for us that does not let us wander about in our zeal for righteousness.

There are in Scripture very many and excellent reasons for commending righteousness, not a few of which we have already noted in various places. And we shall briefly touch upon still others here. From what foundation may righteousness better arise than from the Scriptural warning that we must be made holy because our God is holy? [Lev. 19:2; 1 Peter 1:15-16]. Indeed, though we had been dispersed like stray sheep and scattered through the labyrinth of the world, he has gathered us together again to join us with himself.

---

[19] John Calvin, *Institutes of the Christian Religion*, ed. John T. McNeill, trans. Ford Lewis Battles (Louisville: Westminster/John Knox, 1960), 2.5.15.

When we hear mention of our union with God, let us remember that holiness must be its bond; not because we come into communion with him by virtue of our holiness! Rather, we ought first to cleave unto him so that, infused with his holiness, we may follow whither he calls. But since it is especially characteristic of his glory that he have no fellowship with wickedness and uncleanness, Scripture accordingly teaches that this is the goal of our calling to which we must ever look if we would answer God when he calls [Isa. 35:8, etc.].[20]

Richard Sibbes (1577–1635), Puritan pastor and author:

When we are drawn to duties out of wrong motives or fear or custom, and not from a new nature, this is not from the Spirit, and their performance is not from the true liberty of the Spirit. For under the liberty of the Spirit, actions come off naturally, not forced by fear or hope or any extra motives. A child does not need other motives to please his father. When he knows he is the child of a loving father, it is natural. So there is a new nature in those who have the Spirit of God to stir them up to duty, though God's motives of sweet encouragement and rewards may help. But the principal is to do things naturally, not out of fear or to appease other people.[21]

Flesh and blood as it is, ... the corrupted nature of man, cannot enter into heaven (1 Cor. 15:50). We must have new judgments and new desires, new esteem, new affections, new joys and delights, new company. The whole frame and bent of the soul must be new. The face of the soul must look altogether another way. Whereas before it looked to the world, to things below, now it must look to God and heaven. Those still in their natural

---

[20] *Institutes* 3.6.2.

[21] Richard Sibbes, *Glorious Freedom* (Edinburgh: Banner of Truth Trust, 2000), 55-56. This is a book-length reflection on 2 Cor. 3:18.

state, who feel no change in themselves, are not in the state of grace, for there must be a change.[22]

Actions correspond to powers and abilities, and no holy action can come from an unchanged ability. A change in the soul's faculties must precede a change in life and conduct.

In nature, there is first the form, living, and being of a thing; then there are powers and, finally, actions issuing from the powers. In nature we live, and we have the power to move; being and moving go together. So if we have a being in grace, we have a power to move. In the life of grace and sanctification there is an ability to believe in God, to be holy, and to love God; and then the actions of love spring from that power. Consider, then, the necessity of a change in the inward man, of the powers of the soul. Can the eye see without a power of seeing? or the ear hear without a faculty of hearing? Can the soul perform sanctified actions without a sanctified power? It is impossible.

And the change is especially in the will, which some would say is not touched. They would say the will is free and would give grace no more credit than necessary. But grace works upon the will most of all. For the bent and desires of the will carry the whole man with it. If the choice, and bent, and bias are the right way, by the Spirit, it is good. If the will is not inclined and formed to go the best way, there is no work of grace at all. Though all grace first comes in through the understanding being enlightened, it then goes into the will. That is, it passes. through the understanding into the will, and it puts a new taste and relish upon the will and affections.

You see, then, that the grace in the gospel is not mere persuasion and entreaty, but a powerful work of the Spirit entering into the soul and changing it, and altering the

---

[22] Ibid, 103.

inclination of the will heavenward, whereas corruption of nature turns the soul downward to things below. The soul is carried up and is shut to things below. We must have great notions of the work of grace. The Scripture has great words in it. It is an alteration, a change, a new man, a new creature, a new birth.[23]

Whenever the knowledge of God in Christ is real, there is a change and conversion of the whole person. There is a new judgment and new affections. The bent and bias is another way than they were before.[24]

Richard Baxter (1615–1691), Puritan pastor and author:

The word regeneration also signifies the same thing with conversion, but with this small difference. 1st. The term is metaphorical, taken from our natural generation; because there is so great a change, that a man is as it were another man. 2d. The word is, in scripture sense, I think more comprehensive than conversion, repentance or vocation; for it signifies not only the newness of our qualities, but also of our relations, even our whole new state.[25]

The second part of the work of conversion is upon the heart or will,[26] to which this change of the mind or understanding is preparative: and in this change of the heart, there are these several parts observable. (1.) The will is brought to like what it disliked, and to dislike what it liked before. (2.) It is brought to choose what it refused; and to consent to that which it would not consent to. (3.) It is brought to resolve, where it was either resolved on the contrary; or unresolved. (4.) The several affections are

---

[23] Ibid, 105-06.

[24] Ibid, 129.

[25] 'A Treatise on Conversion,' in *The Practical Works of Richard Baxter: Select Treatises* (Grand Rapids: Baker, 1981), 291.

[26] The first part has to do with a change of mind (293-96), and the third with a change of life (302-35).

changed, of love and hatred; desire and aversion; delight and sorrow; hope and despair; courage and fear; and anger with content and discontent.

1. The first change that God maketh on the heart or will in the work of conversion ... is in the complacency or displacency of it: he causeth that to savour or relish as sweet to the will, which before was as bitter: the soul receiveth a new inclination; it liketh that which before it disliked, not only by a mere approbation, but by a willing agreement of the heart therewith.... Before conversion the very bent of man's mind is toward the things below, and his heart is against the things of God: he relisheth the things below as sweet: and it pleaseth him to possess them, or to think of possessing them, but he hath no pleasure in God, nor in thinking or hearing of the life to come: all things please or displease a man, according as they agree or disagree to his inclination; and as they seem to him either suitable or unsuitable....

Yet a wonderful change is made on them: they that had no savour of God and glory before, do now savour nothing else so much; they can truly say, as David, though perhaps not so feelingly as he, 'Whom have I in heaven but thee, and there is none on earth that I can desire besides thee?'[27]

Well, if ever God will have mercy on your souls, he will show you another kind of pleasure and felicity; he will acquaint you with that which shall be worth your labour, he will bring those sick, distempered souls to another relish than now they have: he will make you abandon those guilty pleasures, and thirst for the living water that shall spring up in you to everlasting life. Instead of your over-eager seeking the food that perisheth, he will make you hunger after the bread of life.[28]

---

[27] 'Treatise on Conversion,' in *Works of Baxter*, 296-97.
[28] Ibid, 299.

Beloved hearers, you may easily conceive that it is a very great change that causes a man to have other ends than ever he had before; that entirely turns the very bent of his heart and life, and makes him have a quite contrary business in the world than before he had: that sets a man's face another way, so that he who before went one way, doth now go the contrary. Alas! it is not the restraint of a wicked work or two, or the outward civilizing of your lives, that is true conversion. It is such a change as I am now describing to you, that turns you quite another way.[29]

John Owen (1616–1683), Puritan theologian, military chaplain, and congregational Nonconformist pastor:

We do not ... suppose that the *motives of the word* [preached] are left unto a mere *natural operation*, with respect unto the ability of them by whom it is dispensed, but, moreover, that it is blessed of God, and *accompanied with the power of the Holy Spirit*, for the producing of its effect and end upon the souls of men. Only, the operation of the Holy Ghost on the minds and wills of men in and by these means is supposed to extend no farther but unto motives, arguments, reasons, and considerations, proposed unto the mind, so to influence the will and the affections. Hence his operation is herein moral, and so metaphorical, not real, proper, and physical.

Now, concerning this whole work I affirm these two things –

1. That the Holy Spirit doth make use of it in the *regeneration* or conversion of all that are *adult*, and that either immediately in and by the preaching of it, or by some other application of light and truth unto the mind derived from the word; for by the reasons, motives, and persuasive arguments which the word affords are

---

[29] Ibid, 301.

our minds affected, and our souls wrought upon in our conversion unto God, whence it becomes our *reasonable* obedience. And there are none ordinarily converted, but they are able to give some account by what considerations they were prevailed on thereunto. But –

2. We say that the whole work, or the *whole of the work* of the Holy Ghost in our *conversion*, doth not consist herein; but there is a real physical work, whereby he infuseth a gracious principle of *spiritual life* into all that are effectually converted and really regenerated, and without which there is no deliverance from the state of sin and death which we have described....[30]

If the Holy Spirit works no otherwise on men, in their regeneration or conversion, but by proposing unto them and urging upon them *reasons*, *arguments*, and *motives* to that purpose, then after his whole work, and notwithstanding it, the will of man remains absolutely indifferent whether it will admit of them or no, or whether it will *convert itself* unto God upon them or no; for the *whole* of this work consists in proposing *objects* unto the will, with respect whereunto it is left *undetermined* whether it will choose and close with them or no.[31]

[M]oral persuasion, however advanced or improved, and supposed to be effectual, yet confers no new *real supernatural strength* unto the soul; for whereas it worketh, yea, the Spirit or grace of God therein and thereby, by reasons, motives, arguments, and objective considerations, and no otherwise, it is able only to excite and draw out the strength which we have, delivering the mind and affections from prejudices and other moral impediments. Real aid, and internal spiritual strength, neither are nor can be conferred thereby. And he who

---

[30] *The Works of John Owen*, ed. William H. Goold, reprint (London: Banner of Truth Trust, 1966), 3:307.

[31] Ibid, 3:307-08.

will acknowledge that there is any such internal spiritual strength communicated unto us must also acknowledge that there is another work of the Spirit of God in us and upon us than can be effected by these persuasions.[32]

The most effectual persuasions cannot prevail with such [unregenerate] men to *convert themselves*, any more than arguments can prevail with a blind man *to see*, or with a dead man to rise from the grave, or with a lame man to walk steadily.[33]

[Regeneration] consists in a new, spiritual, supernatural, vital principle or habit of grace, infused into the soul, the mind, will, and affections, by the power of the Holy Spirit, disposing and enabling them in whom it is unto spiritual, supernatural, vital acts of faith and obedience.[34]

Francis Turretin (1623–1687), Swiss theologian known for his scholastically formulated Calvinism:

Habitual or passive conversion takes place by the infusion of supernatural habits by the Holy Spirit.... Therefore this is the first degree of efficacious grace by which God regenerates the minds of the elect by a certain intimate and wonderful operation and creates them as it were anew by infusing his vivifying Spirit, who, gliding into the inmost recesses of the soul, reforms the mind itself, healing its depraved inclinations and prejudices, endues it with strength and elicits the formal principle to spiritual and saving acts.... Also we obtain the new birth, from which acts of faith and love flow forth (1 John 4:7; 5:1). Thus this habitual conversion consists in principles of action which God confers upon the faculties of corrupt man.[35]

[32] Ibid, 3:309.
[33] Ibid, 3:313.
[34] Ibid, 3:329.

'The movement of efficacious grace is properly to be called neither physical nor ethical, but supernatural and divine (which in a measure includes both these relations).' It is not simply physical because it is concerned with a moral faculty which ought to be moved in a way appropriate to its nature; nor is it simply ethical, as if God acted only objectively and used mild suasion (as the Pelagians maintain). Rather it is supernatural and divine, rising above all these classes. In the meantime, it partakes somewhat of the ethical and the physical because the Spirit in our conversion operates both powerfully and sweetly, pleasingly and invincibly. It pertains to a physical mode that God by his Spirit creates, regenerates, gives us a heart of flesh and infuses into us efficiently the supernatural habits of faith and love. It pertains to a moral mode in that it teaches, inclines, persuades and draws to itself by various reasons as if by the chains of love. Hence Augustine is accustomed everywhere to express it by the phrase 'delightful conqueror' who has conjoined with the highest pleasantness and sweetness, the greatest efficacy and power which expels all the obstinacy of the heart. Thus neither that strength nor efficacy compels the man unwillingly, nor sweetly moves him now running spontaneously; but each joined together both strengthens the weakness of man and overcomes the hatred of sin. It is powerful that it may not be frustrated; sweet that it may not be forced. Its power is supreme and inexpugnable that the corruption of nature may be conquered, as well as the highest impotence of acting well and the necessity of doing evil. Yet still it is friendly and agreeable, such as becomes an intelligent and rational nature....

---

[35] Francis Turretin, *Institutes of Elenctic Theology, Vol. 2: Eleventh Through Seventeenth Topics*, trans. George Musgrave Giger, ed. James T. Dennison, Jr. (Phillipsburg, NJ: Presbyterian & Reformed, 1994), 2:522-23.

[U]nless that grace by which we are converted were furnished with the highest power, sin (which has struck its roots so deeply in us) could not be overcome and rooted out. Unless the same would yield fruit of the sweetest joy so that the most loathsome delight of sin might be overcome by the opposite pleasure, the man would be drawn not voluntarily, but unwillingly and in a manner little suited to his nature.[36]

And such and so great is the corruption introduced into the soul by sin that although there always remains in it a natural power of understanding and willing, still the moral habit or disposition of judging and willing properly has so failed that it can no longer be moved to a right exercise of itself by the presentation of the object (as it usually can in the natural order and in the instituted state of man) unless the faculty itself is first renovated. On this account, there is always need for a twofold grace in the conversion of man: the one objective and extrinsic, consisting in the proposition of the object; the other subjective, acting immediately upon the faculty to render it capable of receiving the object, not only that it may be able rightly to elicit its own acts in reference to it, but also to elicit them actually. Each depends upon the Holy Spirit working in two ways – both in the word and in the heart; in the word as the objective cause; in the heart as the efficient cause of faith. In the word, acting morally by the revelation of the object and suasion; in the heart, working efficaciously and hyperphysically by an infusion of good habits, the creation of a new heart and the powerful impression of the proposed object.[37]

[Sanctification] does not consist in a correction of life and morals alone (as the Socinians maintain, who, denying original corruption and whatever taint and

---

[36] Ibid, 2:524-25.
[37] Ibid, 2:526-27.

depravity is in us, say it has been contracted by frequent acts of sin and by a certain habit of sinning, and contend that regeneration and sanctification are nothing else than 'a change of a bad habit and of life, and reformation according to the doctrine of Christ'). Rather it consists in a change and renovation of the nature itself (corrupted by original sin) by which depraved qualities and habits are cast out and good ones infused so that the man desists from evil acts and strives for good.[38]

Stephen Charnock (1628–1680), chaplain to Henry Cromwell and Puritan pastor in London:

[Regeneration] is a universal change of the whole man. It is a new creature, not only a new power, or new faculty: this ... extends to every part, understanding, will, conscience, affections, all were corrupted by sin, all are renewed by grace. Grace sets up its ensigns in all parts of the soul, surveys every corner, and triumphs over every lurking enemy.[39]

It is principally an inward change. It is as inward as the soul itself. Not only a cleansing the outside of the cup and platter, a painting over the sepulcher, but a casting out the dead bones, and putrefied flesh; of a nature different from a pharisaical and hypocritical change.... If it were not so, there could be no outward rectified change.[40]

[T]his new creation consist[s] in gracious qualities and habits, which beautify and dispose the soul to act righteously and holily.... God hath put into all creatures such forms and qualities, whereby they may be inclined

---

[38] Ibid, 2:689-90.

[39] Stephen Charnock, *The Doctrine of Regeneration* (Welwyn, Hertford-shire: Evangelical, 1980), 103. Reprint.

[40] Ibid, 106.

of themselves to motions agreeable to their nature, in an easy and natural way. Much more doth God infuse into those that he moves to the obtaining a supernatural good, some spiritual qualities, whereby they may be moved rationally, sweetly, and readily to attain that good: he puts into the soul a spirit of love, a spirit of grace, whereby as their understandings are possessed with a knowledge of the excellency of his ways, so their wills are so seasoned by the power and sweetness of this habit, that they cannot, because they will not, act contrary thereunto.[41]

Henry Scougal (1630–1657), Professor of Divinity at the University of Aberdeen:

[R]eligion may be designed by the name of life; because it is an inward, free and self-moving principle; and those who have made progress in it, are not acted only by external motives, driven merely by threatenings, nor bribed by promises, nor constrained by laws; but are powerfully inclined to that which is good, and delight in the performance of it.

The love which a pious man bears to God and goodness, is not so much by virtue of a command enjoining him to do so, as by a new nature instructing and prompting him to it; nor doth he pay his devotions as an unavoidable tribute, only to appease the Divine justice, or quiet his clamorous conscience; but those religious exercises are the proper emanations of the Divine life, the natural employments of the new-born soul. He prays, and gives thanks, and repents, not only because these things are commanded, but rather because he is sensible of his wants, and of the Divine goodness, and of the folly and misery of a sinful life; his charity is not forced, nor his alms extorted from him, his love makes him willing

---

[41] Ibid, 123-24.

to give; and though there were no outward obligation, his 'heart would devise liberal things'; injustice or intemperance, and all other vices, are as contrary to his temper and constitution, as the basest actions are to the most generous spirit, and impudence and scurrility to those who are naturally modest: so that I may well say with St John, 'Whoever is born of God doth not commit sin: for his seed remaineth in him, and he cannot sin because he is born of God' (1 John 3:9).[42]

The love of God is a delightful and affectionate sense of the Divine perfections, which makes the soul resign and sacrifice itself wholly unto him, desiring above all things to please him, and delighting in nothing so much as in fellowship and communion with him, and being ready to do or suffer any thing for his sake, or at his pleasure. Though this affection may have its first rise from the favours and mercies of God toward ourselves, yet doth it, in its growth and progress, transcend such particular considerations, and ground itself on his infinite goodness, manifested in all the works of creation and providence.[43]

When we have said all that we can, the secret mysteries of a new nature and divine life can never be sufficiently expressed; language and words can not reach them; nor can they be truly understood but by those souls that are enkindled within, and awakened unto the sense and relish of spiritual things ...[44]

The exercises of religion, which to others are insipid and tedious, do yield the highest pleasure and delight

---

[42] Henry Scougal, *The Life of God in the Soul of Man* (Fearn, Scotland: Christian Focus, 2001), 43-44. This little book, originally written as a letter to a friend, was instrumental in the conversion of the British evangelist George Whitefield.

[43] Ibid, 53.

[44] Ibid, 55.

to souls possessed with divine love; they rejoice when they are called 'to go up to the house of the LORD ...' (Ps. 63:2).[45]

John Howe (1630–1705), English Moderatist pastor:

[T]hat holy rectitude which is effected by regeneration, or this new birth, takes place in every thing belonging to the nature of man. Therefore be not so vague as to imagine, that if there be somewhat done in some one faculty, this is regeneration, or that this speaks a man new born. If now and then there be a right thought injected and cast in, if there be an inclination, some motion or desire; if something of convictive light be struck into a man's conscience; is this regeneration? Is this being new born? No, that makes all things new: 'If any man is in Christ, he is a new creature; old things are done away, all things are become new.' There is a new mind, a new judgment, a new conscience, a new will, new desires, new delights, new love, new fear, every thing new.[46]

Pray think with yourselves what you say, when you say you believe Jesus to be the Christ; for every one that so believes is born of God, and hath that mighty universal change wrought in the very habit of his soul, that makes him imitate God, that conforms him to God, and inclines him to God, and makes him value communion with God above all things in this world.[47]

---

[45] Ibid, 77.

[46] *The Works of the Rev. John Howe*, ed. Edmund Calamy, (London: William Ball, 1838), 895. These quotes are from a series of thirteen sermons on regeneration, based on 1 John 5:1. See Hughes Oliphant Old's comments on this series (*The Reading and Preaching of the Scriptures in the Worship of the Christian Church: Moderatism, Pietism, and Awakening* [Grand Rapids: Eerdmans, 2004], 5:14).

[47] *Works of Howe*, 896.

Here is a change to be wrought in his nature, a nature that is corrupt, depraved, averse from God, alienated from the divine life; this nature is now to be attempered to God, made suitable to him, made propense and inclined towards him. This might be done, it is true, by an immediate exertion of Almighty power, without any more ado. But God will work upon men suitably to the nature of man. And what course doth he therefore take? He gives 'exceeding great and very precious promises,' and in them he declares his own good will, that he might win theirs. In order to the ingenerating grace in them, he reveals grace to them by these great and precious promises. And what is grace in us? Truly grace in us is good will towards God, or good nature towards God; which can never be without a transformation of our vicious, corrupt nature. It will never incline towards God, or be propense towards God, till he make it so by a transforming power. But how doth he make it so? By discovering his kindness and goodness to them in 'exceeding great and precious promises,' satisfying and persuading their hearts.... Thus the 'exceeding great and precious promises' are instruments to the communicating a divine nature to us, though that divine nature be ingenerated by a mighty power.[48]

[T]here are two motive principles, and each of them called spirit, the spirit which is of this world, and the Spirit which is of God.... We have not received the spirit of this world, but the Spirit that is from God. It is not a mundane spirit; that spirit that now comes upon us is another spirit, and is to work out the former impress, and introduce a new one ... and he will do so in all that are regenerate.

And hereby it is that spirits are distinguished, which spirit is regular; they that are regenerate of God, and

---

[48] Ibid, 898.

then they hear the things of God, the word of God, with gust, with savour and relish.[49]

It is a creature of a very peculiar benignity and goodness.... This goodness shows itself in ... an habitual propension thereunto, so as to do good with complacency and delight; so this goodness imitates the Divine goodness; he exerciseth loving-kindness in the earth, because he delights therein; so doth the good man do good even with delight, tasting and relishing his own act in what he doth. Oh, how sweet is it to do good! He tastes and the relish of it more than the receiver of it doth, incomparably more; according to that motto of our Lord, 'It is more blessed to give than to receive.' A more blessed thing, a thing that carries more sweet and savour in it.... Oh, what a pleasant savour hath grace and goodness! Oh, the sweet relishes of it! ... when regeneration makes a man good, produceth a divine creature, his delight is in doing good as God's own is.[50]

Peter Van Mastricht (1630–1706), Dutch theologian whose theological writings Edwards said he preferred to any other books in the world outside the Bible itself:

[R]egeneration, strictly so called, finds man spiritually dead (Eph. 2:2, 5), into whom it infuses the first act or principle of the spiritual life, by which he has a power or ability to perform spiritual exercises.[51]

[A] man who is spiritually dead can hear spiritual truth; he can also, grammatically at least, understand what he hears. He can moreover approve in his judgment, at least speculatively, what he understands; and lastly he can, in a general manner, have some kind of affection toward

---

[49] Ibid, 900-01.
[50] Ibid, 908-10.
[51] Peter Van Mastricht, *A Treatise on Regeneration*, trans. Brandon Withrow (Morgan, PA: Soli Deo Gloria, 2002), 7. First published 1699.

what he approves. Nor does the Holy Spirit in the work of regeneration and spiritual quickening treat the elect as stocks or brutes, but as rational creatures, to whose reception, the Redeemer, with the terms of salvation, has been already offered by the external call. To receive this, the Spirit has invited them by the most pressing motives. Yea, it is possible that persons who are as yet spiritually dead may, if not by the powers which they naturally possess, yet by the assistance of common grace arrive to certain attainments not accompanying salvation (Heb. 6:4-5, 9), or that are not inseparably connected therewith. So that we are not to think that there is nothing to be done with the unregenerate. However, while they perform all these things, they do nothing at all which is spiritual, or at least nothing in a spiritual manner (1 Cor. 2:13-14).[52]

As this spiritual life, bestowed in regeneration, is seated in the will, it is called a new heart (Ps. 51:12), a heart of flesh, or a heart easily affected (Ezek. 36:26), a heart on which God has written His fear (Jer. 32:39-40; Heb. 8:10), by which the regenerate walk in His statutes (Ezek. 11:19-20). For the Holy Ghost implants in the heart or will by regeneration a new inclination or propensity towards spiritual good. For although the will naturally has a kind of propensity toward moral good in general (Rom. 2:14-15) and toward external religious duties (Luke 18:10-12; Phil. 3:5-6), whereby in duties with which salvation is not connected an unregenerate person may sometimes perform things that are really wonderful (Mark 10:19-21; Heb. 6:4-5), yet as for their propensity towards spiritual and saving good, mankind has utterly lost it by sin; hence they are said to be dead in sin (Eph. 2:1, 5), and insufficient to think even the least thought that spiritually good (2 Cor. 3:5). Wherefore it is absolutely necessary that

---

[52] Ibid, 10-11.

a new propensity toward spiritual good be restored to the will (Rom. 7:22; 2 Thess. 3:5). For although the will naturally follows the last dictate of the practical understanding, so that were the understanding but sufficiently illuminated an immediate renovation of the will might seem unnecessary, yet this is to be admitted as truth only when the understanding, in its last dictate, judges agreeably to the inclination of the will.[53]

Matthew Henry (1662–1714), Nonconformist English pastor known for his commentary on the entire Scripture:

What it is that is required: to be *born again*. We must *live a new life*. Birth is the beginning of life; to be *born again* is to begin anew. We must not think to patch up the old building, but begin from the foundation. We must *have a new nature*, new principles, new affections, new aims. We must be born *anothen*, which signifies both *again*, and *from above*. We must be born *anew*. Our souls must be *fashioned* and *enlivened* anew. We must be born *from above*. This new birth has its rise *from heaven*, it is to be born to a *divine* and *heavenly* life.[54]

To be born of God is to be inwardly renewed, and restored to a holy rectitude of nature by the power of the Spirit of God. Such a one committeth not sin, his seed remaineth in him. Renewing grace is an abiding principle. Religion is not an art, an acquired dexterity and skill, but a new nature. And thereupon the consequence is the regenerate person cannot sin. He cannot continue in the course and practice of sin. And the reason is because he is born of God. There is that light in his mind which shows him the evil and malignity of sin. There is that bias upon his heart which disposes him

[53] Ibid, 23-24.
[54] *Matthew Henry's Commentary,* ed. Leslie F. Church (Grand Rapids: Zondervan, 1960), 1517. Henry is commenting on John 3:3-8.

to loathe and hate sin. There is the spiritual disposition, that breaks the force and fullness of the sinful acts. It is not reckoned the person's sin, in the gospel account, where the bent and frame of the mind and spirit are against it. The unregenerate person is morally unable for what is religiously good. The regenerate person is happily disabled for sin.[55]

August Hermann Francke (1663–1727), German Lutheran and a leader of Pietism:

Nor is it enough to explain that first and mighty Change, which is at once made in a Sinner at his Conversion, when he comes to love that God which before he hated, and to hate the Evil which he before loved; when from being an Unbeliever he becomes a Believer; or when his false and dead Faith is changed into a true and saving one: But that further progressive Change should also be much recommended, in which the Christian must be improving to the very End of his Life.[56]

[N]o doctrine in Christianity is more necessary than the doctrine of rebirth. This is the very ground upon which Christianity stands. A person without this is not to be called a Christian. Just as the article of creation is the first, without which the others would not be (for if man were not created, how could his redemption and sanctification occur?), so if the person is not created anew or born of God, it does not help at all that Christ died for him; nor does it help at all that he has sent the Holy Spirit, and so forth. But when new birth occurs, we enjoy all the more the heavenly Father, our Savior, and the dear Holy Spirit.[57]

---

[55] Ibid, 1958-59, commenting on 1 John 3:4-10.

[56] Quoted in Dale Brown, *Understanding Pietism* (Grand Rapids: Eerdmans, 1978), 96.

[57] Gary R. Sattler, *God's Glory, Neighbor's Good: A Brief Introduction to the Life and Writings of August Hermann Francke* (Chicago: Covenant, 1982), 135, 142.

John Wesley (1703–1791), itinerant preacher, organizational genius, founder of Methodism, and key figure in the Great Awakening of the 1740s:

> But as soon as he is born of God, there is a total change in all these particulars. The 'eyes of his understanding are opened' (such is the language of the great Apostle); and, He who of old 'commanded light to shine out of darkness shining on his heart, he sees the light of the glory of God,' His glorious love, 'in the face of Jesus Christ.' His ears being opened, he is now capable of hearing the inward voice of God, saying, 'Be of good cheer; thy sins are forgiven thee'; 'Go and sin no more....' He 'feels in his heart,' to use the language of our Church, 'the mighty working of the Spirit of God' ... he feels, is inwardly sensible of, the graces which the Spirit of God works in the heart. He feels, he is conscious of, a 'peace which passeth all understanding.' He many times feels such a joy in God as is 'unspeakable, and full of glory.' He feels 'the love of God shed abroad in his heart by the Holy Ghost which is given unto him'; and all his spiritual senses are then exercised to discern spiritual good and evil.[58]

> From hence it manifestly appears, what is the nature of the new birth. It is that great change which God works in the soul when He brings it into life; when He raises it from the death of sin to the life of righteousness. It is the change wrought in the whole soul by the almighty Spirit of God when it is 'created anew in Christ Jesus'; when it is 'renewed after the image of God in righteousness and true holiness'; when the love of the world is changed into the love of God; pride into humility; passion into meekness; hatred, envy, malice, into a sincere, tender, disinterested love for all mankind. In a word, it is that

---

[58] *Wesley's Standard Sermons*, ed. Edward H. Sudgen (London: Epworth, 1951), 2:233-34.

change whereby the earthly, sensual, devilish mind is turned into the 'mind which was in Christ Jesus.' This is the nature of the new birth: 'so is every one that is born of the Spirit.'[59]

For the same reason, except he be born again, none can be happy even in this world. For it is not possible, in the nature of things, that a man should be happy who is not holy.... The reason is plain: all unholy tempers are uneasy tempers: not only malice, hatred, envy, jealousy, revenge, create a present hell in the breast; but even the softer passions, if not kept within due bounds, give a thousand times more pain than pleasure.... Therefore, as long as they must reign in any soul, happiness has no place there. But they must reign till the bent of our nature is changed, that is, till we are born again; consequently, the new birth is absolutely necessary in order to happiness in this world, as well as in the world to come.[60]

A ... scriptural mark of those who are born of God, and the greatest of all, is love; even 'the love of God shed abroad in their hearts by the Holy Ghost which is given unto them' (Rom. v. 5). 'Because they are sons, God hath sent forth the Spirit of His Son into their hearts, crying, Abba, Father!' (Gal. iv. 6). By this Spirit, continually looking up to God as their reconciled and loving Father, they cry to Him for their daily bread, for all things needful, whether for their souls or bodies. They continually pour out their hearts before Him, knowing 'they have the petitions which they ask of Him' (1 John v. 15). Their delight is in Him. He is the joy of their heart; their 'shield,' and their 'exceeding great reward.' The desire of their soul is toward Him; it is their 'meat and drink to do His will'; and they are

---

[59] Ibid, 2:234.
[60] Ibid, 2:236.

'satisfied as with marrow and fatness, while their mouth praiseth Him with joyful lips' (Ps. lxiii. 5).[61]

George Whitefield (1714–1770), Calvinist Methodist evangelist and key leader on both sides of the Atlantic in the Great Awakening:[62]

Third argument, which shall be founded on the consideration of the nature of that happiness God has prepared for those that unfeignedly love him. To enter indeed on a minute and particular description of heaven, would be vain and presumptuous, since we are told that 'eye hath not seen, nor ear heard, neither hath it entered into the heart of man to conceive, the things that are prepared' for the sincere followers of the holy Jesus, even in this life, much less in that which is to come. However, this we may venture to affirm in general, that as God is a spirit, so the happiness he has laid up for his people is spiritual likewise: and consequently, unless our carnal minds are changed and spiritualized, we can never be made meet to partake of that inheritance with the saints in light.

It is true, we may flatter ourselves, that supposing we continue in our natural corrupt state, and carry all our lusts along with us, we should, notwithstanding, relish heaven, was God to admit us therein. And so we might, was it a Mahometan paradise, wherein we were to take our full swing in sensual delights. But since its joys are

---

[61] 'The Marks of the New Birth,' in Sudgen, *Wesley's Standard Sermons*, 1:292.

[62] Though I have exerted the utmost strength in refraining from commenting on or commending secondary literature in this appendix, here I must give in to the temptation. My personal favorite biography is that of the Canadian pastor Arnold Dallimore on Whitefield, entitled *George Whitefield: The Life and Times of the Great Evangelist of the 18th Century Revival* (2 vols.; Edinburgh: Banner of Truth Trust, 1970, 1980). It is as heart-expanding as anything I have ever read.

only spiritual, and no unclean thing can possibly enter those blessed mansions, there is an absolute necessity of our being changed, and undergoing a total renovation of our depraved natures, before we can have any taste or relish of those heavenly pleasures. It is, doubtless, for this reason, that the apostle declares it to be the irrevocable decree of the Almighty, that 'without holiness, (without being made pure by regeneration, and having the image of God thereby reinstamped upon the soul,) no man shall see the Lord.' And it is very observable, that our divine Master, in the famous passage before referred to, concerning the absolute necessity of regeneration, does not say, Unless a man be born again, he *shall not*, but 'unless a man be born again, he *cannot* enter into the kingdom of God.' It is founded in the very nature of things, that unless we have dispositions wrought in us suitable to the objects that are to entertain us, we can take no manner of complacency or satisfaction in them. For instance, what delight can the most harmonious music afford to a deaf, or what pleasure can the most excellent picture give to a blind, man? Can a tasteless palate relish the rich dainties, or a filthy swine be pleased with the finest garden of flowers? No: and what reason can be assigned for it? An answer is ready: Because they have neither of them any tempers of mind correspondent or agreeable to what they are to be diverted with. And thus it is with the soul hereafter: for death makes no alteration in the soul, than as it enlarges its faculties, and makes it capable of receiving deeper impressions either of pleasure or pain. If it delighted to converse with God here, it will be transported with the sight of his glorious majesty hereafter....

It is necessary ... in order to make Christ's redemption complete, that we should have a grant of God's Holy Spirit to change our natures, and so prepare us for the enjoyment of that happiness our Saviour has purchased by his precious blood. Accordingly, the holy scriptures inform us, that whom Christ justifies, or whose sins he forgives, and to whom he imputes his perfect obedience, those he also sanctifies, purifies, and cleanses, and totally changeth their corrupted natures....

The sum of the matter is this: Christianity includes morality, as grace does reason; but if we are only mere moralists, if we are not inwardly wrought upon, and changed by the powerful operations of the Holy Spirit, and our moral actions proceed from a principle of a new nature, however we may call ourselves Christians, we shall be found naked at the great day, and in the number of those who have neither Christ's righteousness imputed to them for their justification in the sight, nor holiness enough in their souls as the consequence of that, in order to make them meet for the enjoyment, of God.'[63]

[B]efore you or I can have any well-grounded, scriptural hope, of being happy in a future state, there must be some great, some notable, and amazing change pass upon our souls. I believe, there is not one adult person in the congregation, but will readily confess, that a great change hath past upon their bodies, since they came first into the world, and were infants dandled upon their mothers' knees. It is true, ye have no more members than ye had then; but how these are altered! Though you are in one respect the same ye were, for the number of your limbs, and as to the shape of your body, yet if a person that knew you when ye were in your cradle, had been absent from you for some years, and saw you when grown up, ten thousand to one if he would know you at all, ye are so altered, so different from what ye were, when ye were little ones. And as the words [of Matt. 18:3] plainly imply, that there has a great change

---

[63] 'On Regeneration,' in George Whitefield, *Sermons on Important Subjects* (London: Henry Fisher, 1832), 547-50.

passed upon our bodies since we were children, so before we can go to heaven, there must as great a change pass upon our souls; our souls considered in a physical sense are still the same, there is to be no philosophical change wrought upon them; but then, as for our temper, habit, and conduct, we must be so changed and altered, that those who knew us the other day, when in a state of sin, and before we knew Christ, and are acquainted with us now, must see such an alteration, that they may stand as much amazed at it, as a person at the alteration wrought on any person he has not seen for twenty years from his infancy.[64]

Samuel Hopkins (1721–1803), student of Edwards' and New England pastor:

This regeneration of which I am speaking consists in a change of the will or heart. The truth of this observation appears from the foregoing, as it is a plain consequence from it. If the depravity and corruption of the heart is the only ground of the necessity of regeneration, then regeneration consists in removing this depravity, and introducing opposite principles, and so laying a foundation for holy exercises. But depravity or sin lies wholly in the heart, and not in the intellect or faculty of understanding, considered as distinct from the will, and not including that. So far as the will is renewed or set right, the whole mind is right; for sin and holiness lie wholly in this. If moral depravity does not lie in, or properly belong to, the faculty of the understanding or the intellect, as distinguished from the will, or heart, then that operation of the Spirit of God, by which this is in some measure removed and moral rectitude introduced, does not immediately respect the understanding, but the will or heart, and immediately produces a change in the

---

[64] 'Marks of a True Conversion,' Whitefield, *Sermons*, 270.

latter, not in the former. It is allowed by all, I suppose, that regeneration does not produce any new *natural* capacity or faculty in the soul. These remain the same after regeneration that they were before, so far as they are *natural*. The change produced is a moral change, and, therefore, the will or heart must be the immediate subject of this change, and of the operation that effects it; for every thing of a moral nature belongs to the will or heart.

As depravity or sin began in the will, and consists wholly in the irregularity and corruption of that, so regeneration, or a recovery from sin in the renovation of the mind, must begin here, and wholly consists in the change and renewal of the will. There is not, nor can there be, any need of any other change, in order to the complete renovation of the depraved mind, and its recovery to perfect holiness. Therefore, I think I have good grounds to assert, that in regeneration the will or heart is the immediate subject of the divine operation, and so of the moral change that is effected hereby. The Spirit of God in regeneration gives a new heart, an honest and good heart. He begets a right and good taste, temper, or disposition, and so lays a foundation for holy exercises of heart.[65]

Archibald Alexander (1772–1851), American Presbyterian theologian and founder of Princeton Theological Seminary:

[W]hat are the precise effects of regeneration, or the exercises of a newly converted soul? As the restoration of depraved man to the image of God, lost by the fall,[66]

---

[65] From the sermon 'Regeneration and Conversion,' on John 1:13 (*Introduction to Puritan Theology: A Reader*, ed. Edward Hindson [Grand Rapids: Baker, 1976], 179-80).

[66] I would differ with Alexander here, asserting not that the image of God was 'lost' in the fall, but *corrupted*. This is seen in the Bible in places such as Genesis 9:6, where God, speaking to Noah, prohibits the shedding of man's

is the grand object aimed at in the whole economy of salvation, it can easily be said, in the general, that by this change a principle of holiness is implanted, spiritual life is communicated, the mind is enlightened, the will renewed, and the affections purified and elevated to heavenly objects.... [S]ome suppose, that there can be no other method of influencing a rational mind but by the exhibition of truth, or the presentation of motives: any physical operation, they allege, would be unsuitable. Their theory of regeneration, therefore, is, that it is produced by the moral operation of the truth, contemplated by the understanding, and influencing the affections and the will, according to the known principles of our rational nature.... Now, in my judgment, this theory is defective, only in one point, and that is, it supposes the mind, which is already in possession of doctrinal knowledge of the truth, to have this same truth presented to it in an entirely new light, without any operation on the soul itself. Just as if a man was blind, but standing in the clear shining of the sun's rays. These he feels, and can talk philosophically about the sensation of light and colours; while he has not in his mind the first simple perception of any object of sight. Could this man be made to perceive the visible objects around him, without an operation on the eyes to remove the obstruction, or to rectify the organ? The case of the soul is entirely analogous. Here is light enough; the truth is viewed by the intellect of unregenerate man, but has no transforming efficacy. The fault is not in the truth, which is perfect, but the blindness is in the mind, which can only be removed by an influence on the soul itself; that is, by the power of God creating 'a new heart,' to use the language of Scripture.[67]

---

blood because man is created in the image of God. Evidently there remains some vestige of the *imago dei*, then, even after the fall.

[67] Archibald Alexander, *Thoughts on Religious Experience* (Philadelphia: Presbyterian Board of Publication, 1844), 79-81. Reprint.

Thomas Chalmers (1780–1847), Scottish mathematician and leader of the Free Church of Scotland:

> There are a thousand things which, in popular and understood language, man can do. It is quite the general sentiment, that he can abstain from stealing, and lying, and calumny – that he can give of his substance to the poor, and attend church, and pray, and read his Bible, and keep up the worship of God in his family. But, as an instance of distinction between what he can do, and what he cannot do, let us make the undoubted assertion, that he can eat wormwood, and just put the question, if he can also relish wormwood. That is a different affair. I may command the performance; but have no such command over my organs of sense, as to command a liking, or a taste for the performance.... I may accomplish the doing of what God bids; but have no pleasure in God himself. The forcible constraining of the hand, may make out many a visible act of obedience, but the relish of the heart may refuse to go along with it.... The poor man has no more conquered his rebellious affections, than he has conquered his distaste for wormwood. He may fear God; he may listen to God; and, in outward deed, may obey God. But he does not, and he will not, love God; and while he drags a heavy load of tasks, and duties, and observances after him, he lives in the hourly violation of the first and greatest of the commandments.[68]

> [T]he love of gratitude differs from the love of moral esteem.... There is a real distinction of cause between these two affections, and there is also between them a real distinction of object. The love of moral esteem finds its complacent gratification, in the act of dwelling contemplatively on that Being, by whom it is excited; just as a tasteful enthusiast inhales delight from the act

---

[68] 'An Estimate of the Morality that is Without Godliness,' in Thomas Chalmers, *Sermons and Discourses, Vol. II* (New York: Robert Carter, 1846), 2:34.

of gazing on the charms of some external scenery. The pleasure he receives, emanates directly upon his mind, from the forms of beauty and loveliness, which are around him. And if, instead of a taste for the beauties of nature, there exists within him, a taste for the beauties of holiness, then will he love the Being, who presents to the eye of his contemplation the fullest assemblage of them, and his taste will find its complacent gratification in dwelling upon him, whether as an object of thought, or as an object of perception. 'One thing have I desired,' says the Psalmist, 'that I may dwell in the house of the LORD all the days of my life, to behold the beauty of the LORD, and to inquire in his temple.' Now, the love of gratitude is distinct from this in its object. It is excited by the love of kindness; and the feeling which is thus excited, is just a feeling of kindness back again.[69]

[W]e are not perfect and complete in the whole of God's will, till the love of moral esteem be in us, as well as the love of gratitude – till that principle, of which, by nature, we are utterly destitute, be made to arise in our hearts, and to have there a thorough establishment, and operation – till we love God, not merely on account of his love to our persons, but on account of the glory, and the residing excellence, which meets the eye of the spiritual beholder, upon his own character....

[T]he chief end of man is to glorify God, and to enjoy him for ever. This is the real destination of every individual who is redeemed from among men. This should be the main object of all his prayers, and all his preparations. It is this which fits him for the company of heaven; and unless there be a growing taste for God, in the glories of his excellency – for God, in the beauties of his holiness – there is no ripening, and no perfecting, for the mansions of immortality.[70]

---

[69] 'The Principle of Love to God,' in Chalmers, *Sermons and Discourses*, 2:64-65.

Charles Hodge (1797–1878), American Presbyterian theologian of Princeton Seminary:

> A beautiful object in nature or art may be duly apprehended as an object of vision by an uncultivated man, who has no perception of its aesthetic excellence, and no corresponding feeling of delight in its contemplation. So it is with the unrenewed man. He may have an intellectual knowledge of the facts and doctrines of the Bible, but no spiritual discernment of their excellence, and no delight in them.[71]

> Out of the heart proceed all conscious, voluntary, moral exercises. A change of heart, therefore, is a change which precedes these exercises and determines their character. A new heart is to a man what goodness is to the tree in the parable of our Lord.
>
> In regeneration, therefore, there is a new life communicated to the soul; the man is the subject of a new birth; he receives a new nature or new heart, and becomes a new creature. As the change is neither in the substance nor in the mere exercises of the soul, it is in those immanent dispositions, principles, tastes, or habits which underlie all conscious exercises, and determine the character of the man and of all his acts.[72]

William Anderson (1799–1872), Scottish pastor:

> The change of Regeneration ... is effected, not on the faculties of the Understanding, but on the passions and affections of the Will. Of these two departments of mind – the powers of Knowledge, and the Passions, the latter

---

[70] 'The Affection of Moral Esteem Towards God,' in Chalmers, *Sermons and Discourses*, 2:75, 82.

[71] Charles Hodge, *Systematic Theology* (3 vols.; Grand Rapids: Eerdmans, 1946), 3:33.

[72] Ibid, 3:35.

is by far the more important; and to its rectification is the regenerative work directed. For although ... it is through an enlightened understanding that the heart is changed; yet is this change of heart the great object ultimately contemplated; and the intellectual powers, through which the rectifying light is transmitted, remain in their former condition. If previously to his being regenerated, the man's memory was unretentive, his judgment obtuse, and his imagination sluggish; now that he is regenerated they will be found equally sluggish, obtuse, and unretentive, as the general rule.[73]

If regenerated, you will feel nothing new beyond what you can clearly comprehend, viz., that whereas you once regarded God, and his Son, and his Spirit, and his Saints, and his Book, and his Heaven, with aversion and despite, you now regard them with reverence, with love, and ardent desire. There may be mystery – I shall afterwards exert myself to prove that there is deep and unfathomable mystery – in the Agency by which the change is produced; but mystery there is none in the nature of the change itself. It is the old love of the old heart with which it loved things earthly, *newly directed* to the loving of things divine and heavenly.[74]

The primary characteristic of Regeneration is a change of heart from a state of carelessness about God, or slavish fear of Him, or enmity against Him: of despite to his Person and his government, to his law and his love, to his promises and his threatenings, to his family, and to his inheritance – *into* a state of filial reverence, confidence, and obedience – of admiration of Him, as being of all who are called great the most excellent; of gratitude towards Him as being of all benefactors the

---

[73] William Anderson, *Treatise on Regeneration* (Philadelphia: Smith, English & Company, 1871), 28.
[74] Ibid, 40.

most bountiful; of dependence on Him, as being of all friends the most tender, faithful, and powerful; and of loyalty towards Him, as being of all Sovereigns, the most rightful, glorious, and gracious – as being One in the contemplation of whom the soul finds all its demands of perfection answered, and in whom it reposes satisfied with the vision; whose favor it seeks after and enjoys as the chief good; to serve whom it regards its highest honor; to advance the interests of whose kingdom engages its warmest patriotism; in whose family it finds its most endeared kindred; and whose house is its longed-for home.[75]

J. C. Ryle (1816–1900), Anglican Bishop of Liverpool, England:

True Christians are what they are, because they are regenerate, and formal Christians are what they are, because they are not. The heart of a Christian in deed has been changed. The heart of the Christian in name only has not been changed. The change of heart makes the whole difference.[76]

Scripture describes regeneration as a great radical change of heart and nature – a thorough alteration and transformation of the whole inner man, a participation in the resurrection life of Christ, or, to borrow the words of the Church Catechism, 'a death unto sin and a new birth unto righteousness'.

This change of heart in a true Christian is so complete that no word could be chosen more fitting to express it than that word 'regeneration' or new birth. Doubtless it is no outward, bodily alteration, but undoubtedly it is an entire alteration of the inner man. It adds no

<hr />

[75] Ibid, 44.
[76] J. C. Ryle, *Regeneration* (Fearn, Scotland: Christian Focus, 2003), 12. Reprint.

new faculties to a man's mind, but it certainly gives an entirely new bent and bias to all his old ones. His will is so new, his taste so new, his opinions so new, his views of sin, the world, the Bible, and Christ so new, that he is to all intents and purposes a new man. The change seems to bring a new being into existence. It may well be called being *born again*.[77]

William G. T. Shedd (1820–1894), American systematizer of Calvinist theology and professor at Union Seminary:

Regeneration is to be defined as the origination of a new inclination by the Holy Spirit, not as the exertion of a new volition or making a new choice as a sinner. Keeping this distinction in mind, we say that in regeneration God inclines man to holiness and disinclines him to sin. This change of the disposition of the will is attributable solely to the Holy Spirit. The sinner discovers, on making the attempt, that he is unable to reverse his determination to self and the creature. He cannot start a contrary disposition of his will. He is unable to incline himself to God as the chief end of his existence. He can choose the antecedents or preparatives to inclining, but cannot incline. By a volition he can read his Bible. This is a preparative or antecedent to supreme love of God, but it is not supreme love and cannot produce it. By volitions he can listen to preaching and can refrain from vicious actions. These also are preparatives or antecedents to a holy inclination of the will, but are not this inclination itself and cannot produce it. It is a fact of consciousness that while the sinner can put forth single volitions or particular choices that are favorable to a new voluntary disposition because they evince the need of it, he cannot begin the new disposition itself. He cannot incline himself by any volition whatsoever.

---

[77] Ibid, 14.

By the operation of the Holy Spirit in regeneration, the man is enabled to incline to holiness instead of sin. In the scriptural phraseology, he is 'made willing' (Ps. 110:3). God 'works in him to will' (Phil. 2:13).... By renewing the sinful and self-enslaved will, the Holy Spirit empowers it to self-determine or incline to God as the chief good and the supreme end. This new self-determination expels and takes the place of the old sinful self-determination. From this new self-determination or inclination or disposition or principle, holy volitions or choices proceed, and from the holy choices, holy actions.[78]

Robert Lewis Dabney (1820–1898), American Presbyterian theologian sympathetic to the South and professor at Union Seminary:

Let us consider, and we shall see that the change of a godless, self-willed, worldly soul into a sincere, believing, joyful Christian, is as truly above the laws of his natural heart as the living again of a corpse is above the powers of matter....

[T]he saving change of the soul is God's own almighty work, and is, in that sense, supernatural.

What is this change? Some, from shallow observation, answer: It is only the sinner's change of purpose concerning his duty to God. But the Scriptures answer, that it is a change of the dispositions of heart, which prompt and regulate man's purposes concerning this duty. Note, I pray you, my words, and apprehend the difference, for it is that between light and darkness.... That new birth, I repeat, which is necessary to salvation, is some deeper thing than the mere making of a new resolution by the sinner. It is the fundamental revolution of the very dispositions of soul, out of which his purposes were all prompted. Hence, it is not the work

---

[78] William G. T. Shedd, *Dogmatic Theology, 3rd ed.*, ed. Alan W. Gomes (Phillipsburg, NJ: Presbyterian & Reformed, 2003), 765-66.

merely of reasonings and inducements presented to the mind, but of God's almighty power, through his Holy Ghost, quickening the soul to feel those reasonings and inducements....

Well, this heart is, in different degrees and phases, universal among natural men, in all races and ages, under all religions and forms of civilization, whatever religious instincts men may have, and to whatever pious observances they may be driven by remorse, or self-righteousness, or spiritual pride. We perceive that this disposition of soul begins to reveal itself in all children as early as any intelligent moral purpose is disclosed. We observe that while it is sometimes concealed, or turned into new directions by the force of circumstances, it is always latent, and is a universal and controlling principle of conduct towards God. We find that it holds its evil sway in spite of all light and rational conviction in men's own minds, and of inducements drawn from conscience and heaven and hell, which ought to be omnipotent. Such is every man's inward history, until *grace* reverses his career....

There is, there can be, no case in which mere inducements work in man a permanent purpose contrary to the natural dispositions of the soul. But ungodliness is a native, a universal, a radical propensity. Hence, when we see such a revolution in this as the gospel requires in the new birth, we must believe that it is above nature. This great change not only reforms particular vices; it revolutionizes their original source, ungodliness. It not only causes the renewed sinner to submit to obedience, as the bitter, yet necessary medicine of an endangered soul; it makes him prefer it for itself as his daily bread.... Such is the change which makes the real Christian. It is a spiritual resurrection; it is the working of that 'mighty power of God which he wrought in Christ when he raised him from the dead.'[79]

---

[79] 'The Believer Born of Almighty Grace,' in Robert L. Dabney, *Discussions: Evangelical and Theological, Vol. 1* (London: Banner of Truth Trust, 1967), 484-89.

Charles Haddon Spurgeon (1834–1892), Baptist pastor of the Metropolitan Tabernacle in London:

[R]egeneration consists in this, God the Holy Spirit, in a supernatural manner – mark, by the word supernatural I mean just what it strictly means; supernatural, more than natural – works upon the hearts of men, and they by the operations of the divine Spirit become regenerate men; but without the Spirit they never can be regenerated. And unless God the Holy Spirit, who 'worketh in us to will and to do,' should operate upon the will and the conscience, regeneration is an absolute impossibility, and therefore so is salvation.... in the salvation of every person there is an actual putting forth of divine power, whereby the dead sinner is quickened, the unwilling sinner is made willing, the desperately hard sinner has his conscience made tender; and he who rejected God and despised Christ, is brought to cast himself down at the feet of Jesus.... If you like it not, quarrel with my Master, not with me; I do but simply declare his own revelation that there must be in your heart something more than you can ever work there. There must be a divine operation, call it a miraculous operation if you please; it is in some sense so. There must be a divine interposition, a divine working, a divine influence, or else do what you may, without that you perish, and are undone – 'For except a man be born again he cannot see the kingdom of God.' The change is radical; it gives us new natures, makes us love what we hated and hate what we loved; sets us in a new road; makes our habits different, our thoughts different, makes us different in private, and different in public.[80]

Regeneration is not the reforming of principles which were there before, but the implantation of a something

[80] *The Metropolitan Tabernacle Pulpit: Sermons Preached and Revised by C. H. Spurgeon* (London: Passmore & Alabaster, 1857), 3:188.

which had no existence; it is the putting into a man of a new thing called the Spirit, the new man – the creation not of a soul, but of a principle higher still – as much higher than the soul, as the soul is higher than the body.... In the bringing of any man to believe in Christ, there is as true and proper a manifestation of creating power, as when God made the heavens and the earth.[81]

The absolute necessity of the new birth is ... a certainty. We come down with demonstration when we touch that point. We shall never poison our people with the notion that a moral reformation will suffice, but we will over and over again say to them, 'Ye must be born again.'[82]

Benjamin Breckinridge Warfield (1851–1921), New Testament professor at Princeton Theological Seminary:

From that moment of the first divine contact the work of the Spirit never ceases: while man is changing his mind and reforming his life, it is ever God who is renewing him in true righteousness. Considered from man's side the new dispositions of mind and heart manifest themselves in a new course of life. Considered from God's side the renewal of the Holy Spirit results in the production of a new creature, God's workmanship, with new activities newly directed.... At the root of all lies an act seen by God alone, and mediated by nothing, a direct creative act of the Spirit, the new birth. The new birth ... becomes visible to his fellow-men only in a turning to God in external obedience, under the constant leading of the indwelling Spirit (Rom. viii. 14). A man must be born again by the Spirit to become God's son. He must be born again by the Spirit and Word to

---

[81] Ibid, 9:566. See the discussion of Spurgeon on regeneration in Iain H. Murray, *The Forgotten Spurgeon* (Edinburgh: Banner of Truth Trust, 1966), 95-97.

[82] *Lectures to My Students*, 222.

become consciously God's son. He must manifest his new spiritual life in Spirit-led activities accordant with the new heart which he has received and which is ever renewed afresh by the Spirit, to be recognized by his fellow-men as God's son....

Salvation consists in its substance of a radical subjective change wrought by the Holy Spirit, by virtue of which the native tendencies to evil are progressively eradicated and holy dispositions are implanted, nourished and perfected.[83]

Adolf Schlatter (1852–1938), conservative German New Testament scholar and professor at Tübingen University:

Jesus did not have in mind a technique or method by which the conversion of Capernaum, Galilee, and Jerusalem could be affected. Technique can only regulate and enhance human performance; but in conversion to God, Jesus did not see merely a human decision. For Jesus, conversion pointed to God, who gives his grace to the individual. The forgiveness Jesus offered to the guilty nation was God's action having its ground in God's own will.[84]

Faith is not a single act of thought or a flawless set of teachings about God or Christ but moves the individual in his inner condition of life and turns him to Christ. It does so not merely by a transformation of his thoughts but also by a movement of his will that controls the person entirely and uniformly since he trusts in the veracity and goodness of Jesus.[85]

The call to repentance and the promise of new birth by the Spirit did not have in common merely that both

[83] B. B. Warfield, *Biblical Doctrines* (New York: Oxford University Press, 1929), 457, 460.

[84] Adolf Schlatter, *The History of the Christ*, trans. Andreas J. Köstenberger (Grand Rapids: Baker, 1997), 113.

[85] Ibid, 202-03.

condemned the existing condition of human life, but also that both promised as attainable a new form of life....

Conversion does not merely alter individual thoughts and aspirations; if so, it would reveal itself only as long as the sole focus were the performance of the repentant person. It produces an effect that transcends this, since God accepts and forgives the repentant person and makes him his own son. Jesus did not base this on the repentant person's performance according to a doctrine of merit, nor did he conceive of a change of human nature by a person's own will power. He rather invested repentance with the effect of granting salvation and life, since God's gracious act upon man answered it and gave him a share in the divine sonship and eternal life. This occurred by the Spirit.'[86]

Why did Paul ... see in the change effected by faith not merely relative progress, not merely a lessening of the reprehensible element in man and an increase in what was good in man, but rather a new beginning, which made something qualitatively different out of man, the old man becoming subject to death together with Christ? This assessment resulted for him from God's changed relationship with us that arises through the emergence of faith. Through allegiance to Christ, God's grace becomes for Paul the potency that determines human existence. The gift of grace entails the power of shaping man completely in soul and body, in spirit and nature, according to God's will.[87]

Louis Berkhof (1873–1957), Dutch professor of theology at Calvin Theological Seminary:

Regeneration consists in the implanting of the principle of the new spiritual life in man, in a radical change of

---

[86] Ibid, 338.

[87] *The Theology of the Apostles*, trans. Andreas J. Köstenberger (Grand Rapids: Baker, 1998), 281.

the governing disposition of the soul, which, under the influence of the Holy Spirit, gives birth to a life that moves in a Godward direction. In principle this change affects the whole man....

Regeneration is that act of God by which the principle of the new life is implanted in man, and the governing disposition of the soul is made holy ... and the first holy exercise of this new disposition is secured.[88]

C. S. Lewis (1898–1963), British professor of literature author across literary genres:

But what man, in his natural condition, has not got, is Spiritual life – the higher and different sort of life that exists in God. We use the same word *life* for both: but if you thought that both must therefore be the same sort of thing, that would be like thinking that the 'greatness' of space and the 'greatness' of God were the same sort of greatness. In reality, the difference between Biological life and spiritual life is so important that I am going to give them two distinct names. The Biological sort which comes to us through Nature, and which (like everything else in Nature) is always tending to run down and decay so that it can only be kept up by incessant subsidies from Nature in the form of air, water, food, etc., is *Bios*. The Spiritual life which is in God from all eternity, and which made the whole natural universe, is *Zoe*. *Bios* has, to be sure, a certain shadowy or symbolic resemblance to *Zoe*: but only the sort of resemblance there is between a photo and a place, or a statue and a man. A man who changed from having *Bios* to having *Zoe* would have gone through as big a change as a statue which changed from being a carved stone to being a real man.

And that is precisely what Christianity is about. This world is a great sculptor's shop. We are the statues and

---

[88] Louis Berkhof, *Systematic Theology* (Edinburgh: Banner of Truth Trust, 1958), 468, 469.

there is a rumor going round the shop that some of us are some day going to come to life.[89]

I can to some extent control my acts: I have no direct control over my temperament. And if (as I said before) what we are matters even more than what we do – if indeed, what we do matters chiefly as evidence of what we are – then it follows that the change which I most need to undergo is a change that my own direct, voluntary efforts cannot bring about. And that applies to my good actions too. How many of them were done for the right motive? How many for fear of public opinion, or a desire to show off? How many from a sort of obstinacy or sense of superiority which, in different circumstances, might equally have led to some very bad act? But I cannot, by direct moral effort, give myself new motives. After the first few steps in the Christian life we realize that everything which really needs to be done in our souls can be done only by God.[90]

There are three kinds of people in the world. The first class is of those who live simply for their own sake and pleasure, regarding Man and Nature as so much raw material to be cut up into whatever shape may serve them. In the second class are those who acknowledge some other claim upon them – the will of God, the categorical imperative, or the good of society – and honestly try to pursue their own interests no further than this claim will allow. They try to surrender to the higher claim as much as it demands, like men paying a tax, but hope, like other taxpayers, that what is left over will be enough for them to live on (this idea is also in Mere Xianity). Their life is divided, like a soldier's or a schoolboy's life, into time 'on parade' and 'off parade', 'in

---

[89] C. S. Lewis, *Mere Christianity* (New York: MacMillan, 1943), 139-40. *Bios* and *Zoe* are transliterations of two different Greek words, both used in the New Testament, for 'life.'

[90] Ibid, 166.

school' and 'out of school'. But the third class is of those who can say like St Paul that for them 'to live is Christ'. These people have got rid of the tiresome business of adjusting the rival claims of Self and God by the simple expedient of rejecting the claims of Self altogether. The old egoistic will has been turned round, reconditioned, and made into a new thing. The will of Christ no longer limits theirs; it is theirs. All their time, in belonging to Him, belongs also to them, for they are His.

The price of Christ is something, in a way, much easier than moral effort – it is to want Him.[91]

John Murray (1898–1975), Scottish professor of systematic theology at Westminster Theological Seminary:

'A new heart also will I give you, and a new spirit will I put within you' (Ezek. 36:26). God effects a change which is radical and all-pervasive, a change which cannot be explained in terms of any combination, permutation, or accumulation of human resources, a change which is nothing less than a new creation by him who calls the things that be not as though they were, who spake and it was done, who commanded and it stood fast. This, in a word, is regeneration.[92]

The regenerate person cannot live in sin and be un-converted. And neither can he live any longer in neutral abstraction. He is immediately a member of the kingdom of God, he is spirit, and his action and behaviour must be consonant with that new citizenship. In the language of the apostle Paul, 'if any man be in Christ, he is a new creature; the old things have passed away, behold they have become new' (2 Cor. 5:17). There are numerous

[91] C. S. Lewis, *Present Concerns* (London: Fount, 1986), 21-22.

[92] John Murray, *Redemption Accomplished and Applied* (Grand Rapids: Eerdmans, 1955), 96.

other considerations derived from the Scripture which confirm this great truth that regeneration is such a radical, pervasive, and efficacious transformation that it immediately registers itself in the conscious activity of the person concerned in the exercises of faith and repentance and new obedience. Far too frequently the conception entertained of conversion is so superficial and beggarly that it completely fails to take account of the momentous change of which conversion is the fruit.... Regeneration is at the basis of all change in heart and life. It is a stupendous change because it is God's recreative act.[93]

The Holy Spirit is the controlling and directing agent in every regenerate person. Hence the fundamental principle, the governing disposition, the prevailing character of every regenerate person is holiness – he is 'Spiritual' and he delights in the law of the Lord after the inward man (1 Cor. 2:14, 15; Rom. 7:22). This must be the sense in which John speaks of the regenerate person as not doing sin and as unable to sin (1 John 3:9, 5:18).[94]

Anthony A. Hoekema (1913–1988), professor of systematic theology at Calvin Theological Seminary:

It is at the moment of regeneration that the dead sinner becomes spiritually alive, that resistance to God is changed to non-resistance, and that hatred for God is changed to love. Regeneration means that the person who was outside of Christ is now in Christ. Hence this is a radical, not just a superficial change....

[R]egeneration is a total change – a change which involves the whole person. In Scriptural terms, regeneration means the giving of a new heart. And the heart in

---

[93] Ibid, 104-05.
[94] Ibid, 142.

Scripture stands for the inner core of the person, the center of all activities, the fountain out of which all the streams of mental and spiritual exercises flow: thinking, feeling, willing, believing, praying, praising, and so on. It is this fountain which is renewed in regeneration. It should be added, however, that this does not mean the removal of all sinful tendencies. Though regenerated persons are new, they are not yet perfect.[95]

John R. W. Stott (1921–), Anglican theologian, clergyman, author, and international statesman of a unified and theologically mature evangelicalism:

[C]an human nature be changed? Is it possible to make a sour person sweet, a proud person humble, or a selfish person unselfish? The Bible declares emphatically that these miracles can take place. It is part of the glory of the gospel. Jesus Christ offers to change not only our standing before God but our very nature. He spoke to Nicodemus of the indispensable necessity of a new birth, and his words are still applicable to us: 'Truly, truly, I say to you, unless one is born anew, he cannot see the kingdom of God ... Do not marvel that I said to you, "You must be born anew".'

Paul's statement is in some ways even more dramatic, for he blurts out, in a sentence which has no verbs: 'If anyone in Christ – new creation!' Here then is the possibility of which the New Testament speaks – a new heart, a new nature, a new birth, a new creation.

This tremendous inward change is the work of the Holy Spirit. The new birth is a birth 'from above'...[96]

---

[95] Anthony A. Hoekema, *Saved by Grace* (Grand Rapids: Eerdmans, 1989), 103-04.

[96] John R. W. Stott, *Basic Christianity* (Downers Grove, IL: InterVarsity, 1958), 99.

This is not arid theological theorizing; it is the daily experience of every Christian. We continue to be conscious of sinful desires which are tugging us down; but we are now also aware of a counteracting force pulling us upwards to holiness.[97]

Regeneration or new birth ... is the inward work of the Holy Spirit, who then remains as a gracious indwelling presence, transforming the believer into the image of Christ, which is the process of sanctification.[98]

J. I. Packer (1926–), Anglican theologian, author, and professor at Regent College, Vancouver:

Regeneration is ... God renovating the heart, the core of a person's being, by implanting a new principle of desire, purpose, and action, a dispositional dynamic that finds expression in positive response to the gospel and its Christ....
Regeneration is a transition from spiritual death to spiritual life, and conscious, intentional, active faith in Christ is its immediate fruit, not its immediate cause.[99]

[Sanctification is] a divinely wrought character change freeing us from sinful habits and forming in us Christlike affections, dispositions, and virtues.
Regeneration is birth; sanctification is growth. In regeneration, God implants desires that were not there before: desire for God, for holiness, and for the hallowing and glorifying of God's name in this world; desire to pray, worship, love, serve, honor, and please God; desire to show love and bring benefit to others. In sanctification, the Holy Spirit 'works in you to will and to

---

[97] Ibid, 101.
[98] John R. W. Stott, *The Cross of Christ* (Downers Grove, IL: InterVarsity, 1986), 188.
[99] J. I. Packer, *Concise Theology: A Guide to Historic Christian Beliefs* (Wheaton: Tyndale House, 1993), 157, 158.

act' according to God's purpose; what he does is prompt you to 'work out your salvation' (i.e. express it in action) by fulfilling these new desires (Phil. 2:12-13).[100]

Iain H. Murray (1931–), Scottish pastor, author, and founder of the Banner of Truth Trust publishing company:

> [O]nce the Biblical doctrine of regeneration is grasped it means that no man can be a *true* believer who does not possess a new life 'created in righteousness and true holiness' (Eph. 4:24). According to Scripture it is quite impossible to be justified by faith and not to experience the commencement of true sanctification, because the spiritual life communicated by the Spirit in the act of regeneration (which introduces the new power to believe) is morally akin to the character of God and contains within it the germ of all holiness. Thus saving faith is never found in isolation.[101]

> To claim as the work of the Holy Spirit anything that does not show itself first by purity of life is to undermine the real meaning of Christianity. What made the revivals of the early nineteenth century so powerful in the conviction and silencing of unbelief was their indisputable effects in changing men's habits, subduing their selfishness and pride, and rendering visible the apostolic assertion, 'if any man be in Christ, he is a new creature: old things are passed away; behold, all things are become new' (2 Cor. 5:17). Joshua Bradley, writing in 1819, gives testimony to this:

>> God has delivered his cause from reproach, and laid waste the systems of infidels. These are confounded, and stand with silent astonishment,

---

[100] Ibid, 169, 170.
[101] Iain H. Murray, *The Forgotten Spurgeon* (Edinburgh: Banner of Truth Trust, 1966), 108-09.

to see such a striking alteration, as evidently appears in many old hardened sinners, who they thought, were inaccessible to the influences of religion. But they are not more astonished than many of the converts are themselves, to find such a change in their own feelings, views, motives, and desires. Who can behold the blessed effects of the religion of Jesus, and not be convinced of its divine original?[102]

Men not only need the light of the truth, they need the capacity to *see* it; they need a removal of the enmity which causes them by nature to 'receive not the things of the Spirit of God' (1 Cor. 2.14); they need to be *made* willing. The voice of the preacher leads people to the exercise of faith, but the *ability* to believe comes only as 'the dead hear the voice of the Son of God' himself (John 5.25). This is a voice which the unsaved do not hear (John 10.16-27); it is the 'calling' which brings faith and justification (Rom. 8.30); and it is much more than the outward hearing of the words of the gospel. Regeneration is the putting forth of creative power in the implanting of a new nature. There can be no *exercise* of faith until men hear the gospel (Rom. 10.14) but it is the power of the Holy Spirit with the gospel which first gives men a believing nature. Salvation is through faith, not *because* of it. Men are not renewed because they believe, rather they 'see' and 'hear' because they are reborn (John 3.3; Acts 16.14; Eph. 2.4-9).[103]

---

[102] Murray, *Revival and Revivalism*, 217.
[103] Ibid, 364.

THE CREEDS

BELGIC CONFESSION – 1561, NETHERLANDS

Article 24: *The Sanctification of Sinners*

We believe that this true faith,
  produced in man by the hearing of God's Word
  and by the work of the Holy Spirit,
regenerates him and makes him a 'new man,'
  causing him to live the 'new life'
  and freeing him from the slavery of sin.

Therefore,
far from making people cold
toward living in a pious and holy way,
this justifying faith,
quite to the contrary,
so works in them that
  apart from it
they will never do a thing out of love for God
but only out of love for themselves
and fear of being condemned.

So then, it is impossible
for this holy faith to be unfruitful in a human being,
seeing that we do not speak of an empty faith
but of what Scripture calls
'faith working through love,'
  which leads a man to do by himself
  the works that God has commanded
  in his Word.[1]

---

[1] *Ecumenical Creeds and Reformed Confessions* (Grand Rapids: CRC, 1988), 101.

HEIDELBERG CATECHISM – 1563, GERMANY

8 Q. But are we so corrupt that we are totally unable to do any good and inclined toward all evil?

A. Yes, unless we are born again by the Spirit of God.[2]

88 Q. What is involved in genuine repentance or conversion?

A. Two things:
> the dying-away of the old self,
> and the coming-to-life of the new.

89 Q. What is the dying-away of the old self?

A. It is to be genuinely sorry for sin, to hate it more and more, and to run away from it.

90 Q. What is the coming-to-life of the new self?

A. It is wholehearted joy in God through Christ and a delight to do every kind of good as God wants us to.[3]

---

[2] Ibid, 15.
[3] Ibid, 54.

CANONS OF DORT – 1618–19, NETHERLANDS

The Third and Fourth Main Points of Doctrine
*Human Corruption, Conversion to God,
and the Way It Occurs*

Article 11: *The Holy Spirit's Work in Conversion*
Moreover, when God carries out this good pleasure in his chosen ones, or works true conversion in them, he not only sees to it that the gospel is proclaimed to them outwardly, and enlightens their minds powerfully by the Holy Spirit so that they may rightly understand and discern the things of the Spirit of God, but, by the effective operation of the same regenerating Spirit, he also penetrates into the inmost being of man, opens the closed heart, softens the hard heart, and circumcises the heart that is uncircumcised. He infuses new qualities into the will, making the dead will alive, the evil one good, the unwilling one willing, and the stubborn one compliant; he activates and strengthens the will so that, like a good tree, it may be enabled to produce the fruits of good deeds.

Article 12: *Regeneration a Supernatural Work*
And this is the regeneration, the new creation, the raising from the dead, and the making alive so clearly proclaimed in the Scriptures, which God works in us without our help. But this certainly does not happen only by outward teaching, by moral persuasion, or by such a way of working that, after God has done his work, it remains in man's power whether or not to be reborn or converted. Rather, it is an entirely supernatural work, one that is at the same time most powerful and most pleasing, a marvelous, hidden, and inexpressible work, which is not lesser than or inferior in power to that of creation or of raising the dead, as Scripture

(inspired by the author of this work) teaches. As a result, all those in whose hearts God works in this marvelous way are certainly, unfailingly, and effectively reborn and do actually believe. And the will, now renewed, is not only activated and motivated by God but in being activated by God is also itself active. For this reason, man himself, by that grace which he has received, is also rightly said to believe and to repent.

Article 16: *Regeneration's Effect*
However, just as by the fall man did not cease to be man, endowed with intellect and will, and just as sin, which has spread through the whole human race, did not abolish the nature of the human race but distorted and spiritually killed it, so also this divine grace of regeneration does not act in people as if they were blocks and stones; nor does it abolish the will and its properties or coerce a reluctant will by force, but spiritually revives, heals, reforms, and – in a manner at once pleasing and powerful – bends it back. As a result, a ready and sincere obedience of the Spirit now begins to prevail where before the rebellion and resistance of the flesh were completely dominant. It is in this that the true and spiritual restoration and freedom of our will consists. Thus, if the marvelous Maker of every good thing were not dealing with us, man would have no hope of getting up from his fall by his free choice, by which he plunged himself into ruin when still standing upright.[4]

Rejection of the Errors
Having set forth the orthodox teaching, the Synod rejects the errors of those

VI

Who teach that in the true conversion of man new qualities, dispositions, or gifts cannot be infused or poured into his

---

[4] Ibid, 134-36. Article 11 is cited by Francis Turretin in *Institutes of Elenctic Theology*, 2:528.

will by God, and indeed that the faith by which we first come to conversion and from which we receive the name 'believers' is not a quality or gift infused by God, but only an act of man, and that it cannot be called a gift except in respect to the power of attaining faith....

IX

Who teach that grace and free choice are concurrent partial causes which cooperate to initiate conversion, and that grace does not precede – in the order of causality – the effective influence of the will; that is to say, that God does not effectively help man's will to come to conversion before man's will itself motivates and determines itself....[5]

---

[5] Ibid, 136-38.

Westminster Confession of Faith – 1640s, England

IX. *Of Free-Will*

4. When God converts a sinner, and translates him into the state of grace, He freeth him from his natural bondage under sin; and, by His grace alone, enables him freely to will and to do that which is spiritually good; yet so, that by reason of his remaining corruption, he doth not perfectly, nor only, will that which is good, but doth also will that which is evil.[6]

X. *Of Effectual Calling*

1. All those whom God hath predestined unto life, and those only, He is pleased, in His appointed and accepted time, effectually to call, by His word and Spirit, out of that state of sin and death, in which they are by nature to grace and salvation, by Jesus Christ; enlightening their minds spiritually and savingly to understand the things of God, taking away their heart of stone, and giving unto them an heart of flesh; renewing their wills, and, by His almighty power, determining them to that which is good, and effectually drawing them to Jesus Christ: yet so, as they come most freely, being made willing by His grace.[7]

XIII. *Of Sanctification*

1. They, who are once effectually called, and regenerated, having a new heart, and a new spirit created in them, are further sanctified, really and personally, through the virtue of Christ's death and resurrection, by His Word and Spirit

---

[6] 'The Westminster Confession of Faith,' in *The Westminster Confession of Faith Together with the Larger Catechism and the Shorter Catechism* (Atlanta: Committee for Christian Education and Publications, 1990), 35.

[7] Ibid, 36.

dwelling in them, the dominion of the whole body of sin is destroyed, and the several lusts thereof are more and more weakened and mortified; and they more and more quickened and strengthened in all saving graces, to the practice of true holiness, without which no man shall see the Lord.[8]

XVI. *Of Good Works*

3. [Believers'] ability to do good works is not at all of themselves, but wholly from the Spirit of Christ. And that they may be enabled thereunto, beside the graces they have already received, there is required an actual influence of the same Holy Spirit to work in them to will, and to do, of His good pleasure: yet are they not hereupon to grow negligent, as if they were not bound to perform any duty unless upon a special motion of the Spirit; but they ought to be diligent in stirring up the grace of God that is in them.[9]

---

[8] Ibid, 43-44.
[9] Ibid, 50-51.

The Larger Catechism

Q. 67. What is effectual calling?

A. Effectual calling is the work of God's almighty power and grace, whereby (out of his free and special love to his elect, and from nothing in them moving him thereunto) he doth, in his accepted time, invite and draw them to Jesus Christ, by his word and Spirit; savingly enlightening their minds, renewing and powerfully determining their wills, so as they (although in themselves dead in sin) are hereby made willing and able freely to answer his call, and to accept and embrace the grace offered and conveyed therein.[10]

---

[0] 'The Larger Catechism,' in *The Westminster Confession of Faith*, 35-36.

SELECT BIBLIOGRAPHY

PRIMARY WORKS

Miller, Perry, John E. Smith, and Harry S. Stout, eds. *The Works of Jonathan Edwards. 23 Volumes.* New Haven: Yale University Press, 1957–.

Vol. 1, *Freedom of the Will.* Paul Ramsey, ed., 1957.

Vol. 2, *Religious Affections.* John E. Smith, ed., 1959.

Vol. 3, *Original Sin.* Clyde A. Holbrook, ed., 1970.

Vol. 4, *The Great Awakening.* C. C. Goen, ed., 1972.

Vol. 5, *Apocalyptic Writings.* Stephen J. Stein, ed., 1977.

Vol. 6, *Scientific and Philosophical Writings.* Wallace E. Anderson, ed., 1980.

Vol. 7, *The Life of David Brainerd.* Norman Pettit, ed., 1985.

Vol. 8, *Ethical Writings.* Paul Ramsey, ed., 1989.

Vol. 9, *A History of the Work of Redemption.* John F. Wilson, ed., 1989.

Vol. 10, *Sermons and Discourses, 1720–1723.* Wilson H. Kimnach, ed., 1992.

Vol. 11, *Typological Writings.* Wallace E. Anderson and Mason I. Lowance, Jr., with David Watters, eds., 1993.

Vol. 12, *Ecclesiastical Writings.* David D. Hall, ed., 1994.

Vol. 13, *The 'Miscellanies,' Entry nos. a-z, aa-zz, 1-500.* Thomas A. Schafer, ed., 1994.

Vol. 14, *Sermons and Discourses, 1723–1729.* Kenneth P. Minkema, ed., 1997.

Vol. 15, *Notes on Scripture.* Stephen J. Stein, ed., 1998.

Vol. 16, *Letters and Personal Writings.* George S. Claghorn, ed., 1998.

Vol. 17, *Sermons and Discourses, 1730–1733.* Mark Valeri, ed., 1999.

Vol. 18, *The 'Miscellanies,' Entry nos. 501-832.* Ava Chamberlain, ed., 2000.

Vol. 19, *Sermons and Discourses, 1734–1738*. M. X. Lesser, ed., 2001.

Vol. 20, *The 'Miscellanies,' Entry nos. 833-1152*. Amy Plantinga Pauw, ed., 2002.

Vol. 21, *Writings on the Trinity, Grace, and Faith*. Sang Hyun Lee, ed., 2003.

Vol. 22, *Sermons and Discourses, 1739–1742*. Harry S. Stout and Nathan O. Hatch, with Kyle P. Farley, eds., 2003.

Vol. 23, *The 'Miscellanies,' Entry nos. 1153-1360*. Douglas A. Sweeney, ed., 2004.

Vol. 24, *The Blank Bible*. Stephen J. Stein, ed., 2006.

Vol. 25, *Sermons and Discourses, 1743-1758*. Wilson H. Kimnach, ed., 2006

The Works of Jonathan Edwards. 2 vols. Edited by Edward Hickman. London, 1834. Edinburgh: Banner of Truth Trust, 1974. Reprint.

Grossart, Alexander B., ed. *Selections from the Unpublished Writings of Jonathan Edwards of America*. Ligonier, PA: Soli Deo Gloria, 1992. Reprint from 1865.

SECONDARY WORKS

Alexander, Archibald. *Thoughts on Religious Experience*. Philadelphia: Presbyterian Board of Publication, 1844. Reprint.

Alexander, Donald L., ed. *Christian Spirituality: Five Views of Sanctification*. Downers Grove, IL: InterVarsity, 1988.

Anderson, William. *Treatise on Regeneration*. Philadelphia: Smith, English & Company, 1871.

Aquinas, St. Thomas. *Summa Theologica*. Translated by Fathers of the English Dominican Province. 3 vols. New York: Benziger Brothers, 1947-48.

Augustine, Saint. *The Works of Saint Augustine, Vol. 23: Answer to the Pelagians*. Edited by John E. Rotelle, translated by Roland J. Teske. New York: New City, 1997.

Bailey, Richard A. and Gregory A Wills, eds. *The Salvation of Souls: Nine Previously Unpublished Sermons on the Call of Ministry and the Gospel by Jonathan Edwards*. Wheaton: Crossway, 2002.

Baxter, Richard. *The Practical Works of Richard Baxter: Select Treatises*. Grand Rapids: Baker, 1981. Reprint.

Berkhof, Louis. *Systematic Theology*. Edinburgh: Banner of Truth Trust, 1958.

Best, W. E. *Regeneration and Conversion*. Grand Rapids: Guardian, 1975.

Bombaro, John J. 'Dispositional Peculiarity, History, and Edwards's Evangelistic Appeal to Self-Love.' *Westminster Theological Journal* 66 (2004): 121-57.

_____. 'Jonathan Edwards's Vision of Salvation.' *Westminster Theological Journal* 65 (2003): 45-67.

Brown, Dale. *Understanding Pietism*. Grand Rapids: Eerdmans, 1978.

Byrne, Herbert W. *Motivating Church Workers*. N.p., 1982.

Calamy, Edmund, ed. *The Works of the Rev. John Howe*. London: William Ball, 1838.

Calvin, John. *Institutes of the Christian Religion*. Edited by John T. McNeill. Translated by Ford Lewis Battles. Louisville: Westminster John Knox Press, 1960.

_____. *Sermons on the Ten Commandments*. Edited by Benjamin Wirt Farley. Grand Rapids: Baker, 2001.

Chalmers, Thomas. *Sermons and Discourses*. 2 vols. New York: Robert Carter, 1846.

Chapell, Bryan. *Holiness by Grace: Delighting in the Joy That Is Our Strength*. Wheaton: Crossway, 2001.

Charnock, Stephen. *The Doctrine of Regeneration*. Welwyn, Hertfordshire: Evangelical, 1980. Reprint.

Church, Leslie F., ed. *Matthew Henry's Commentary*. Grand Rapids: Zondervan, 1960.

Citron, Bernhard. *New Birth: A Study of the Evangelical Doctrine of Conversion in the Protestant Fathers*. Edinburgh: Edinburgh University Press, 1951.

Conforti, Joseph A. *Samuel Hopkins and the New Divinity Movement*. Grand Rapids: Christian College Consortium.

Dabney, Robert L. *Discussions: Evangelical and Theological*. 2 vols. London: Banner of Truth Trust, 1967.

Dallimore, Arnold A. *George Whitefield: The Life and Times of the Great Evangelist of the Eighteenth Century Revival*. 2 vols. Edinburgh: Banner of Truth Trust, 1970, 1980.

Duffield, George. *Spiritual Life: or, Regeneration*. Carlisle, Pennsylvania: Fleming, 1832.

Fairweather, A. M., ed. *Nature and Grace: Selections from the Summa Theologica of Thomas Aquinas*. Philadelphia: Westminster Press, 1954.

Ferguson, Sinclair B. *Children of the Living God*. Edinburgh: Banner of Truth Trust, 1989.

_____. *John Owen on the Christian Life*. Edinburgh: Banner of Truth Trust, 1987.

Ferm, Robert L. *Jonathan Edwards the Younger: 1745–1801*. Grand Rapids: Eerdmans, 1976.

Filson, David Owen. 'Fit Preaching: "Fitness" in the Preaching of Jonathan Edwards.' *Presbyterion* 31/2 (2005): 89-100.

Fuller, Daniel P. *Gospel and Law: Contrast or Continuum? The Hermeneutics of Dispensationalism and Covenant Theology*. Grand Rapids: Eerdmans, 1980.

_____. *The Unity of the Bible*. Grand Rapids: Zondervan,1992.

Gerstner, John H. *Jonathan Edwards: A Mini-Theology*. Wheaton: Tyndale House, 1987.

_____. 'Outline of the Apologetics of Jonathan Edwards.' *Bibliotheca Sacra* 133/1 (1976): 3-10, 99-107.

_____. *The Rational Biblical Theology of Jonathan Edwards*. 3 vols. Orlando: Ligonier Ministries, 1991.

Gerstner, John H., and Jonathan Neil Gerstner. 'Edwardsean Preparation for Salvation.' *The Westminster Theological Journal* 42/3 (1979): 5-71.

Gonzalez, Justo. *The Story of Christianity, Volume 1: The Early Church to the Reformation*. San Francisco: Harper, 1984.

_____. *The Story of Christianity, Volume 2: The Reformation to the Present Day*. San Francisco: Harper, 1985.

Goold, William H., ed. *The Works of John Owen*. London: Banner of Truth Trust, 1966. Reprint.

Gundry, Stanley N., ed. *Five Views on Sanctification*. Grand Rapids: Academie, 1987.

Gura, Philip F. *Jonathan Edwards: America's Evangelical*. New York: Hill and Wang, 2005.

Hafemann, Scott J. *The God of Promise and the Life of Faith: Understanding the Heart of the Bible*. Wheaton: Crossway, 2001.

Haykin, Michael A. G. *Jonathan Edwards: The Holy Spirit in Revival*. Darlington: Evangelical, 2005

Hindson, Edward, ed. *Introduction to Puritan Theology*. Grand Rapids: Baker, 1976.

Hodge, Charles. *Systematic Theology*. 3 vols. Grand Rapids: Eerdmans, 1946.

Hoekema, Anthony A. *Saved by Grace*. Grand Rapids: Eerdmans, 1989.

Holbrook, Clyde A. *The Ethics of Jonathan Edwards: Morality and Aesthetics*. Ann Arbor, MI: University of Michigan Press, 1973.

Holmes, Stephen R. *God of Grace and God of Glory: An Account of the Theology of Jonathan Edwards*. Grand Rapids: Eerdmans, 2000.

Hunsinger, George. 'Dispositional Soteriology: Jonathan Edwards on Justification by Faith Alone.' *Westminster Theological Journal* 66 (2004): 107-120.

Jones, David Clyde. *Biblical Christian Ethics*. Grand Rapids: Baker, 1994.

Kimnach, Wilson H., Kenneth P. Minkema and Douglas A. Sweeney, eds. *The Sermons of Jonathan Edwards: A Reader*. New Haven: Yale University Press, 1999.

Knight, Janice. *Orthodoxies in Massachusetts: Rereading American Puritanism*. Cambridge, MA: Harvard University Press, 1994.

Ladd, George Eldon. *A Theology of the New Testament*. Revised edition. Edited by Donald A. Hagner. Grand Rapids: Eerdmans, 1993.

Lewis, C. S. *Mere Christianity*. New York: MacMillan, 1943.

_____. *Present Concerns*. London: Fount, 1986.

Lloyd-Jones, Martyn. 'Jonathan Edwards and the Crucial Importance of Revival.' In *The Puritan Experiment in the New World*. Huntington, Cambs.: Westminster Conference, 1976.

Logan, Samuel T. 'The Doctrine of Justification in the Theology of Jonathan Edwards.' *Westminster Theological Journal* 46/2 (1984): 26-52.

Lull, Timothy F., ed. *Martin Luther's Basic Theological Writings*. Minneapolis: Fortress, 1989.

Luther, Martin. *Commentary on the Epistle to the Romans*. Translated by J. Theodore Mueller. Grand Rapids: Kregel, 1954.

Marsden, George M. *Jonathan Edwards: A Life*. New Haven: Yale University Press, 2003.

McDermott, Gerald R. *Jonathan Edwards Confronts the Gods: Christian Theology, Enlightenment Religion, and Non-Christian Faiths*. Oxford: Oxford University Press, 2000.

_____. 'Jonathan Edwards on Justification: Closer to Luther or Aquinas?' *Reformation & Revival Journal* 14/1 (2005): 119-38.

McMullen, Michael D., ed. *The Blessing of God: Previously Unpublished Sermons of Jonathan Edwards*. Nashville: Broadman & Holman, 2003.

_____. *The Glory and Honor of God: Volume 2 of the Previously Unpublished Sermons of Jonathan Edwards*. Nashville: Broadman & Holman, 2004.

McReynolds, Paul. *Four Early Works on Motivation*. Gainesville: Scholars' Facsimiles and Reprints, 1969.

Miller, Perry. *Jonathan Edwards*. New York: William Sloane, 1949.

Minkema, Kenneth P. 'Jonathan Edwards in the Twentieth Century.' *Journal of the Evangelical Theological Society* 47/4 (2004): 659-87.

Murray, Iain. *The Forgotten Spurgeon*. Edinburgh: Banner of Truth Trust, 1966.

_____. *Jonathan Edwards: A New Biography*. Edinburgh: Banner of Truth Trust, 1987.

_____. *Pentecost – Today? The Biblical Basis for Understanding Revival*. Edinburgh: Banner of Truth Trust, 1998.

_____. *Revival and Revivalism: The Making and Marring of American Evangelicalism, 1750–1858*. Edinburgh: Banner of Truth Trust, 1994.

_____. *Spurgeon v. Hyper-Calvinism: The Battle for Gospel Preaching*. Edinburgh: Banner of Truth Trust, 1995.

_____. *Wesley and Men Who Followed*. Edinburgh: Banner of Truth Trust, 2003.

Murray, John. *Collected Writings*. Edinburgh: Banner of Truth Trust, 1976 – . 4 vols.

_____. *Redemption Accomplished and Applied*. Grand Rapids: Eerdmans, 1955.

Nichols, Stephen J. *An Absolute Sort of Certainty: The Holy Spirit and the Apologetics of Jonathan Edwards*. Phillipsburg, NJ: Presbyterian & Reformed, 2003.

_____. *Jonathan Edwards: A Guided Tour of His Life and Thought*. Phillipsburg, NJ: Presbyterian & Reformed, 2001.

_____. *Heaven on Earth: Capturing Jonathan Edwards's Vision of Living in Between*. Wheaton, IL: Crossway, 2006.

Nichols, William C., ed. *Seeking God: Jonathan Edwards' Evangelism Contrasted With Modern Methodologies*. Ames, IA: International Outreach, 2001.

Noll, Mark A. 'Jonathan Edwards, Moral Philosophy, and the Secularization of American Christian Thought.' *Reformed Journal* 33/2 (1983): 22-28.

_____. *The Rise of Evangelicalism: The Age of Edwards, Whitefield, and the Wesleys*. Downers Grove, IL: InterVarsity, 2003.

Odeberg, Hugo. *Pharisaism and Christianity*. Translated by J. M. Moe. St. Louis: Concordia Publishing House, 1964.

Old, Hughes Oliphant. *The Reading and Preaching of the Scriptures in the Worship of the Christian Church*. 5 vols. Grand Rapids: Eerdmans, 1998-2004.

Packer, J. I. *Concise Theology: A Guide to Historic Christian Beliefs*. Wheaton: Tyndale House, 1993.

_____. *Keep in Step With the Spirit*. Old Tappan, NJ: Revell, 1984.

_____. *A Quest for Godliness: The Puritan Vision of the Christian Life*. Wheaton: Crossway, 1990.

_____. *Rediscovering Holiness*. Ann Arbor, MI: Servant, 1992.

Peterson, David. *Possessed by God: A New Testament Theology of Sanctification and Holiness*. Grand Rapids: Eerdmans, 1995.

Peterson, Robert A., and Sean Michael Lucas, eds. *All for Jesus: A Celebration of the 50th Anniversary of Covenant Theological Seminary*. Fearn, Scotland: Christian Focus, 2006.

Piper, John. *Desiring God: Meditations of a Christian Hedonist*. 3rd ed. Sisters, OR: Multnomah, 2003.

_____. *The Purifying Power of Living by Faith in Future Grace*. Sisters, OR: Multnomah, 1995.

Piper, John and Justin Taylor, eds. *A God Entranced Vision of All Things: The Legacy of Jonathan Edwards*. Wheaton: Crossway, 2004.

Ricker, Marilla M. *Jonathan Edwards: The Divine Who Filled the Air with Damnation and Proved the Total Depravity of God*. New York: American Freethought Tract Society, 1918.

Ryle, J. C. *Regeneration*. Fearn, Scotland: Christian Focus, 2003. Reprint.

Sattler, Gary R. *God's Glory, Neighbor's Good: A Brief Introduction to the Life and Writings of August Hermann Francke*. Chicago: Covenant, 1982.

Schlatter, Adolf. *The History of the Christ*. Translated by Andreas J. Köstenberger. Grand Rapids: Baker, 1997.

_____. *The Theology of the Apostles*. Translated by Andreas J. Köstenberger. Grand Rapids: Baker, 1998.

Scougal, Henry. *The Life of God in the Soul of Man*. Fearn, Scotland: Christian Focus, 2001. Reprint.

Shedd, William G. T. *Dogmatic Theology*. 3rd edition. Edited by Alan W. Gomes. Phillipsburg, NJ: Presbyterian & Reformed, 2003.

Sibbes, Richard. *Glorious Freedom*. Edinburgh: Banner of Truth Trust, 2000. Reprint.

Simonson, Harold. *Jonathan Edwards: Theologian of the Heart*. Grand Rapids: Eerdmans, 1974.

Smith, Timothy L. *Whitefield and Wesley on the New Birth*. Grand Rapids: Francis Asbury Press, 1986.

Sproul, R. C. *The Mystery of the Holy Spirit*. Wheaton: Tyndale House, 1990.

Spurgeon, C. H. *Lectures to My Students*. Grand Rapids: Zondervan, 1954.

_____. *The Metropolitan Tabernacle Pulpit: Sermons Preached and Revised by C. H. Spurgeon*. 63 vols. London: Passmore & Alabaster, 1855-60. Pasadena, TX: Pilgrim, 1969-80.

Stein, Stephen J. 'The Quest for the Spiritual Sense: The Biblical Hermeneutics of Jonathan Edwards.' *Harvard Theological Review* 70/1 (1977): 99-113.

Storms, Sam. *Chosen for Life: The Case for Divine Election*. Wheaton: Crossway, 2007.

_____. *One Thing: Developing a Passion for the Beauty of God*. Fearn, Scotland: Christian Focus, 2004.

_____. *Pleasures Evermore: The Life-Changing Power of Enjoying God*. Colorado Springs: NavPress, 2000.

Stott, John R. W. *Basic Christianity*. Downers Grove, IL: InterVarsity, 1958.

_____. *The Cross of Christ*. Downers Grove, IL: InterVarsity, 1986.

Sudgen, Edward H., ed. *Wesley's Standard Sermons*. London: Epworth, 1951.

Sweeney, Douglas A. *The American Evangelical Story: A History of the Movement*. 2 vols. Grand Rapids: Baker, 2005.

Turretin, Francis. *Institutes of Elenctic Theology*. Translated by George Musgrave Giger, edited by James T. Dennison, Jr. 3 vols. Phillipsburg, NJ: Presbyterian & Reformed, 1994.

Van Mastricht, Peter. *A Treatise on Regeneration*. Edited by Brandon Withrow. Morgan, PA: Soli Deo Gloria, 2002. Reprint.

Waddington, Jeffrey C. 'Jonathan Edwards's "Ambiguous and Somewhat Precarious" Doctrine of Justification?' *Westminster Theological Journal* 66 (2004): 357-72.

Wainwright, William. 'Jonathan Edwards and the Sense of the Heart.' *Faith and Philosophy* 7 (1990): 43-62.

Warfield, B. B. *Biblical Doctrines*. New York: Oxford University Press, 1929.

_____. 'Edwards and the New England Theology.' *Biblical and Theological Studies*, Vol. 10: 515-38.

Wells, David F. *Above All Earthly Pow'rs: Christ in a Postmodern World*. Grand Rapids: Eerdmans, 2005.

_____. *God in the Wasteland: The Reality of Truth in a World of Fading Dreams*. Grand Rapids: Eerdmans, 1994.

_____. *Losing Our Virtue: Why the Church Must Recover Its Moral Vision*. Grand Rapids: Eerdmans, 1998.

_____. *No Place for Truth: Or Whatever Happened to Evangelical Theology?* Grand Rapids: Eerdmans, 1993.

Whitefield, George. *Sermons on Important Subjects*. London: Henry Fisher, 1832.

Winiarski, Douglas L. 'Jonathan Edwards, Enthusiast? Radical Revivalism and the Great Awakening in the Connecticut Valley.' *Church History* 74/4 (2005): 683-739.

Yarbrough, Robert W. 'Biblical Authority and the Ethics Gap: The Call to Faith in James and Schlatter.' *Presbyterion* 22/2 (1996): 67-75.

SCRIPTURE INDEX

General Index

A Call to United,
Extraordinary Prayer...

(An humble attempt...)

Jonathan Edwards

A CALL TO UNITED
EXTRAORDINARY PRAYER...

An Humble Attempt...

Jonathan Edwards

Too often Prayer is a small, dusty compartment of our lives. This book shows that if we really believe that Prayer is communicating with all powerful, holy, loving and just God - then it will be - it has to be - something entirely different.

Luis Palau

The name of Jonathan Edwards is synonymous with revival. And when it comes to renewal and revival in the church, I can't think of a better way to get one's heart beating in rhythm with the Saviour's than to spend time with Jonathan Edwards through his excellent treatise, *"An Humble Attempt"*. The words may be from another century, but his passion and zeal, fervor and devotion to God are as fresh and first-hand as though he were preaching today.

Joni Eareckson Tada

Since Edwards, American evangelicals have not thought about life from the ground up as Christians because their entire culture has ceased to do so. ... there is no successor to his God-entranced world-view.

Mark Noll

For all his intellectual might, Edwards was the farthest thing from a cool, detached, neutral, disinterested academician.

John Piper

If you prayerfully read these pages, the ripples of blessing just might go to 'the edge of the pond,' and then drift on to eternity.

Erwin W. Lutzer

ISBN 978-1-85792-860-0

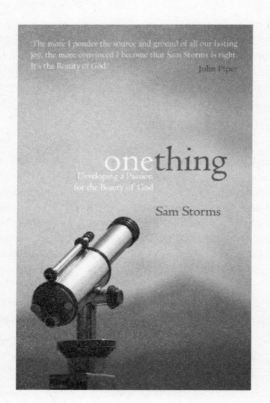

'The more I ponder the source and ground of all our lasting joy, the more convinced I become that Sam Storms is right. It's the Beauty of God.'
John Piper

onething
Developing a Passion for the Beauty of God

Sam Storms

ONE THING

Developing a Passion for the Beauty of God

Sam Storms

The goal of our creation was not simply that we might be happy, but happy in appreciating God's own glory. Not in reviewing our own accomplishments or in the enjoyment of our own sensual appetites. Not in the development of a healthy self-esteem or in the acquisition of a four-bedroom home with a three-car garage. We were made to glorify God and enjoy him forever. Nothing is more important than understanding this truth. This inspiring work helps us see that beauty has the power to convince the inquiring mind of truth. The soul's contact with God's beauty elicits love and forges in us a new affection that no earthly power can overcome. Enjoying God in the revelation of his beauty is the solution to our struggle with sin, the catalyst for substantive and lasting change and is the soul's satisfaction, with which no rival pleasure can hope to compete.

So what is it about God that when known and seen and experienced empowers the human soul to feel sickened in the presence of sin and satisfied in the divine embrace? That word again: Beauty.

Apatheism affects not just those outside the church but those inside the church who can't be bothered with their own religion let alone someone else's.

The more I ponder the source and ground of all our lasting joy, the more convinced I become that Sam Storms is right. It's the Beauty of God. In all his gifts we are to see him. Especially in the gospel.... Let Sam Storms guide you biblically and waken your heart to the Treasure of Christ who is the image of the Beauty of God.

John Piper
Bethlehem Baptist Church.

Sam Storms founded Enjoying God Ministries (www.enjoyinggodministries. com) in 2004. It exists "to proclaim the power of truth and the truth about power."

ISBN 978-1-85792-952-2

"...this remarkable book."

John Piper

The
LIFE OF GOD
in the
SOUL OF MAN

Henry Scougal

Introduced by
J. I. Packer

THE LIFE OF GOD
IN THE
SOUL OF MAN

Introduction by J.I. Packer

Henry Scougal

Henry Scougal died in 1657 at the age of 27 but by then he was already Professor of Divinity at Aberdeen University.

This timeless classic was originally written to encourage a friend and stimulate his spiritual life. It was so appreciated that it was later published as a book for a wider readership.

A hundred years later a copy was sent to George Whitefield by his friend, Charles Wesley - it was instrumental in Whitefield's conversion. This book provided much of the stimulation behind the Methodist Revival of Britain and the Great Awakening in America.

In it Scougal explains the four essential characteristics of divine life, their excellence, their advantages and the practical steps that you can take in realising them as your personal experience.

This book has an extensive introduction by J.I. Packer and contains, as an appendix, the 'Rules and instructions for a holy life' by Archbishop Robert Leighton of Glasgow.

There are some books whose vision is so deep and clear that truth rings from the page like the toll of a large bell, perfectly obvious, but rare and precious. They unfold the heart of man and God with such forceful illumination that the truth is not just shown to my mind but created in my heart... so it went as I grazed in the green pasture of this remarkable book.

John Piper,
Bethlehem Baptist Church, Minneapolis,

ISBN 978-1-85792-105-2

studies in romans eight

supernatural

living for natural people

Raymond C. Ortlund Jr.

'an outstanding scholar and gifted expository preacher...
a book of such practical and spiritual riches as we seldom read today.'
Eric Alexander

SUPERNATURAL LIVING
FOR NATURAL PEOPLE

Studies in Romans Eight

Raymond C. Ortlund Jr

Romans 8 is a favourite of many Christians. Verse after verse is pure spiritual gold. It opens up to us the power of God's goodness. In this thoughtful and perceptive book Ray Ortlund delves deeply into Romans 8. Our appreciation and understanding of the chapter will be thoroughly revitalised.

There is meat for the hungry soul here. There is refreshing water for the thirsty spirit. Ray's confidence in the power of the Spirit-energized Word of God shows forth on every page of this wonderful, Christ-exalting study of Romans 8. Get it. Then let it get you!

Sam Storms,
Enjoying God Ministries

Ray Ortlund in his exposition of Romans 8 has succeeded in weaving together both truth and application, both theology and the realities of everyday life. He shows that Romans 8 speaks to many of our deepest needs, such as the need for forgiveness, power, assurance, and security.

Thomas R. Schreiner,
Southern Baptist Theological Seminary, Louisville, Kentucky

This is a choice study of the eighth chapter of Romans by an outstanding scholar and gifted expository preacher. Dr. Ortlund mines the depths of this chapter, but what he produces is a book of such practical and spiritual riches as we seldom read today.

Eric Alexander

Raymond C. Ortlund Jr. serves as Senior Minister at First Presbyterian Church, Augusta, Georgia. He was formerly Professor of Old Testament at Trinity Evangelical Divinity School in Deerfield, Illinois.

ISBN 978-1-85792-694-1

Christian Focus Publications

publishes books for all ages

Our mission statement –

STAYING FAITHFUL

In dependence upon God we seek to help make His infallible Word, the Bible, relevant. Our aim is to ensure that the Lord Jesus Christ is presented as the only hope to obtain forgiveness of sin, live a useful life and look forward to heaven with Him.

REACHING OUT

Christ's last command requires us to reach out to our world with His gospel. We seek to help fulfil that by publishing books that point people towards Jesus and help them develop a Christ-like maturity. We aim to equip all levels of readers for life, work, ministry and mission.

Books in our adult range are published in three imprints.

Christian Focus contains popular works including biographies, commentaries, basic doctrine and Christian living. Our children's books are also published in this imprint.

Mentor focuses on books written at a level suitable for Bible College and seminary students, pastors, and other serious readers. The imprint includes commentaries, doctrinal studies, examination of current issues and church history.

Christian Heritage contains classic writings from the past.

Christian Focus Publications Ltd
Geanies House, Fearn,
Ross-shire, IV20 1TW, Scotland, United Kingdom
info@christianfocus.com

Our titles are available from quality bookstores and
www.christianfocus.com